T0396833

Implementation of Basel Accords in Bangladesh

A K M Kamrul Hasan · Yasushi Suzuki

Implementation of Basel Accords in Bangladesh

The Role of Institutions

A K M Kamrul Hasan
Ritsumeikan Asia Pacific University
Beppu, Oita, Japan

Yasushi Suzuki
Ritsumeikan Asia Pacific University
Beppu, Oita, Japan

ISBN 978-981-16-3471-0 ISBN 978-981-16-3472-7 (eBook)
https://doi.org/10.1007/978-981-16-3472-7

This Palgrave Macmillan imprint is published by the registered company Springer Nature Singapore Pte Ltd.
The registered company address is: 152 Beach Road, #21-01/04 Gateway East, Singapore 189721, Singapore

To our parents

PREFACE

Despite very significant discussions in the literature on the effectiveness of Basel Accords for enhancing the resilience of internationally active banks, less has been done to investigate the universal applicability of Basel Accords to local banks particularly in developing countries. As a matter of facts, Bangladesh, one of the least developed countries has introduced the Basel-type 'capital to risk-weighted assets based approach' for assessing the capital adequacy of banks, having abandoned the 'capital to liabilities approach' in 1996 and formally introduced the Basel Accords II and III in 2009 and 2015, respectively. The chief objective of the introduction of the Basel Accords in Bangladesh was to bring its financial stability and make its bank capital more shock absorbent. However, during our investigated period of 2009–2018, the banking industry has accumulated huge non-performing loans which eroded its profitability. This adverse effect was the motivation of writing this book, partly because the first author was in the financial instability in Bangladesh as a bank staff.

The book has nine chapters which can be categorized into three tracts. First tract (chapter 2 and 3) deals with the historical and theoretical issues on Basel Accords, banking theories and academic debate on banking regulations. The second tract (chapter 4 to chapter 7) offers a comprehensive discussion on the Bangladeshi regulations on external credit assessment institutions (ECAIs), subordinated debt and cases on bank distress in Bangladesh. The third tract (Chapter 8 and 9) offers a set of pragmatic way out to the decision makers to build a resilience capital regulation and reaping the potential benefits from implementation of Basel Accords in Bangladesh, summary of the entire study and future research issues.

This book challenges the conventional explanations of Bangladeshi financial instability and suggests a different set of failures that affected the Bangladeshi banking system. In this book, we analyze a funding and liability structure of Bangladeshi banks; to maintain the minimum capital adequacy ratio, Bangladeshi private commercial banks were forced to tap into subordinated debts (sub-debt) as Tier 2 capital on the one hand, and the bulk of public money was injected constantly to recapitalize the state-owned commercial banks on the other hand. This practice in funding in this decade (2009–2018) undermined the banking resilience and increased the systemic risk of the financial system. In fact, Bangladeshi banks were not able to build sustainable retained earnings due partly to the loan loss provisioning and the payout pressure of cash dividends to their equity holders. We shed an analytical light on the ill-by-product of Basel Accords such that the banks tend to increase sub-debt as Tier 2 capital just to maintain the minimum capital to risk-weighted assets ratio (CRAR). In this book, we also analyze that the naïve and excess reliance on ECAIs' credit rating in the process of adopting the Basel-type capital adequacy amounted to a risky strategy for the Bangladeshi banking industry. As an endorsement for our discussions, we raise several cases of bank distresses for understanding the Bangladeshi banking sector malaise from the Basel Accord perspective. We believe that this book will contribute to further discussions on the possible ill-by-product of the internationally standardized Accords which do not necessarily have the universal applicability.

Beppu, Japan   A K M Kamrul Hasan
February 2021   Yasushi Suzuki

Acknowledgments

The authors thank Vishal Daryanomel, Commissioning Editor at the Palgrave Macmillan for his enthusiasm and help. We also would like to thank the anonymous referees for their comments and suggestions on manuscript. We would be more than happy if this book encourages further studies in the Institutional Economics of Banking and Financial Institutions.

A K M Kamrul Hasan would like to express gratitude to his honorable supervisor Professor Dr. Yasushi Suzuki for rigorous supervision and intellectual guidance throughout the research. Words are not enough to express the gratitude toward the Professor. Special thanks to the senior officials of various public bodies, corporates, professionals and academics who shared their valuable times for this academic research.

Yasushi Suzuki would like to acknowledge that several years of the Finance and Economics postgraduate seminar members, including Dr. Kamrul Hasan, at Ritsumeikan Asia Pacific University incubated some arguments in this book. Their enthusiasm, support, comments and criticism were invaluable.

CONTENTS

ABOUT THE AUTHORS

A K M Kamrul Hasan received his Ph.D. (Focusing on Banking and Financial Institutions) from Ritsumeikan Asia Pacific University, Beppu, Oita, Japan. His research interest includes banking regulations, financial stability, venture capital, corporate governance, etc.

Yasushi Suzuki is a Professor of Finance at Ritsumeikan Asia Pacific University, Japan. His research interest focuses on theories of banking, Islamic finance, public finance, institutional political economy, philosophy of economics, etc.

Abbreviations

ALCO	Asset and liability management committee
BB	Bangladesh bank
BDT	Bangladesh taka
BIS	Bank for international settlements
BSEC	Bangladesh securities and exchange commission
CRAR	Capital to risk-weighted assets ratio
CRAs	Credit rating agencies
CRC	Credit rating company
ECAIs	External credit assessment institutions
IRB	Internal ratings-based approach for credit risk
NPL	Non-performing loans
ROA	Return on assets
ROE	Return on equity
RWA	Risk-weighted assets
SA	Standardised approach for credit risk
Sub-debt	Subordinated debt
USD	United States Dollar

LIST OF FIGURES

LIST OF TABLES

CHAPTER 1

Introduction

1.1 INTRODUCTION

The classical definition of 'risk' and 'uncertainty' that was provided by Frank Knight for an imperfect market is still relevant to understand systemic risk in the modern financial sector. According to Knight, risk is quantifiable by mathematical probability for success or failure whereas in the case of uncertainty it is not possible to know the outcome—rather, subjective judgment is applied to deal with uncertainty as the situation is unique in each case and decisions vary from case to case (Knight, 1921). However, Stockhammer and Ramskogler (2007) point out that John Maynard Keynes viewed the world as having different degrees of uncertainty rather than as a 'dichotomy of uncertainty' and 'probabilistic certainty' as identified by Knight. The 'fundamental uncertainty' is a key concept in the post-Keynesian discussion. Meaningful economic activities are considered as those for reducing and mitigating 'uncertainty' in the post-Keynesian tradition. On the other hand, institutional economists believe that institutions as rules can reduce uncertainty. North (2005) argues that the institutional framework can create the incentives structure which would matter for reducing uncertainties. All business and investments are subject to fundamental uncertainties in the sense that the future is unknown. Therefore, the credit risk undertaken by bankers cannot be reduced to 'risk' as measurable uncertainties. In this context, the regulatory framework as a formal institution would be required to encourage

A K M K. Hasan and Y. Suzuki, *Implementation of Basel Accords in Bangladesh*, https://doi.org/10.1007/978-981-16-3472-7_1

banks to challenge themselves to absorb fundamental uncertainties while preventing them from taking excess risk and uncertainty.

The Basel Accord was first introduced in 1988 by the Bank for International Settlement (BIS) as a regulatory tool to respond to frequent bank failures in Western economies in 1980s. Capital to risk-weighted assets ratio (CRAR) is the core method in the Basel Accord, the primary objective of which is to encourage banks to maintain a certain capital buffer to prevent them from taking a 'leveraging' strategy (Suzuki, 2011). In this framework, the regulated banks are expected to maintain the minimum CRAR. The theoretical implication of Basel regulation is that it would discourage banks to take excess credit risk, perhaps having a 'negative' impact on loan growth, consequently having a 'positive' impact on the constraint or reduction of NPL. One of the big puzzles is that although Bangladesh adopted the Basel Accords many years ago, the case of the Bangladeshi banking industry does not endorse the above implication. In the following sub-section, we portray the realities faced by the Bangladeshi banking sector during 2009 and 2018.

1.2   STATE OF BANGLADESHI BANKING SECTOR REALITIES IN 2009–2018 AND BASEL ACCORD

Bangladesh has achieved a steady GDP growth (more than 6% on an average) during the last decade (MoF, 2019) and met the graduation criteria to leave the least developed countries (LDCs) categories in 2018 and potentially graduate to a lower-middle income country in 2024 (UN, 2018). However, the financial condition of the banking sector continues to deteriorate despite steady GDP growth. According to 'Global Competitiveness Report 2019', the macroeconomic stability and financial system of the country have been downgraded in the last decade and Bangladesh has been ranked as the 105th out of 141 countries in overall global competitiveness index (WEF, 2019). As per the 'Doing Business Report-2020' of the World Bank which measures business regulations and their enforcements on 11 parameters, the country has ranked at 168th out of 190 countries across the globe in 2020 from the 110th in 2009 (WB, 2019). Indeed, country's overall performance, competitiveness of financial system and quality of institutions are reflected in those global indices. Besides taking cross country scenario into account, the CRAR of the country's banking sector was weak compared to the ratios of major South Asian Economies in last decade (see Fig. 1.1; Table 1.1 in Annexure for

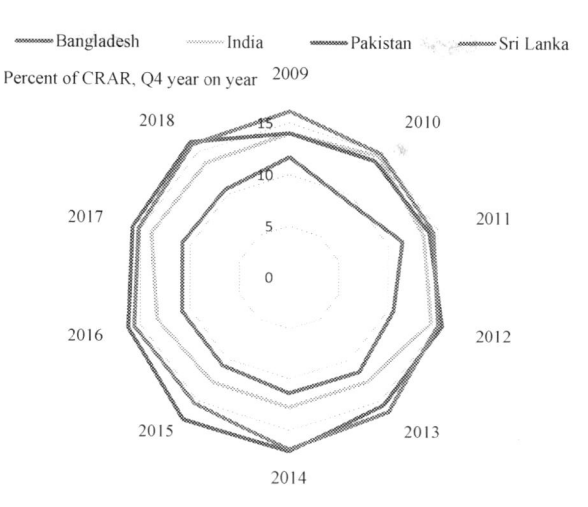

Percent of CRAR, Q4 year on year 2009

Fig. 1.1 Comparisons of CRAR among major South Asian Economies between 2009 and 2018 (*Source* IMF, Financial Soundness Indicators (FSIs). Retrieved on 26 June 2020)

financial soundness indicators (FSIs) of banking sector of the major South Asian economies and few advanced economies such as Japan, the US and the UK between 2016 and 2019). As of December 2018, the Tier 1 capital ratio of Bangladesh, India, Pakistan and Sri Lanka were 6.8, 11.9, 13.3 and 12.0%, respectively (see Table 1.1 in Annexure), which reveals that the country's banking sector core capital ratio is exceptionally thin and vulnerable compared to its South Asian peers.

In fact, Bangladesh introduced the 'capital to risk-weighted assets'-based approach for assessing the capital adequacy of banks, replacing the 'capital to liabilities' approach in 1996. More specifically, the Basel-type risk-based capital adequacy framework (hereafter, Basel Accords), the Basel Accords II and III were formally introduced in 2009 and 2015, respectively. Nevertheless, among 57 scheduled banks, only 34 banks were able to maintain the 10% minimum 'Capital to risk-weighted assets ratio' (hereafter CRAR) plus the conservation buffer of 1.875% in addition to CRAR at the end of December 2018. The banking system resilience found itself vulnerable to credit defaults after stress tests at different levels (BB, 2018). The country's non-performing loans (NPL) to total loans and advances ratio stood at 10.3% as of December 2018 whereas the shortfall of loan loss provisions was BDT 66.1 billion during the same period (BB, 2018). The situation became worse in 2019Q3, when the NPL ratio reached 11.99% which amounted BDT 1.16 trillion in levels, and the shortfall of loans loss provisioning stood at BDT 81.3 billion (BB, 2019). In particular as on 2019Q3, the state-owned commercial banks' NPLs were around 30% of total loans, with an additional 20% classified as rescheduled and restructured whereas private commercial banks have a total of around 5% NPLs and 10% classified as rescheduled and restructured (Moody, 2020). It is argued that the loan default has created a significant risk to the country's financial stability by lowering the CRAR of its banking sector (IMF, 2019; WB, 2019) whereas the central bank opined that the negative relationship between bank performance and NPL is a vicious cycle which the banking sector fails to break (BB, 2018). See Table 1.2 in Annexure which compares the indicators of profitability, NPL and CRAR between 2009 and 2018.

Indeed, several initiatives have been taken by the central bank (Bangladesh Bank) to enhance the sustainability of the banking sector; however, its overall performance has not improved. For example, in order to deal with the huge NPL, BDT 164.1 billion default loans, which was 17.4% of total NPL, were restructured and stretched for another 12 years under a special scheme in 2015. In addition, the banks were encouraged to write off a total of BDT 410.71 billion in bad loans during 2009 and 2018 which was expected to help to downsize the RWA as well as to improve the CRAR. But the NPL soared over the years. We observe that the Bangladeshi private commercial banks as well as state-owned commercial banks (SCBs) tend to issue subordinated debt (sub-debt) as Tier 2 capital to maintain minimum CRAR. The sub-debt is a kind of debt instrument which is subordinated to deposits and other liabilities of the bank and it is recognized as Tier 2 regulatory capital under the Basel framework in 1988. In fact, a total of BDT 242.75 billion sub-debt has been issued by commercial banks as Tier 2 capital to maintain the minimum CRAR between 2009 and 2018. In parallel, the government has injected a total of BDT 157.05 billion from the public funds into SCBs for their recapitalization between FY 2009 and 2017.

The weak performance of the banking sector may have adversely affected the country's Gross Domestic Product (GDP). For instance, the share of the banking sector's contribution to the country's Gross Domestic Product (GDP) dropped to 7.38% in FY 2018–19 from 12.98% in FY 2010–11. Since the banking industry per se is a large sector in the

Bangladeshi economy, when the banking sector's profits were hampered by the accumulation or writing-off of NPL, in turn, its contribution to GDP would decrease. Besides, the lost opportunity to mediate financial resources to the corporate sector must have been huge. If the Bangladeshi banking sector had improved its performance earlier, the private corporate sector would have borrowed more loans to realize their investments. We should note that recent Bangladeshi economic growth comes to depend more on public investment instead of private investment. Probably bad loans shrink the lending capacity of the commercial banks.

What brought the huge accumulation of NPL in the Bangladeshi banking sector? Some scholars explain it referring to the crony capitalism and rent-seeking theory contributed by Aligica and Tarco (2014), Khan (2000, 2017), Krueger (1974, 2002), Roberts (2010), Tullock (2005), and so on. Some scholars attempt to explain it referring to the corporate governance theory contributed to by Alchian and Demstez (1972), Aoki (2001), Fama (1980), Fitch (2019), Jensen and Meckling (1976), Williamson (1984), and so on. Suzuki and Hasan (2018) suggest that the weak corporate governance system embedded in the fundamental structure of ownership concentration in the Bangladeshi banking sector amplified its malaise.

This study aims to raise another discourse such that the Basel framework has given Bangladeshi banks an ill-incentive or moral hazard in their credit risk management, leading to the huge accumulation of NPL. This hypothesis is drawn from the contributions by the 'Regulation' school of economics including Freixas et al. (2015), analyzing the relationship between the systemic risk in banking and microprudential regulations. Also, this study applies an institutional approach to understanding how the Basel regulations as formal institutions (rules) have created ill-incentives (or weak mechanism of giving adequate sanctions) for the economic players in the Bangladeshi banking sector, consequently deteriorating the overall outcomes of the rules. Little in the academic debate has been addressed to shed analytical light on the impact of Basel regulations on the Bangladeshi banking sector as one of the root causes of the huge accumulation of NPL.

1.3   Scope of Research
and Anomalies in the Banking Sector

CRAR is the amount of regulatory capital (RC) divided by the amount of risk-weighted assets (RWA) [e.g., CRAR = RC/RWA]. Hence, to understand the impact of the Basel Accords, it is required to understand how RWA is computed in the regulatory and operational context of Bangladesh and what the components that constitute RC are. Under the regulations upon Basel Accord II and III, the 'standardized approach' (SA) was promoted by the Bangladesh Bank (BB) while computing the credit risk. Hence, it is reasonable to investigate what the standardized approach (SA) is like and how it is implemented in Bangladesh. Since the regulator encouraged all the banks to adopt the SA, aiming to standardize the method of measuring credit risk in each bank, we should check the viability and quality of the standardized method. In addition, even if the method is considerably viable, we should check whether the homogenization of credit information contributed to improving the resilience of the banking sector in Bangladesh. We should note that under SA, ECAIs rating notches on exposures are allowed while assigning the credit risk weight on the bank's credit portfolio for the purpose of calculating capital adequacy. Hence, in this study, we are concerned with the impact of the implementation of the Basel Accords in Bangladesh, looking at the incentives created by the Basel regulations in particular, credit rating agencies (CRAs)/external credit assessment institutions (ECAIs). In addition, we should ask how the Bangladeshi banks could expand their loan exposure so extraordinarily fast under the Basel regulations. This is another puzzle because the primary objective of Basel regulation is to prevent banks from taking the 'leveraging' strategy by asking them to maintain a capital buffer. In order to tackle the puzzle, we investigate the impact of subordinated debt which is allowed as a component of regulatory capital under Tier 2 capital in Basel framework. In the Accord, the funding of sub-debt is expected to enhance the market discipline facilitating the control of the risk appetite in banks. However, it is apparent that the expected market discipline has not yet been achieved in Bangladesh. We are concerned about the regulatory framework of subordinated debt as a Tier 2 regulatory capital, which is considered an ill-incentive for Bangladeshi banks to leave their dismal credit portfolio unresolved. To wrap up, this research shed analytical light on three pillars to discuss the issues mentioned above. First, we critically assess the Basel regulatory framework, institutions regarding the CRAs and ECAIs as well as subordinated debt in Bangladesh (this pillar will be discussed in Chapter 4). Then, we examine the CRAs/ECAIs incentive and liability regime and their limited quality of rating which is reflected in the computation of RWA (this pillar will be discussed in Chapter 5). Next, we analyze the role of subordinated debt as a regulatory capital to explain as a unique problem observed in the case of Bangladesh (this pillar will be discussed in Chapter 6). Lastly, we offer several cases on bank distress as an evidence of the discussion on three pillars.

Anomalies in the Bangladeshi Banking Sector

Finally, from the above discussion, we wish to summarize the following anomalies/puzzles observed in the Bangladeshi banking industry under the implementation of Basel regulations since 2009.

(i) The Basel Accord aims to constrain the risk appetite in banks, discouraging them from expanding loan exposure (expecting a negative relationship with loan growth) and consequently contributing to financial stability. As was observed earlier, the Bangladeshi case suggests that the adoption of Basel regulations had a positive relationship with loan growth in Bangladeshi banks and the resulting negative impact on its financial stability. NPLs have been constantly accumulated in accordance with the rapid expansion of loan exposure in banks.

(ii) In spite of the financial turmoil, generally, ROE (especially in case of private commercial banks; see Table 1.2 in Annexure) tends to be increased while CRAR is maintained in Bangladeshi banks.

How can we make sense of the anomalies related to the above (i)? What kinds of incentives were given to the bank managers since the adoption of Basel regulations in Bangladesh? We assume that the ill-designed adoption of Basel regulations in Bangladesh is the root cause of the anomalies. The computation of RWA for credit risk is crucial as it is the denominator part in the calculation of required CRAR. As was mentioned earlier, under the regulations upon Basel Accords II and III, the 'standardized approach' (SA) was promoted by BB to compute credit risk. We should review *the role of ECAIs in the adoption of Basel regulations in Bangladesh and* hypothesize that *the rating offered by ECAIs fails to capture the accurate credit risk, consequently deteriorating the credit portfolio in Bangladeshi banks.*

How can we make sense of the anomaly related to the above (ii)? We hypothesize that *the lack of prudence in funding sub-debt may allow the Bangladeshi banks to take the 'leveraging' strategy and to write off NPL without paying efforts to improve their credit risk screening.* As a result, the above anomaly is considered to occur. So far as the regulatory capital (RC) as the numerator of capital adequacy ratio remains unchanged, a higher RWA would lead to a lower ratio. The objective of setting the minimum CRAR under Basel regulations is to encourage banks to increase the RC base as a cushion for unexpected loss. We should note that retained earnings are one of the major sources for Tier 1 capital. One of the alternative options for banks is to increase Tier 2 capital (for instance issuance of sub-debt) to keep the CRAR, as retained earnings were not built up due to loan loss provisioning. Besides, presumably, many Bangladeshi banks tapped into sub-debt for the purpose of writing off the NPL without paying efforts to improve their credit risk screening. Rather, we assume that the lack of prudence in funding the sub-debt may allow the Bangladeshi banks to take the 'leveraging' strategy. We name this vicious cycle as the 'sub-debt trap.'

1.4   Silent Contributions of the Research

Several rounds of research have been conducted on the economic development and financial sector performance of the country from a political economy perspective. Some scholars mentioned that financial crimes related to trade-based money laundering (Habib, Ahmed, et al., 2017; Habib, Zareen, et al., 2017) heighten non-performing loans, while some adopt the 'financial restraint model' to explain the inefficiencies in managing credit risks by Bangladeshi banks (Suzuki & Adhikary, 2009) and some identified the poor enforcement of laws regarding the settlements of NPLs aggravated the financial malaise (Adhikary, 2006). However, the discussion on quality of credit risk quantification using ECAIs rating notch (i.e., ECAIs rating accuracy under a Basel Accord perspective) is almost overlooked in the Bangladesh context by the contemporary researchers. On the other hand, in the international context a significant amount of academic research has been conducted on the effect of the Basel Accords comprised of single country study to multi-country study from different perspectives but 'sub-debt trap' was not discussed anywhere. Besides truly little in the way of academic research has been addressed to explain the disastrous realities of the Bangladeshi banking sector from the institutional economics perspective. Hence, this study fills a lacuna in the existing debate on the Bangladeshi banking resilience from Basel Accord perspective and the study concentrates on the ECAIs 'incentive' and 'liability regime' in the existing regulations and the role of subordinated debt as a regulatory capital. In summary, the study provides the curious readers a clear understanding on how the ill-designed adoption of Basel regulations in Bangladesh, leaving the poor quality of Bangladeshi ECAIs unsolved. The case of Bangladesh would help them mapping the ECAIs rating accuracy of developing countries context. Also, we believe that this study sheds an analytical light on the new concept of the 'sub-debt trap' to explain the anomaly in the Bangladeshi banking sector and examines the fallacy of sub-debt with empirical analyses with special reference to Bangladesh.

On top of that, the book also provides practical solutions to several stakeholders. For instance, it will provide a message to the global and national regulators of CRAs that the existing institutions need to review to the installation of appropriate incentives and create a liability regime for ECAIs. It will be helpful for policy makers while reforming the dubious regulatory capital components like sub-debt to avoid 'sub-debt trap' that we observed in case of Bangladesh.

1.5   Organization of the Chapters

This book consists of nine chapters including introduction and conclusion. Chapter 2 discusses the historical backgrounds of establishment of BIS. It also sheds light on the historical events that lead to initiation of the Basel Accords by BIS. Chapter 3 presents the modern economic theories on banking business model and banking regulations. It helps the readers to understand the theoretical framework of the capital regulation as a microprudential regulation and how it contributes to stop bank runs and enhance the resilience of the financial system. Besides, existing academic debate on reliance on CRA ratings for banking regulations and sub-debt's role in the Basel framework is also discussed in this chapter to aid the discussion on Chapters 5 and 6. Chapter 4 briefly discusses on an institutional economist view on regulations. Then, it proceeds on details of credit risk quantification approaches that advocate in Basel framework. The chapter also offers a comprehensive institutional analysis of Basel Accord associated institutions in Bangladesh, i.e., ECAIs regulations and sub-debt regulations in Bangladesh context. Chapter 5 contains a thorough discussion on the incentive issues of ECAIs in Bangladesh. It helps to understand how ECAIs' business model affects their rating accuracy and quality under these two issues. Chapter 6 presents the discussion on the subordinated debt. It also discusses the lack of prudence in funding sub-debt by banks which creates systemic risk in the financial sector. In addition, to what extent the 'sub-debt trap' will last in the Bangladeshi financial sector is briefly discussed in this part. Chapter 7 offers several bank distress cases in Bangladesh as an evidence of prior discussions in the study. It offers an inclusive discussion on the central bank act from institutional perspectives. Finally, Chapter 8 provides policy recommendations for designing a robust capital regulation considering Bangladesh context. It offers pragmatic policy prescriptions on how to utilize the sub-debt under the Basel Accord philosophy efficiently. It also offers policy implications to the Bangladeshi regulators to ensure potential benefit from ECAIs exposure rating. The book ends with the summary of this academic work and with providing future research thoughts based on Basel Accord in Chapter 9.

1.6   Concluding Remarks

The chapter provides a quick snapshot of the entire research work. It discussed the role of institutions to tackle the fundamental uncertainties in business. It also discussed the economic realities in the Bangladeshi banking sector, the anomalies that observed during Basel Accord implementation phase and the research scope of the study. We also specify the silent contributions of the book which would expect to fill the research gaps in the banking regulations literature. Finally, the chapter presented a brief outline of the entire book chapters. In a word, this chapter clearly highlights that the contemporary debate on Bangladeshi banking sector malaise can be explained from institutional perspectives because institutions matter.

REFERENCES

Adhikary, B. K. (2006). Nonperforming loans in the banking sector of Bangladesh: Realities and challenges. *Ritsumeikan Journal of Asia Pacific Studies, 21*, 75–95.

Alchian, A., & Demsetz, H. (1972). Production, information costs, and economic organization. *The American Economic Review, 62*(5), 777–795.

Aligica, P. D., & Tarco, V. (2014). Crony capitalism: Rent seeking, institutions and ideology. *Kyklos, 67*(2), 156–176. https://doi.org/10.1111/kykl.12048.

Aoki, M. (2001). *Towards a comparative institutional analysis*. The MIT Press.

Bangladesh Bank (BB). (2018). *Financial Stability Report, 2018, Issue 9*. Financial Stability Department, Bangladesh Bank. https://www.bb.org.bd/pub/index.php.

Bangladesh Bank (BB). (2019). *Bangladesh Bank Quarterly, July–September 2019, Volume XVII, No. 1*. Bangladesh Bank.

Fama, E. F. (1980). The agency problem and the theory of firms. *Journal of Political Economy, 88*(2), 288–307.

Fitch Ratings (Fitch). (2019). *Sovereigns Bangladesh: Rating Report 30 December 2019*. Retrieved June 18 2020 from Bangladesh Bank: https://www.bb.org.bd/.

Freixas, X., Leven, L., & Peydro, J. (2015). *Systemic risk, crises, and macroprudential regulation*. The MIT Press.

Habib, S. M. A., Ahmed, N., Pandit, A. C., Nayn, Z., & Hossain, M. K. (2017). *Addressing financial crime in the banking sector of Bangladesh* (Banking Research Series 2016—Paper One). Bangladesh Institute of Bank Management (BIBM).

Habib, S. M. A., Zareen, A., Ahmed, T., Rahman, M. A., Hossain, K., Rahman, M., & Hoque, A. T. M. N. (2017). *Trade services operations of banks* (Banking Research Series 2017—Paper Two). Bangladesh Institute of Bank Management (BIBM).

International Monetary Fund (IMF). (2019). *2019 Article IV Consultation: Staff Report*. International Monetary Fund.

Jensen, M., & Meckling, W. H. (1976). Theory of the firm: Managerial behavior, agency costs, and capital structure. *Journal of Financial Economics, 3*, 305–360.

Khan, M. (2000). Rent seeking as a process. In M. Khan & K. S. Jomo (Eds.), *Rent, Rent- seeking and economic development* (pp.70–144). Cambridge University Press.

Khan, M. (2017). Debate: Political settlements and analysis of institutions. *African Affairs, 117*(696), 636–655.

Knight, F. H. (1921). *Risk, uncertainty and profit*. Sentry Press.

Krueger, A. O. (1974). The political economy of the rent-seeking society. *American Economic Review, 64*(3), 291–303.

Krueger, A. O. (2002). *A new approach to Sovereign debt restructuring*. International Monetary Fund.

Ministry of Finance (MoF). (2019). *Bangladesh economic review*. Finance Division, Ministry of Finance, Government of the people's Republic of Bangladesh. https://mof.portal.gov.bd/site/page/28ba57f5-59ff4426-970a-bf014242179e/Bangladesh-Economic-Review.

Moody's Investors Service (Moody). (2020). *Government of Bangladesh: Annual credit analysis: issuer in-depth 18 May 2020*. Retrieved June 25, 2020 from Bangladesh Bank: https://www.bb.org.bd/.

North, D. C. (2005). *Understanding the process of economic change*. Princeton University Press.

Roberts, J. M. (2010). Cronyism: Undermining economic freedom and prosperity around the world. *Backgrounder, 2447*. http://thf_media.s3.amazonaws.com/2010/pdf/bg2447.pdf.

Stockhammer, E., & Ramskogler, P. (2007). *Uncertainty and exploitation in history* (Working Paper No. 104). Department of Economics, Vienna University of Economics and Business Administration. https://doi.org/10.1.1.334.4248.

Suzuki, Y. (2011). *Japan's Financial Slump: Collapse of the monitoring system under institutional and transitional failures*. Palgrave Macmillan.

Suzuki, Y., & Adhikary, B. K. (2009, April). *A "Bank Rent" approach to understanding the development of the banking system in Bangladesh* (Working Paper Series, RCAPS Working Paper No. 09). Ritsumeikan Center for Asia Pacific Studies, Ritsumeikan Asia Pacific University.

Suzuki, Y., & Hasan, A. K. M. K. (2018). An analysis of codified corporate governance practice in the banking industry: The case study of Bangladesh. *Financial Internet Quarterly e-Finanse, 14*(3), 60–75. https://doi.org/10.2478/fiqf-2018-0020.

Tullock, G. (2005). *The selected works of Gordon Tullock: Vol. 5. The rent-seeking society*. Liberty Fund.

United Nations (UN). (2018, March 12–16). *Committee for Development Policy: Report on the twentieth session*. United Nations Economic and Social Council (ECOSOC), United Nations.

Williamson, O. E. (1984). Corporate governance. *The Yale Law Journal, 93*, 1197–1230.

World Bank (WB). (2019). *Doing business 2020*. The World Bank.

World Economic Forum (WEF). (2019). *The Global Competitiveness Report 2019*. The World Economic Forum.

CHAPTER 2

BIS and the Basel Accord: Looking Back at History

2.1 Introduction

The Bank for International Settlements (BIS) was officially inaugurated in Rome on February 27, 1930 (Toniolo, 2005), with signing the agreements by seven nations (Belgium, France, Germany, Italy, Japan, the UK and Switzerland) and now sixty-two central banks are members of the BIS (BIS, 2019a). The core objectives of the establishment of the BIS were to manage reparation payments required to be made by Germany under the Treaty of Versailles following World War I (BIS, 2019b; Seabrooke, 2006). Other reasons for the establishment of this institution include the dominance of the dollar that surpassed sterling as a source of trade credit during and after World War I (WW I), which created the necessity for acceptance of bills in dollars for European countries (Eichengreen & Flandreau, 2011). On the other hand, Basel Accord first initiated by the BIS in response to the several chaos observed in the international banking arena in 1980s. The chapter comprehensively discusses those issues of BIS and Basel Accords from historical grounds. The structure of the chapter is as follows. Section 2.2 provides a summary of the historical background of the establishment of the BIS and its role on bringing financial stability in the Western European market. Section 2.3 discusses the establishment of

BCBS by BIS, turmoil of global financial industry in the 1980s and initiation of the Basel Accord by the BIS. Section 2.4 highlights the role of capital in Basel Accord and key reasons for reforms in the Basel Accords. Section 2.5 presents concluding remarks.

2.2 Initiation of BIS and Its Role in Western Financial System

Gold standard and Central bank cooperation in the pre-BIS era:

Economic historian Toniolo (2005) categorized nineteenth-century monetary standards into three: (i) gold standard bloc, (ii) silver-standard bloc and (iii) bimetallic bloc. Gold standard bloc was dominated by the UK, its colonies and Portugal which mainly was based on the concept of convertibility of paper money into gold at the price set by Sir Isaac Newton in 1717. The US, France, Belgium, Switzerland and Italy adopted the bimetallic standard which has the dual option of conversion of paper notes (either gold or silver, at a fixed rate between two), whereas the rest of the European countries, Scandinavian countries and major parts of Asia, adopted the silver standard (Toniolo, 2005). In the late nineteenth century (1860s), there was observed a trend to switch to the gold standard mainly due to the UK's power in the global financial industry and the trend continued until World War I, which was termed by Toniolo (2005) as the 'classical period' of the gold standard (1870s to 1914). On the other hand, historical events and documents provide evidence that there existed some mistrust and less transactions among European central banks like Britain, France and Russia during the period of 1800s to 1914 (Flandreau, 1997). There was no 'predominant pattern' for cooperative transaction among major central banks; rather, it was on an ad hoc basis and a non-institutionalized one (Flandreau, 1997). For example, Toniolo (2005) while quoting from Clapham (1944) mentions that the 'Baring crisis' of 1890 in the UK has lowered the gold reserve in the Bank of England (BOE), and consequently, to prevent the occurrence of a 'run of gold', the BOE had borrowed gold from the central banks of France and Russia. Similarly, the US had borrowed gold from the BOE during the US 'bankers' panic' in 1907 (Eichengreen, 1992). Therefore, such an ad hoc type of cooperation among central banks was not a product of bilateral interest rather unilateral interest (Flandreau, 1997). However, during World War I, the US and European countries put an embargo on international gold transactions, resulting in suspending the gold standard during wartime (Brown, 1940). After World War I, there was a generally agreed upon point to return to the international gold standard; however, the main dispute was on whether it would be 'pre-war parities' or 'new gold parities' (p. 227). The debate continued, and both the US and Britain had significantly increased their gold reserve through imports (Brown, 1940). British economists Keynes and Hawtrey and Swede economist Cassell recommended to fix the new gold parities based on the current purchasing power of each national currency, and the countries whose currencies had depreciated far more than the pound had supported the proposition (Toniolo, 2005). At the end, the result of the race between the US and European countries was decentralization of the global financial system from London and France to New York between 1924 and 1928.

These historical events evidence that there was absence of a truly multilateral cooperation among developed economies' central banks till World War I; rather, European nations' states were engaged to maximize their own nation states' economic interest through unilateral cooperation. We shall note that the agenda for the establishment of an international body to cooperate with central banks was first raised in the International Monetary Conference in Paris in 1881; however, no resolution was made in the conference. Rather, some theoretical and practical issues regarding cooperation among central banks were discussed (Toniolo, 2005). The second conference in 1892 in Brussels also failed to bring any meaningful developments on central banks' role on the common ratio between gold and silver standard (Schenk & Straumann, 2014). Professor Julius Wolff proposed to create an international currency in this conference and later published a theoretical paper on the essence of an international clearinghouse (Toniolo, 2005). Luigi Luzzatti, a prominent Italian politician who attended the Paris Conference in 1881, first concisely wrote about the essence of international cooperation among central banks in Europe in the Italian dailies, spoke at various European conferences of central banks between 1907 and 1912. In fact, Europeans were amazed by the establishment of the Federal Reserve in the US in 1913 and many of them had considered the Federal Reserve as a benchmark for the establishment of an international central bank in Europe (Toniolo, 2005). The first post-World War I conference in Brussels in 1920 and second conference in Genoa in 1922 were to act as a perfect foundation to work to establish an international central bank cooperation concept instead of a Federal Reserve-type bank concept (Toniolo, 2005). Although the main concern in Genoa conference was more on bringing economic and political stability to restore the war-effected European economy and its political system (Bakic, 2011), the conference agreed to keep the central bank independent from 'political order' and the BOE was asked to organize a conference of central bankers to adopt the agenda (Toniolo, 2005).

Some scholars argued that the defeat of Germany, at the hands of the Triple Entente in World War I, and the subsequent German reparations to the Entente as per the 'peace treaty' also played an important role in the establishment of the BIS. For instance, Keynes (1919) in his book 'The Economic Consequences of Peace' analyzed the clause of the treaty and its reparation process in detail. He recommends revising the treaty arguing that some of the clauses are quite impossible to fulfill for the German Empire and the reparation system that was fixed is beyond the capacity of Germany (pp. 256–268). It is worth to quote 'the Treaty includes no provisions for the economic rehabilitation of Europe, nothing to make the defeated Central Powers into good neighbors, nothing to stabilize the new states of Europe, nothing to reclaim Russia; nor does it promote in any way a compact of economic solidarity amongst the Allies themselves; no arrangement war reached at Paris for restoring the disordered finances of France and Italy, or to adjust the systems of the Old World and the New' (Keynes, 1919, p. 226). Later, in 1924, through the Dawes plan (in which the US is encouraged to cooperate with the UK, French, Belgium and Italian governments), the allied powers had revised the reparation payment (Toniolo, 2005) which indicated that Keynes was conceptually right to explain the potential outcomes of the treaty and irrational reparation process to Germany in early 1920. The next section illustrates how the Dawes plan leads the European countries to set up the BIS.

German Reparation and Institutionalization of BIS:

As the German economy was turmoil in 1923 and was not strong enough to make reparations to France and Belgium, two ad hoc committees were formed by US persuasion, one was to identify the strategy to balance the German budget and another was to stabilize the exchange rate (Toniolo, 2005). Both committees were chaired by retired American General Charles Dawes (although the US govt. did not directly participate in the committees, it did, however, allow its citizens to participate in the process). The committee's proposal was termed as the 'Dawes

Plan' which was approved on August 30, 1924. The important outcome of the plan was to reschedule the German reparations considering the country's economic strength and ability to pay (Toniolo, 2005). The plan is considered as the first international response to solve the problem of Germany's indebtedness (Bederman, 1988). Indeed, the plan helped Germany to get loans from the other central banks while issuing debt, consequently increasing its currency reserve (Bederman, 1988). Besides, it helped the economy to boom as huge US short-term capital inflows entered the German market (Toniolo, 2005). However, the US's great recession of the 1930s had already started and the Federal Reserve increased the interest rate which adversely affected the entire European economy (a kind of 'contraction effect') including Germany. In turn, Germany defaulted paying the scheduled installment of reparations and France wanted to commercialize German debt while Germany wanted to increase its payment time (Toniolo, 2005). In this situation, the Belgian, UK, French, German, Italian and Japanese delegates met at the League of Nations in Geneva in 1928 and jointly declared to make a committee of experts to work out a final and full settlement of German reparations. Owen D. Young (an experienced American financial diplomat, who also co-author of Dawes plan) was made the Chairman of the committee and finalized the German reparations into 59 annual payments. After being signed by seven participating countries on June 7, 1929, the expert's report was termed as the 'Young Plan' and the plan recommend establishment of a bank for final settlements (Toniolo, 2005).

Scholars agreed that the Young plan in 1929 had opened the door to cooperation among central banks and mutual agreement on the establishment of the BIS (Bederman, 1988; Fratianni & Pattison, 2001; Toniolo, 2005). According to the plan, the Baden-Baden committee fixed the organization structure of the BIS (Bederman, 1988), and later, it was further rectified in the Hague Conference in 1930 (Hughes & Palke, 2019). Finally, under the Hague agreement of 1930, the BIS was established (BIS, 2019b). The inauguration of the BIS was welcomed by major European and US daily commentators. In fact, founding of the BIS served all concerned parties' interests in the 1920s expectation which Fratianni and Pattison (2001) mentioned while quoting from Schloss (1958) 'The French wanted it because they hoped it would help them mobilize their share of the German indemnity, that is, to substitute progressively a debt by Germany to private investors in all countries for a debt to the French Government. The Germans wanted it because they hoped it could help them in bringing about the necessary expansion of their export trade. The British wanted it because they hoped it would help solve the gold problem about which they were already seriously concerned' (Fratianni & Pattison, 2001, pp. 198–199).

The role of BIS in global financial system:

In its first annual report in 1931, the BIS clearly describes its objectives in the following way 'one of the objects of the Bank is to facilitate collaboration between Central Banks whose currencies satisfy the practical requirements of the gold or gold exchange standard - collaboration not only in connection with the maintenance of monetary stability but also in connection with a better organization of credit in the respective markets and the facilitation of international capital transactions......... The Bank is acting as Trustee or Agent in connection with the following international financial settlements and transactions: the receipt, administration and distribution of the German annuity payments specified by the New Plan adopted at The Hague in January 1930; the receipt and distribution of funds payable pursuant to the terms of the Hague Agreements of January 1930, by Bulgaria, by Hungary and by Czechoslovakia; the receipt and distribution, as Fiscal Agent of the Trustees for the German External Loan 1924, of the funds requisite for the service of that Loan; the receipt and distribution of the funds relative to the service of the German Government International 5.5% Loan 1930; the receipt and distribution of the funds necessary for the service of the Austrian Government International Loan 1930' (BIS, 1931, pp. 6–8). Therefore, the BIS works as an international forum of central bank cooperation and settlements since its inception (Hughes & Palke, 2019). In addition, the BIS acted as a 'crisis manager' during the financial panic in Europe in 1931 (Toniolo, 2005), as trustee to emergency loans of Bulgaria, Czechoslovakia and Hungary in 1931 (Bederman, 1988). In 1934, the bank also arranged the short-term loans for the Reichsbank, the National Bank of Hungary, and the National Bank of Austria and organized syndicates for emergency credits to Hungary and Germany (Bederman, 1988). However, there are two failures of the BIS in the 1930s, as noted by Toniolo (2005), such as (i) it could not stop the abandonment of gold standard (due to the failure of the London Conference in 1933 to stabilize the exchange rate) and (ii) full settlement of Germany's reparations (as Hitler stopped the reparations in 1934 while the weak external reserve position as an excuse). Anyway, we should consider the then European political and economic crisis as being largely responsible for these two events. Indeed, as an international settlement institution, the BIS was helpless to produce a meaningful contribution as most of the European countries were engaged in tackling their respective political and economic crisis.

At the beginning of World War II, the BIS had made a public statement on December 18, 1939, regarding its neutrality with refraining from three activities: (i) transaction of central banks of belligerent countries and the countries in a state of war, (ii) disposing of the assets of belligerent countries and the countries in a state of war, and (iii) not holding accounts to preserve gold for belligerent countries and the countries in a state of war (Toniolo, 2005). To be clearer and more transparent to its shareholders, the BIS stated (in its 11th annual report that was published on June 9, 1941) that 'The Bank has adhered to the principles of scrupulous neutrality which is laid down for itself in the autumn of 1939, confining its activities strictly to transactions whereby no question can possibly arise of conferring economic or financial advantages on any belligerent nation to the detriment of any other. Moreover, no operations are carried out which might directly or indirectly run counter to the monetary policy of the central bank in the country concerned or in practice constitute a circumvention of the legal provisions governing the disposal of the currency of that country. When the Bank has been faced with opposing claims to the same assets, it has been careful to examine the legal questions involved, having obtained, in some instances, legal opinions from independent experts, and in case of doubt it has adopted a course of action designed to protect the various interests involved' (BIS, 1941, pp. 184–185). Within these limits, during wartime, the BIS maintained transaction with allied powers (the US and the UK), axis powers (German, Italy, Japan) and neutral powers (Norway, Sweden). The war deterred the financial activities of the BIS and the transactions sharply declined and reduced its profit. For instance, during June 1938–June 1940 and July 1941–May 1945, the gold shipments through the BIS were 276.1 tonnes and 21.3 tonnes, respectively (Toniolo, 2005). Despite the BIS's clear-cut stance during World War II, academics critique the BIS's role during wartime (1939–1945) from two points of view: (i) the Czech gold incident, i.e., after Germany invaded Czechoslovakia in March 1939, Germany ordered that all Czech gold be tendered to German accounts (Reichsbank) and the BIS complied with this (Bederman, 1988), and (ii) the bank settled some gold swaps and payments on behalf of Germany to Axis-dominated countries which breached its neutrality commitments that it declared in 1939 (Toniolo, 2005).

The Role of BIS in Bretton Woods System (BWS) era:

The United Nations Conference at Bretton Woods in 1944 was held mainly to establish two projects: (i) the International Bank for Reconstruction and Development (IBRD) and (ii) the International Monetary Fund (IMF), the brainchildren of John Maynard Keynes, a well-known British economist, and Harry Dexter White, a senior US treasury department official (Temin & Vines, 2014; Toniolo, 2005). Interestingly, the Bretton Woods Conference in July 1944 had passed a resolution to abolish the BIS as soon as possible due to its partisan role in World War II; however, the proposal was dropped considering that the conference is not an appropriate body to liquidate the BIS (Bederman, 1988, p. 103; Toniolo, 2005, p. 260), and Keynes argued to wait until the proposed two institutions (IBRD and IMF) were established (Skidelsky, 2000). Readers may ask why Keynes was interested in designing the IBRD and the IMF. The fact is, when the war began in 1940, Keynes worked with the internal balance of Britain for wartime and full employment of postwar global economy aiming to avoid the global depression that occurred in the 1930s (Temin & Vines, 2014). In fact, the role of the BIS was not substituted by the BWS institutions which was another reason to keep the BIS alive in the post-war era. For instance, during the European Recovery Program (ERP) (commonly known as Marshall Plan) which was announced in 1947, BIS worked to provide technical support to create the European Payment Union (EPU) in 1950. The EPU has three core objectives: (i) remove the obstacle of inconvertibility of European currencies, (ii) remove quantity restrictions and (iii) suppress bilateral commercial practices (OECD, 2011) and the BIS buttressed the EPU to achieve its objectives (Toniolo, 2005). It is worth mentioning here that during the 1950s, the BIS was focused mostly on Western European countries and did not get involved in Eastern European banking issues and hence did not give any clear-cut decision regarding Russian central bank's admission into the BIS (also considering the then political reality) (Toniolo, 2005). To sum up, during the Bretton Woods regime (1947–1971), the main focus of the BIS was the reconstruction of the European economy and attempt to remove the barriers in foreign exchange trade mainly in Western Europe (Felsenfeld & Bilali, 2004).

On the other hand, the BIS's role in the Bretton Woods System (BWS) suspension era was more important as the US dollar and gold convertibility under fixed exchange rate (USD 35 per ounce of gold) was abolished and the international foreign exchange market was more volatile as an adverse outcome. In the academic circle, it is still a debatable issue as to what was the real intention of the US in killing her own brainchild. However, to keep our discussion on track, we will skip those historical discussions and debates. The prime effect of the suspension of BWS was the introduction of a floating exchange rate (instead of fixed dollar exchange rates) which created a new problem such as global economic slowdown and inflation (p. 436). Besides the currency crisis, the first oil shock in 1973 gave the BIS an opportunity to act as an international institution for cooperation among central banks and manage the funds. During this period, the BIS took deposits from oil-producing countries and provided advances to downstream countries which ultimately solved the liquidity crisis in Western economies (Bederman, 1988).

To conclude, it is evident that the cooperation among the European central banks was started in early 1900s mainly on a short-term and ad hoc basis. Although the BIS was established to act as an international settlement institution for German reparation, it played the role of 'crisis manager' in the European financial system and contributed to solving financial disputes among Europeans until World War II. Despite a hostile fired plan at the Bretton Woods Conference, this historical institution was saved. Later, it played a key role in rebuilding war-torn Western Europe by taking several initiatives in 1950s and supporting the post-BWS world order.

2.3 Basel Committee on Banking Supervision (BCBS) and Initiation of Basel Accord

At the end of 1974, the BIS explored a new role as a 'prudential regulation issuer' while setting up the 'Committee on Banking Regulation and Supervisory Practices' (CBS) in response to the Herstatt crisis (Felsenfeld & Bilali, 2004). It was believed that the creation of the CBS was a kind of response to five international banking disturbances in early 1970s such as (i) oil shock; (ii) a wide fluctuation in interest rates in mid-1974; (iii) an international depression that deepened in 1974; (iv) the removal of US controls on capital outflows in January 1974; and (V) the Herstatt Bank failure (Felsenfeld & Bilali, 2004, p. 953). In addition, maturity mismatch (investment in medium-term credit with short-term deposit) in the eurocurrency market in the late 1960s was another motive behind establishing the CBS (Toniolo, 2005). Scholars argue that the Herstatt failure was an example of poor supervision and information asymmetries for national regulators (Mourlon-Drulo, 2015) which created a shock in international banking. To tackle this, the BIS formed the CBS in 1974 as a G10 standing committee to oversee prudential issues and the committee issued a new guideline 'Basel Concordat' in 1975 which aims to enhance supervisory activities of home regulators and host regulators on banks' foreign branches, subsidiaries and joint ventures (BIS, 1975). Later, the CBS was renamed as the 'Basel Committee on Banking Supervision' (BCBS). There were three specific guidelines in the concordat which aimed to reduce information asymmetry related to solvency, liquidity and foreign exchange positions of foreign establishments of G10 countries' domestic banks (BIS, 1975). Later, the guidelines were revised multiple times, included non-G10 and systemically important countries and published the latest version with 29 principles in September 2012 as 'Core Principles for Effective banking Supervision.' However, international banking crises continued and created systemic risk in financial system; especially after the debt crisis in the 1980s, Western economies had serious banking problems which pushed the BCBS to introduce the Basel Accords. In the following sub-section, we describe the debt crisis to better understand the background of the introduction of the Basel Accords by the BIS.

1980s Debt Crisis and Banks Excessive Risk Taking

The debt crisis in the 1980s termed as the 'lost decade' of development for all African and Latin American countries which put stress on international coordination between debtors and creditors for loan repayment (UN, 2017). There are several explanations among academics regarding the source of the crisis such as uncontrolled syndicated loans in other countries, lack of prudential regulation for banks and so on. Davis (1995) mentioned three broad reasons for the rapid expansion of syndicated loans in developing countries by industrialized economies in the early 1980s: (i) free floating exchange rate increases the inflation in the US, leading to a volatile nominal interest rate which created a demand for external finance to LDCs, especially Latin American countries; (ii) Herstatt failure caused the commercial banks to tap into the syndicated loan market and avoid foreign exchange business; and (iii) the second oil shock in 1979 increased the deposit base of Western banks as OPEC nations deposited their petrodollars in the banking system instead of securities market. As a result, there was a form of bull market in the syndicated loan market (which created a low spread for banks) and bank loans were highly concentrated in the 'syndicated credit' market (Davis, 1995). Feldstein (1991) referred the weak institutional arrangements such as the Federal Deposit Insurance Corporation (FDIC) guarantees for depositors and low capital requirements encouraged the banks to take excessive risk in other countries. Consequently, in 1982, Mexico declared that they were too unable to repay their debt (Dick, 1991), followed by Argentina (Adamson, 1985) which created a 'debt crisis' in the international financial market (Davis, 1995). To tackle the debt crisis, the 'Baker Plan' was launched in 1985 through which the IMF provided new funds to commercial banks aiming to extend the loans to the indebted countries (Dick, 1991). In addition, the domestic regulators eased the regulations to record the non-performing loans at book value on balance sheets and write off some loans to maintain the adequate capital ratio (Davis, 1995). To sum up, the 'debt crisis' to some extent had been managed by several initiates; however, to control the excessive risk-taking behavior of banks, the BIS came forward to formulate a uniform capital adequacy ratio for G-10 countries. There is another narrative in the political economy literature regarding introduction of Basel regulations which is described in the next sub-section.

Political Economy Narrative for the Basel Accords

There are arguments from the political economy of regulation (Lütz, 2004; Lyon, 2007; Stubbs & Underhill, 2005; Underhill & Zhang, 2008) that rational politicians have an electoral incentive to propose redistributive international institutions in an open market economy (Oatley & Nabors, 1998). Oatley and Nabors (1998) claim that the US and UK proposal for harmonization in capital ratio in 1980s was motivated to satisfy competing interest group and voter pressure. We summarize the narrative from the very beginning to better understand the US and UK positions in 1980s regarding capital ratio and reasons to support the BIS proposal of Basel Accord I.

From the period of 1914 to World War II, the capital of US banks was maintained based on total deposits and the accepted norm was 10% based on the logic that the function of capital is to protect depositors, and hence, capital should be maintained based on deposits (Goodhart, 2011). However, during World War II, US government securities were held by large banks which made the capital to total deposit ratio absolute; hence, it is further argued that if the role of capital is to cover risks then, it must be related to total assets (Goodhart, 2011). The first initiative was made by the Office of the Comptroller of the Currency (OCC) in 1948 to maintain capital adequacy related to total assets, and further, it was modified in 1952 and in 1956 by the Federal Reserve Board (FRB) in which the standard ratio was considered around 7% although it varied from bank to bank (Goodhart, 2011). In fact until 1975 in the US, the capital ratio was maintained based on bank size; that is, regulators divided the banks into 'peer groups' and established informal target group capital ratios for the banks in each group (Singer, 2007). However, bank failure had increased sharply after 1975 which made a huge burden on the FDIC, and in 1978, to stop bank run and bring discipline in the market, Congress formed the 'Federal Financial Institutions Examination Council (FFIEC)' and the FFIEC first developed uniform capital adequacy standards for US bank regulators (i.e., FRB, OCC and FDIC) (Singer, 2007). In turn, in 1981, the FDIC announced that they would fix the minimum equity capital to asset ratio at a 5% threshold for all banks regardless of asset size which was the first formal capital requirements in the US banking history, and in 1985, the ratio was re-set at 6%, chiefly, as failures of regional banks continued (FDIC, 1997). However, to adjust the additional cost of capital requirements and to increase the return on equity (ROE), banks were aggressively engaged in off-balance sheet transactions (in banking terms, off-balance sheet transactions are contingent liabilities) which increased the bank's risk, and the ultimate situation became worse. For example, a total of 468 banks failed between 1985 and 1987, which is more than the prior thirty years combined, resulting in the FDIC's deposit insurance fund disbursements reaching $12.75 billion (Singer, 2007). To tackle such bank run frequency and bring stability to the domestic financial sector, US regulators proposed introducing so-called 'risk-based capital standards' (Singer, 2007). Their proposal was to assign a 'risk weight' on each asset based on the 'probability of default' or 'financial loss' to encourage banks to hold low risk-weighted assets in their portfolio and refrain from holding more off-balance sheet risk which hoped to reduce the probability of bank failure (Singer, 2007). However, many large US commercial banks having higher international banking exposure expressed their concerns over loss of competitiveness as they would require more capital if the proposed risk weight were to be applied and opined that the Japanese international banks would benefit more from this new rule (Singer, 2007). Mentionable here is that in

1980s international banking assets were dominated by Japanese internationally active banks. For instance, Japan had nine out of the ten largest banks in terms of banking assets in the world in 1987, up from just two banks in 1982, and Japanese banks held 8.7% of US total banking assets at the year-end 1986, up from 5% in 1982 (Singer, 2007). In other words, US regulators faced a dilemma to trade-off between the stability and competitiveness of US banks and thereby quested for an international capital adequacy standard or at least harmonization of capital ratios among industrialized economies (Singer, 2007).

In case of UK, there were no formal minimum regulatory capital ratio requirements that were imposed by the Bank of England (BOE) for British banks before 1979 (Hall, 1999) and the first regulatory reform for capital adequacy was pronounced after the secondary banking crisis in the UK in 1973–1974 (Singer, 2007). In 1980, capital adequacy framework related to a technical paper named 'The measurement of capital' was published by the BOE and the BOE had taken measures to improve the capital adequacy of UK banks based on this framework (Hadjiemannuil, 1996). In addition, the failure of Johnson Matthey Bankers Limited (JMB) in 1984 had pushed the BOE to consider introducing a risk-based capital ratio which was compatible with the US proposal. However, the same logic (as raised by American bankers) was placed from the British banking community against the BOE's proposal. As in 1986 Japan had 26.6% market share (worth of 241.7 billions of pounds) in the UK's total banking assets, the BOE's concern for introducing new tighter capital stringency is that it might harm the competitiveness of British banks compared with Japanese banks (Singer, 2007). Hadjiemannuil (1996, p. 238) notes that, 'increasingly strict requirement has put UK incorporated banks at a disadvantage even in the domestic markets, because the supervision of the capital adequacy of overseas banks was normally left to their home authorities.' In fact, both the US and the UK were eagerly progressing toward a global capital standard targeting Japanese internationally active banks (Oatley & Nabors, 1998) and agreed on a common minimum capital standard at the end of 1986 (Goodhart, 2011).

In contrast, the Japanese financial sector was historically stable and the absence of instability in the Japanese market is attributable to the Ministry of Finance's (MoF) routine intervention in management decisions and its refusal to allow banks to collapse (Singer, 2007). In the academic circle, this uniqueness of the Japanese financial system is referred to as the 'convoy' system (Aoki et al., 1994; Toya, 2006; Vogel, 1996). As a result, structurally, Japanese banks were able to maintain lower capital adequacy (as it is ultimately guaranteed by the MoF), compared with their Western peers. For example, in 1986, Barclays, Chase Manhattan and Citicorp had capital to asset ratios of 4.71, 5.37 and 4.73%, respectively, whereas Japan's Dai-Ichi Kangyo, Sumitomo and Fuji had ratios of 2.38, 2.89, and 2.95%, respectively (Oatley & Nabors, 1998, p. 38). Therefore, Japanese international banks would have to pay a lot compared with their Western peers if the capital ratio is harmonized with active international banks among the industrialized countries. Hence, it is presumed that the US, UK, and other European developed countries had motive to adopt the global capital standard to tackle their domestic financial instability as well as Japan-phobic financial narratives. Readers may ask, what made Japan adopt the Basel Accords? The answer is probably that the BOE and Federal Reserve were able to threaten Japanese banks with exclusion from Western markets and international banking business if they refused to adopt (Singer, 2007). To sum up, from the above discussion, we presume that in addition to continuous debt crisis in the US and UK banking industry, the then global political economy contributed to introducing the Basel Accords in 1988.

Finally, the Basel Committee on Banking Supervision (BCBS) of the BIS published a consultative paper on 'International convergence of capital measurement and capital standards' for all internationally active banks of G10 countries in 1987 (BIS, 1988). Then, the BCBS and the US proposals came on table, then the components of capital were finalized, the risk weights on assets were fixed and the minimum capital ratio was agreed at 8% (from the proposed 7–10%) for internationally active banks primarily to make capital, risk absorbent and bring financial stability in international banking which was finally approved by the G-10 Governors' meeting in December 1987 at the BIS and disclosed as 'Basel Accord I' in 1988 (Goodhart, 2011). The accord fixed the minimum capital adequacy ratio (CAR) at 8% which was to be implemented by 1992 and assigned specific risk weights to bank assets aiming to tackle systemic risk in the internationally active banks (BIS, 1988). Later, the accord was modified into new a version in 2004 and 2017 which were termed as 'Basel Accord II' and 'Basel Accord III,' respectively. Next, we succinctly discuss why Basel Accords were reformed in multiple times. In the following subsection, we discuss the role of capital in the Basel Accords and discussion on rationale to reform the Basel Accord time to time.

2.4   ROLE OF CAPITAL IN THE BASEL ACCORDS AND REFORM OF THE BASEL ACCORDS

In fact, the level of bank capital and the components of bank capital are fundamentally dependent on the purposes said capital is intended to serve in the commercial bank (Goodhart, 2011), in the sense that it depends on the utility of bank capital in each country's regulatory perception, economic condition and overall banking sector scenarios. In general, bank capital is thought to serve three main purposes: '(i) as a cushion to absorb losses and protect depositor and creditors in both an ongoing setting and in liquidation; (ii) as a curb to excessive leveraging and risk-taking by bank management; and (iii) as a protection to earnings for absorbing losses and meeting contractual obligations to depositors and creditors' (Goodhart, 2011, p. 198). However, scholars critique the Basel Accord type minimum capital requirements from two perspectives: (i) the objectives of the minimum capital ratio and (ii) the process of assigning risk weights against bank assets. For example, Aharony et al. (1980), Aharony and Swary (1980), Maisel (1981) did not find any correlation between bank capital and bank failure and argued that minimum capital requirements cannot stop bank failure. Kapstein (1994) further argued that capital serves to absorb the unexpected losses of the bank, and if the banks have higher capital than the historical level of unexpected losses, then the minimum capital adequacy ratio can't refrain banks from risky lending decisions. In addition, he claimed that the Basel Accord provides a strong incentive to the banks to hold strong economies' governmental securities as it assigned minimum risk weights to specific countries' governmental securities which is kind of a 'conspiracy of the central bankers' (Kapstein, 1994).

Reform the Basel Accord I into Basel Accord II

It is argued that the main flaws in Basel Accord I were that it was only focused on credit risk and no other types of risks were considered when computing the RWA, for example, market risk arising from security positions or risk arising from reducing operational profits (Botha & Vuuren, 2009; Davis, 1995). Besides, the arbitrary risk categories and arbitrary weights used in the accord bear no relation with the default rate; that is, all assets within one category are considered the same risk and it doesn't consider sovereign default (Rodríguez, 2003). In fact, the accord gives preferential treatment to governmental securities without considering sovereign defaults; however, the sovereign default of Russia in 1998 and Argentina in 2002 proves that govt. securities are not a risk-free investment (Rodríguez, 2003). Besides, Basel Accord I failed to prevent the global financial systemic risk, such as the Asian financial crisis of 1997–1998 for example. To respond to those limitations the, first-round proposal for revising capital adequacy framework was published in 1999 and the final version was published as Basel Accord II in 2004 (BIS, 2004). Basel Accord II revised the previous accord and offered three pillars: first pillar—minimum capital requirement (MCR); second pillar—supervisory review process (SRP); and third pillar—market discipline concepts in capital regulation (BIS, 2004). In fact, major changes were brought in Basel Accord II while measuring RWA.

Reform of the Basel Accord II into Basel Accord III

A major critique raised after the financial crisis in 2007 from the academics and practitioners' side was that Basel Accord II was procyclical (Goodhart, 2009; Gordy & Howell, 2006; Jokipii & Milne, 2011; Kashyap & Stein, 2004; Repullo & Suarez, 2008). Their point is: (i) risk is assigned on a claim primarily based on the value of collateral in a traditional bank centric system; (ii) it is assumed that the higher value of collateral ensures low risk weight while computing risk-weighted assets and high residual value can be realized if the exposure turns in to default. As a result, during the financial boom, Basel Accord fueled mortgage values upward and inversely refueled them to fall when the financial bubble burst. This tendency is observed in the Lehman shock period, especially on real estate prices in the US. In addition, the 'quality of the rating' by credit rating agencies (CRA) was critically examined in academic circle (Coffee, 2011; Darbellay, 2013; Miglionico, 2019; Partnoy, 2017). In Basel Accord III, those problems were well addressed with two instruments. One is to maintain a counter cyclical buffer at 2.5% (although the BCBS keeps the percentage on national supervisors' discretion) in order to strengthen the risk absorbance capacity of banks against risk-weight assets (BCBS, 2017). Another is to introduce 'Loan to value (LTV) ratio' as a benchmark when assigning risk weights on real estate exposures class (both residential real estate and commercial real estate) (BCBS, 2017). In addition, the International Organization of Securities Commissions (IOSCO) has revised the 'IOSCO CRA code' in 2015 to ensure the rating accuracy

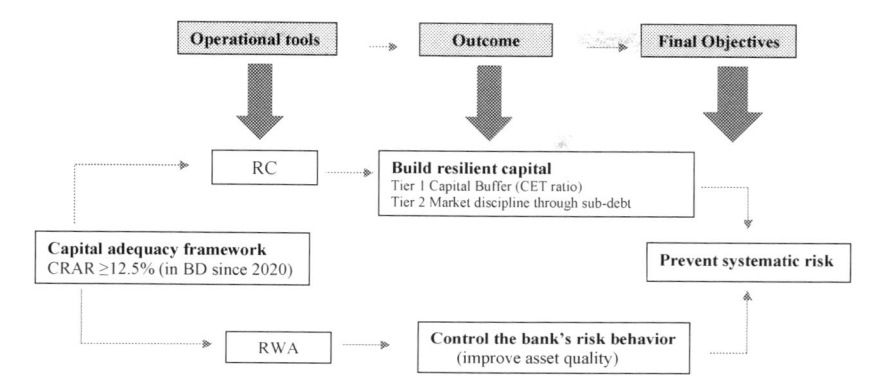

Fig. 2.1 Conceptual Framework of Basel Accord

of CRAs in the case of computation of RWA under the Basel Accords (IOSCO, 2015). Further, to enhance the quality of capital in the CRAR, common equity to Tier 1 capital is fixed at 6% (BCBS, 2017). Ironically, the quality of capital and assurance of liquidity were more pronounced in Basel Accord III.

To sum up, from the above discussion, we can say that the objectives of the Basel Accords are to prevent systemic risk (bank runs) which the banking sector had faced in the 1980s and bring financial stability to the market. It works with two instruments: (i) RC as operational tool to achieve resilient capital and (ii) RWA as a tool to control the bank's risk appetite (through assigning risk weight to the assets) which aids to stop bank run as well as systemic risk in the financial system. Figure 2.1 explains the Basel framework philosophy.

2.5 Concluding Remarks

From our detailed discussion on historical issues on BIS and the Basel Accords, two issues are observed. First, BIS was an emergence response to the cooperation among central banks of the Western European Economics. Second, in response to the harsh realities of the Herstatt failure and Latin American debt crisis, the BIS took several attempts to restore confidence in international banking and finally prepared the Basel framework as an internationally accepted prudential baking regulation. We shall note that, although Basel Accord I was prepared in 1988 for G10 countries' internationally active banks, at present sixty (60) central banks and monetary authorities are members of the BIS and one hundred and twenty (120) countries' central banks are following the Basel Accords as a prudential banking regulation, which shows the general accept-ability of the Basel framework among central banks (BIS, 2019a). On top of that the BIS has reformed the Basel regulations in response to the nature of risk and crises in international banking, and the concerns of the academics regarding the ill-impact of regulation were resolved in the updated versions of the Basel Accords. In other words, we can say that the BIS has formulated the Basel Accords as formal institutions (regulations) to bring financial stability in the banking industry. In Chapter 3, we shall focus on economic theories on banking business model and theories on banking institutions.

REFERENCES

Adamson, A. (1985, December 1). *The international debt problem: The case of Argentina*. Foundation for Economic Education. https://fee.org/articles/the-international-debt-problem-the-case-of-argentina/.

Aharony, J., & Swary, I. (1980). Contagion effects of bank failures: Evidence from capital markets. *The Journal of Business, 56*(3), 305–322.

Aharony, J., Jones, C. P., & Swary, I. (1980). An analysis of risk and return characteristics of corporate bankruptcies using capital market data. *The Journal of Finance, 34*(4), 1001–1016.

Aoki, M., Patrick, H., & Sheard, P. (1994). The Japanese main bank system: An introductory overview. In M. Aoki & H. Patrick (Eds.), *The Japanese main bank system: Its relevance for developing and transforming economics*. Oxford University Press.

Bakic, D. (2011). Great Britain, the little entente and the Genoa Conference of 1922. *Istorija 20. veka, 3*, 9–124.

Bank for International Settlements (BIS). (1931). *First Annual Report*. BIS. https://www.bis.org/publ/arpdf/archive/index.htm.

Bank for International Settlements (BIS). (1941). *Eleventh Annual Report*. BIS. https://www.bis.org/publ/arpdf/archive/index.htm.

Bank for International Settlements (BIS). (1975). *Report to the Governors on the Supervision of Banks' Foreign Establishments, Committee on Banking Regulations and Supervisory Practices, Basle, Switzerland*. https://www.bis.org/publ/bcbs00a.pdf.

Bank for International Settlements (BIS). (1988). *International convergence of capital measurement and capital standards*. BCBS, Bank for International Settlements.

Bank for International Settlements (BIS). (2004). *International convergence of capital measurement and capital standards: A revised framework*. BCBS, Bank for International Settlements.

Bank for International Settlements (BIS). (2019a). *Annual Report 2018/19*. BIS. https://www.bis.org/about/areport/index.htm.

Bank for International Settlements (BIS). (2019b). *The basic texts*. BIS. https://www.bis.org/about/legal.htm?m=1%7C6.

Basel Committee on Banking Supervision (BCBS). (2017). *Basel III: Finalising post-crisis reforms*. Bank for International Settlements. Retrieved from: https://www.bis.org/bcbs/publ/d424.pdf.

Bederman, D. J. (1988). The bank for international settlements and the debt crisis: A new role for the central bankers' bank. *Berkeley Journal of International Law, 6*(1).

Botha, M., & Vuuren, V. G. (2009). Retail credit capital charge optimization and the new Basel Accord. *Risk Management in Financial Institutions, 2*(3), 45–68.

Brown, A. J. (1940). Reviewed Work(s): How to pay for the war: A radical plan for the chancellor of the exchequer by J. M. Keynes; Round Table War Pamphlets, No I. *International Affairs Review Supplement, 19*(1), 34–36.

Clapham, J. H. (1944). *The bank of England: A history 1694–1914*. Cambridge University Press.

Coffee, J. C. (2011). Rating reforms: The good, the bad and the ugly. *Harvard Business Law Review, 1*, 231–278.

Darbellay, A. (2013). *Regulating credit rating agencies*. Edward Elgar.

Davis, E. P. (1995). *Debt financial fragility and systemic risk*. Oxford University Press.

Dick, M. J. (1991). The LDC debt crisis. *Bank of England Quarterly Bulletin, 31*(4), 498–507. Bank of England. https://www.bankofengland.co.uk/sitemap/quarterly-bulletin.

Eichengreen, B. (1992). *Golden fetters: The gold standard and great depression, 1919–1939*. Oxford University Press.

Eichengreen, B., & Flandreau, M. (2011). The federal reserve, the Bank of England and the rise of the dollar as an international currency, 1914–1939. *Open Economic Review, 23*(1), 57–87.

Federal Deposit Insurance Corporation (FDIC). (1997). *History of the eighties: Lessons for the future. Vol. 1, An examination of the banking crises of the 1980s and early 1990s*. FDIC.

Feldstein, M. (1991). Introduction to "The risk of economic crisis". In M. Feldstein (Ed.), *The risk of economic crisis* (pp. 1–18). University of Chicago Press.

Felsenfeld, C., & Bilali, G. (2004). The role of the bank for international settlements in shaping the world financial system. *University of Pennsylvania Journal of International Law, 25*(3), 945–1045.

Flandreau, M. (1997). Central Bank cooperation in historical perspective: A skeptical view. *Economic History Review, 50*, 735–763.

Fratianni, M., & Pattison, J. (2001). The bank for international settlements: An assessment of its role in international monetary and financial policy coordination. *Open Economies Review, 12*, 197–222.

Goodhart, C. (2009). *The regulatory response to the financial crisis.* Elgar.

Goodhart, C. (2011). *The Basel Committee on banking Supervision: A history of the early years 1974–1997.* Cambridge University Press.

Gordy, M. B., & Howell, B. (2006). Procyclicality in Basel II: Can we treat the disease without killing the patient? *Journal of Financial Intermediation, 15*(3), 395–417.

Hadjiemannuil, M. (1996). *Banking regulation and the Bank of England: Discretion and remedies* (Doctoral Thesis, University College London, UK). https://discovery.ucl.ac.uk/id/eprint/10098223/1/Banking_regulation_and_the_Ban.pdf.

Hall, M. J. B. (1999). The reform of UK financial regulation. *Journal of Banking Regulation, 11*(1), 31–75.

Hughes, M. P., & Palke, C. (2019). The bank for international settlements: An evolutionary institution. *Journal of Business Case Studies, 15*(1), 19–28.

International Organization of Securities commissions (IOSCO). (2015). *Code of conduct fundamentals for credit rating agencies: Final Report* (FR05/2015). Madrid, Spain: IOSCO. https://www.iosco.org/library/pubdocs/pdf/IOSCOPD482.pdf.

Jokipii, T., & Milne, A. (2011). Bank capital buffer and risk adjustment decisions. *Journal of Financial Stability, 7*(3), 165–178.

Kapstein, E. B. (1994). *Governing the global economy: International finance and the state.* Harvard University Press.

Kashyap, A. K., & Stein, J. C. (2004). Cyclical implications of the Basel II capital standards. *Economic Perspectives, 8*(Q I),18–31.

Keynes, J. M. (1919). *The economic consequences of the peace.* The Quinn & Boden Company.

Lütz, S. (2004). Convergence within national diversity: The regulatory state in finance. *Journal of Public Policy, 24*(2), 169–197.

Lyon, T. P. (2007). Introduction. In T.P. Lyon (Ed.), *The political economy of regulation* (pp. ix–xxix). Edward Elgar.

Maisel, S. J. (1981). Insolvency and capital adequacy. In S. J. (Ed.), *Risk and capital adequacy in commercial banks* (pp.19–40). University of Chicago Press. https://www.nber.org/books/mais81-1.

Miglionico, A. (2019). *The governance of credit rating agencies regulatory regime and liability issues*. Edward Elgar.

Mourlon-Drulo, E. (2015). 'Trust is good, control is better': The 1974 Herstatt Bank crisis and its implications for international regulatory reform. *Journal Business History, 57*(2), 311–314. https://doi.org/10.1080/000 76791.2014.950956.

Oatley, T., & Nabors, R. (1998). Redistributive cooperation: Market failure, wealth transfers, and the Basle accord. *International Organization, 52*(1), 35–54.

OECD. (2011). *Better policies for better lives: The OECD at 50 and beyond*. Retrieved from https://www.oecd.org/about/.

Partnoy, F. (2017). What's (Still) wrong with credit ratings. *Washington Law Review, 92*(3), 1408–1472.

Repullo, R., & Suarez, J. (2008). The procyclical effects of Basel II. *9th Jacques Polak Annual Research Conference*. International Monetary Fund.

Rodríguez, L. J. (2003). Banking stability and the Basel capital standards. *The Cato Journal, 23*(1), 115–126.

Schenk, C., & Straumann, T. (2014). A century and a half of central banks, international reserves and international currencies. Proceedings of the *Of the Uses of Central Banks: Lessons from History International Monetary Policy Regimes: Historical Perspectives*. https://www.norges-bank.no/en/topics/Res earch/Conferences/.

Schloss, H. H. (1958). *The bank for international settlements: An experiment in central bank cooperation*. North-Holland.

Seabrooke, L. (2006). The bank for international settlements. *New Political Economy, 11*(1), 141–149.

Singer, D. A. (2007). *Regulating capital: Setting standards for the international financial system*. Cornell University Press.

Skidelsky, R. (2000). *John Maynard Keynes, Vol. III, Fighting with Britain: 1937–1946*. Macmillan Publishing.

Stubbs, R., & Underhill, G. R. D. (Eds.). (2005). *Political economy and the changing global order* (3rd ed.). Oxford University Press.

Temin, P., & Vines, D. (2014). *Keynes: Useful economics for the world economy*. The MIT Press.

Toniolo, G. (2005). *Central bank cooperation at the bank for international settlements, 1930–1973*. Cambridge University Press.

Toya, T. (2006). *The political economy of the Japanese Financial big bang: Institutional changes in finance and public policymaking*. Oxford University Press.

Underhill, G. R. D., & Zhang, X. (2008). Setting the rules: Private power, political underpinning, and legitimacy in global monetary and financial governance. *International Affairs, 84*(3), 535–554.

United Nations (UN). (2017). *World Economic and Social Survey 2017: Reflecting on 70 years of development policy analysis*. Department of Economic and Social Affairs Economic Analysis, United Nations. https://www.un.org/development/desa/dpad/publication/world-economic-and-social-survey-2017-reflecting-on-70-years-of-development-policy-analysis/.

Vogel, S. K. (1996). *Freer markets, more rules: Regulatory reform in advanced industrial countries*. Cornell University Press.

CHAPTER 3

Theoretical Discussion on Banking Business Model and Banking Regulations

3.1 Introduction

In the introductory chapter, we have initiated the discussion on the banking industry's systemic risk and the objective of the Basel framework. As the Basel Accords are considered as a prudential banking regulation by the central banks globally, we need to understand three issues, namely: (i) the theoretical foundation of banking business and the limitations of banking business model, (ii) what are the economic rationale to regulate the financial institutions and (iii) contemporary debate on Basel framework. In this chapter, we briefly discuss those three issues. The structure of the chapter is as follows. Section 3.2 discusses the economic theories on banking and the limits of banking business model. Section 3.3 offers a comprehensive discussion on theories on banking regulation and detailed discussion on capital regulation. Section 3.4 presents the existing academic debate on CRAs' roles in the financial industry and the position of this study. Section 3.5 presents the existing academic debate on sub-debt's role in the Basel Accord and the position of the study as well. Section 3.6 contains concluding remarks.

3.2   ECONOMIC THEORIES ON BANKING MODEL AND ITS LIMITATIONS

Bank-money is simply an acknowledgment of private debt expressed in the money of account which is used by passing from one hand to another to settle a transaction (Keynes, 1930, p. 6). A bank is a firm specializing in deposit-taking and dealing with the asymmetric information problem of depositors (Eichberger & Harper, 1997). Eichberger and Harper (1997, p. xiii) have identified financial intermediation in two situations such as (i) symmetric information situation where the household knows the information of the assets that he buys and under equilibrium pricing method the asset price is fixed and (ii) asymmetric information situation where the household uses the contract (debt contract and deposit contract) to avoid market failure in symmetric information. Freixas et al. (2015, p.50) traced the five rationales for banks' existence from contemporary literature: (i) reduction of transaction cost in payment systems and reduction of monitoring cost (in interbank bank markets and lending to firms and households), (ii) asset transformation to borrowers by issuing demand deposits to customers, (iii) liquidity insurance and liquidity management for customers by issuing short-term deposit, (iv) loan monitoring either in ex ante (screening of the loans proposal by skilled loan officers), at interim stage (monitoring of the project) or ex-post phase (enforcements of repayment by borrowers) and (v) risk management by diversification of fund. Based on a long contemporary literature survey, Eichberger and Harper (1997) classified banking business models into two: (i) portfolio model and (ii) monitoring model. The portfolio model considers banks as risk managers, whereas the monitoring model considers banks as financial intermediaries. We discuss below both models in brief and then proceed to the discussion on limitations of banking business model.

Portfolio Model

The concept of 'choice of portfolio' under uncertainty is based on mean and variance of portfolio return theory of Markowitz (1952) and Tobin (1958, 1965). It is widely examined by several authors (Baltensperger, 1980; Benston, 1964; Elyasiani, 1983; Hart & Jaffee, 1974; Porter, 1961; Santomero, 1984) and explained the banking behavior as a deposit-taking financial institution and to explain banking theory based on portfolio choice. Under portfolio theory, banks are considered as an enterprise that transforms indivisible and risky assets issued by firms into assets of small denomination with little or no risk and banks manage small investors' portfolios who seek low-risk investment opportunities but profitable risky business investments (Eichberger & Harper, 1997). Indeed, under the portfolio approach, banks act in a risk averse manner and maximize the expected utility of the wealth (Stiglitz & Greenwald, 2003). The concept of this theory can be outlined as follows: banks are an expertise firm which has the ability to transform a risky asset into a less risky or no risk asset and price their assets according to risk and cost involved with each class of assets and liabilities and in this way maximize their profit (Baltensperger, 1980). Hart and Jaffee (1974) examined the bank portfolio with a different approach, such as imposing certain institutions like reserve requirements and liquidity requirements, and checking the risk averse behavior of banks. The result is similar to previous findings that banks manage the portfolio with less risky assets when imposed restrictions.

However, there are critiques to explain bank behavior based on the model. For instance, banks might want to hold all assets in government securities to make their investment safe or be pessimistic about the returns on loans, which leads the economy into a liquidity trap (Stiglitz & Greenwald, 2003). In addition, Freixas and Rochet (2008) pointed out the deficiencies of the Portfolio model from two perspectives: (i) the model is based primarily on 'portfolio theory' which assumes that all the banks hold colinear (risky) portfolio, and however, in practice, there is diversity in the bank balance sheets and (ii) in this theory bank capital is considered as just another liability (like depositors claim) but in practice bank capital can deviate while choosing banking assets (riskiness of the loans) as solvency ratio (minimum capital regulation) exists. The logic is bank owners wish to take maximum risk with minimum diversification which creates a concentration of asset risk in the sense that all banks invest in the same class of assets to maintain a minimum level of capital.

Monitoring Model

In contrast, the 'monitoring model' of banking firms has a different logic from the 'portfolio model.' It is argued that banks can efficiently monitor the firms and, therefore, are able to maintain a portfolio of assets with lower cost than an individual investor, as they have expertise in ex-ante (screening the loan proposals) and ex-post (monitoring the disbursed loan) activities of the lending business. Freixas and Rochet (2008, p. 30) have expanded the term 'monitoring' into three contexts, such as screening the project in a context of adverse selection, preventing opportunistic behavior of borrowers and punishing or auditing a borrower who fails to meet the contractual obligation. Besides, Diamond (1984) coined and explained the term 'delegated monitoring model' of banking which helps to avoid duplication of monitoring cost, i.e., multiple monitoring by several lenders of a single borrower (Santos, 2006). Diamond (1984, 1996) justified the existence of banks as it can significantly reduce the monitoring cost of borrowers due to economies of scale and scope. Diamond's (1984, 1996) monitoring model is succinctly explained by Matthews and Thompson (2014) in the following way—if we consider that imperfect information exists between lenders and borrowers, there can be three options of contracting: (i) no monitoring, (ii) direct monitoring by lenders (iii) delegated monitoring by intermediaries, i.e., banks. In the case of option (i), the only recourse to the lender in case of a failure by a borrower is to realize his claims through bankruptcy proceedings. Due to information asymmetries between borrowers and lenders, borrowers can manufacture the cash flow of the firm which could only be discovered by lenders in the case of insolvency of the borrower or liquidation of assets. Therefore, the bankruptcy proceedings or liquidation of assets is an 'all or nothing' approach and is clearly expensive and inefficient for lenders (Matthews & Thompson, 2014, p. 49), and thus, we can rule out the first option. In the case of the second option, direct monitoring, it is expensive for lenders because of multiple monitoring costs and thus the option left is monitoring by intermediaries which is cost effective for lenders. Besides this, while analyzing the Arrow-Debreu general equilibrium model in financial intermediation, Suzuki (2011) argued that the delegated monitoring activities of banks help to accumulate the necessary skill and knowledge to monitor the firms' credit risk which give banks comparative advantage (especially in the case of credit risk of SMEs) to lower the monitoring cost than the potential cost of monitoring by an individual.

Limitations of Banking Business Model

A subsequent question is then how to monitor the monitor, i.e., how the depositors would ensure that banks really monitor its borrowers. Diamond (1996) argued that 'liquidation' is the sanction to monitor the bankers' behavior. As if banks reduce monitoring, the bank asset values decrease and banks go to a liquidation process. However, during liquidation, bank borrowers' assets also are to be liquidated to meet the depositors' claims, which ultimately reduces the banker's incentive for collusion with borrowers and this is why banks have incentive to monitor their borrowers. Freixas and Rochet (2008, p. 33) argued that a 'bank run' be a credible sanction mechanism for bank managers who do not monitor their borrowers. Some are view that the demandable features of bank liabilities act as an effective instrument to prevent the opportunistic behavior of bank managers (Diamond & Rajan, 2000; Rajan, 1992). In contrast, Dewatripont and Tirole (1994) argued the existing banking models have two limitations, namely that (i) they cannot explain the existence of outside equity either for banks or for borrowers (firms). It only considers debt and the 'right to audit' as an ex-post strategy when there are insufficient cash flows. In other words, the model did not explain the role of equity in either bankruptcies or liquidation of firms; (ii) the diversification hypothesis is problematic in the sense that the information processing cost is less when a bank's portfolio has homogeneous loan products, and thus by necessity, banks prefer the homogeneous portfolio over a diversified one. In addition, as the systemic (macroeconomic) risk cannot be diversified, the riskless portfolio concept of Diamond does not match with real world, and therefore, bank failure risk cannot be explained by the monitoring model.

In summary, the banking roles as a 'portfolio manager' to manage banking risk and as 'delegated monitoring' activities to monitor their borrower imply that financial institutions (banks) and their role cannot purely eliminate the risk involved in the financial markets. This is because under the portfolio view, banks' deposit taking nature can be explained as: households put their savings into banks as an option, aiming not to absorb the direct risk of investment rather taking indirectly, and banks diversified their portfolio to minimize the default risk. However, ultimately, any default risk of banks has to be borne by the household when bankruptcies occur. On the contrary, the 'Delegated monitoring' model views that a bank is a financial intermediary and argued that banks can monitor the borrowers with low cost of monitoring rather than individuals. However, in the case of systemic risk or bank distress (Carapeto et al., 2010; Flori et al., 2019), banks' monitoring activities prove futile in the sense that the bank fails to capture the macro-economic shock while monitoring the borrowers (which was proven in the financial crisis of 2007–2008). In fact, those limitations of banking business model indicate that banking regulation is essential to ensure financial stability as banking business model cannot stop the chance of bank failure. In next sub-section, we shed lights on various approaches of banking regulation.

3.3   Theories of Banking Regulation

Apart from limitations of banking business model, the essence of banking regulation can be explained from another perspective, i.e., bank investment risk perspective. In fact, the deposit taking nature of a bank has created two types of risk: (i) liquidity risk and (ii) investment risk (Eichberger & Harper, 1997, p. 201). The former risk arises when depositors' withdrawals exceed the cash reserve held by the bank and the latter arises due to the bank losses that come from its' investment decisions (i.e., bad loans are so high that it cannot repay the depositors claim in the long run) (Eichberger & Harper, 1997). Investment risk is common to every firm in the sense that any firm can become bankrupt due to its bad investment decisions. In the banking business, liquidity risk is unique, and in practice, it is quite difficult to distinguish between two risks when financial distress has occurred, because depositors' withdrawal behavior is related to the bank performance (returns of bank investment) and bank investment return depends on the accuracy of its prediction of withdrawal (Eichberger & Harper, 1997, p. 201). This unique nature of banks urges some to regulate banks in a more prudential way. Therefore, to stop the bank run from depositors' sides, provide uninterrupted fund supply to the firms during financial distress and ensure the projected return from firms are key objectives of banking regulation.

There are several institutions which are introduced by the central bank to regulate banks. Suzuki (2011, p. 42), while discussing the instruments of banking regulation, referred to Freixas and Rochet (1997) who had classified banking regulations into six broad types: (i) deposit interest rate ceilings; (ii) entry, branching, network and merger restrictions; (iii) portfolio restrictions, including reserve requirements; (iv) deposit insurance; (v) capital requirements; and (vi) regulatory monitoring including not only closure policy but also the use of market values versus book values. In short, we can classify the banking regulation theories by the following two major approaches:

(i) Depositors' representative approach,
(ii) Systemic risk approach.

Depositors' Representative Approach of Banking Regulation

Dewatripont and Tirole (1994) analyzed the essence of banking regulation from the depositors' representative point of view which mainly focuses on corporate governance issues that arise from separation of ownership and management and the inability of the depositor to monitor the bank (Santos, 2001). Dewatripont and Tirole's (1994) argument is that banks like other firms are subject to incentive problems and governance problems. Small retail depositors lack the skill to interpret the bank balance sheet or they have less incentive to monitor the bank. This incentive problem arises as the retail depositors are considered small liability holders of the bank (Mathew & Thompson, 2014). Besides, as depositors have less technical skill and less liability, they try to free ride on somebody for monitoring banks. Banking regulation, in such a case, can be considered as a monitoring tool for bank managers' behavior. In the depositors' representative approach, capital regulation is considered as another kind of tool that is used by the shareholders to monitor the bank managers' risk-taking behavior. They argued that depositors need to be represented by an entrusted agent (say public regulations) to ensure external intervention in case of poor performance of the bank, and in the absence of such external intervention, managerial behavior depends on its own incentive structure (Dewatripont & Tirole, 1994). However, the missing point in the thesis is how small depositors' hand over their rights and trust to regulation as regulation and regulators can be captured by the regulated (as argued by Stigler (1971) in 'Regulatory capture theory'). Besides, how incentives for depositors can be quantified in the case of delegating their roles to the regulations is not clear in Dewatripont and Tirole's (1994) analysis.

Systemic Risk Approach

'Systemic risk can be characterized by the financial fragility of financial intermediaries, a general lack of confidence in financial intermediaries and markets, and in extreme cases the impairment of payment system, leading to strong negative real effects on economy: ....aggregate output, employment and welfare' (Freixas et al., 2015, p. 52). Systemic risk emerges from information asymmetry between financial intermediaries and retail investors (Davis, 1995; Geneva Report, 2009; Goodhart, 1989), negative externalities associated with spillovers and contagion effect, credit booms and asset price bubbles (Freixas et al., 2015, p. 52). However, Matthews and Thompson (2014) succinctly argued that a bank run is the symptom of systemic risk. Their logic is that banks have monopolistic behavior in the financial market, and they can exploit the information they have about their clients to exercise monopolistic pricing (both deposit and loans). Therefore, uninsured depositors are unable to monitor banks and uninsured depositors are likely to run rather than monitoring which leads to a bankruptcy of a stressed bank. In this aspect, 'bank run' that leads to 'contagion' is considered as a root cause for systemic risk and they advocated for banking regulation that can stop such risk. We briefly discuss below about 'bank runs' to better understand systemic risk and as a rationale of banking regulation.

Bank Runs and their effect:
Diamond and Dybvig (1983) considered bank demand deposits as liquid (in terms of convertibility—of deposit to cash) and fragile in case of run because of their nature of contract and the banks role is to convert the liquid deposits into illiquid assets (loans). Hence, the feature of a bank balance sheet is that the value of liquid assets to provide liquidity service (e.g., cash in hand) is always smaller than the liquidation value of its assets (Santos, 2001). Under this situation, depositor expectations regarding their value of deposit are dependent in line with the time of withdrawal because the payment will be on a first come first served basis (Santos, 2001, p. 46). Suppose if a bank fails to pay its demand depositors' claim in say, period 1, the demand depositors who wish to withdraw their deposit after period 2 will run to the bank to withdraw their deposit. Because they fear that they will not get back their full amount in period 2. It makes panic among depositors, whether they have perfect information of the bank assets or not. This bank run can make a sound bank go into bankruptcy as the bank has already invested in illiquid assets (long-term investments) for period 2 and has no choice but to conduct a fire sale of their assets. However, Bhattacharya and Gale (1987) argued if depositors have information about banks' short-term assets, such liquidity risk can be avoided by interbank lending because both depositors and other banks would be convinced by the problem bank's asset structure. In contrast, Cooper and Ross (2002) argued depositors have no incentive to monitor the bank assets in such a case. Flannery (1996) views that, since banks act as 'delegated monitoring' services, they have to hoard more illiquid assets, and other banks will not lend to a poor bank in case of bank run even

with high interest rate. Rather, they withdraw themselves from the interbank market and try to avoid the 'winners curse effect.' In this situation, banks have no choice except for fire sales of assets to meet depositors' claims. For example, we have mentioned the discussion of the FBL case of Bangladesh in Chapter 7 that the FBL has failed to collect money from the interbank market in November–December 2017 despite offering high interest rates during its cash crunch. The adverse impact of bank runs has been widely discussed in banking and financial literature. Bryant (1980), Diamond and Dybvig (1983) considered that the 'transformation' of illiquid assets into liquid asset during a bank run situation can distort the production system of the economy. Based on this argument, they view that governmental deposit insurance can protect against a bank run to some extent without liquidating the bank assets (Bryant, 1980; Diamond & Dybvig, 1983). However, Calomiris and Gorton (1991)'s critique on this view is that such a type of bank run can occur only when there is demand for money that shocks the entire economy; otherwise, there is no empirical evidence of a bank run.

Jacklin and Bhattacharya (1988) had divided bank runs into two types: information-based bank run and pure panic-based bank run. Santos (2001) advocates that information-based bank run which is triggered by a leak of poor performance of banking assets is good for the banking industry as it punishes the bad banks, acts as a sanction mechanism and is effective for discipline in the market, whereas panic bank run is harmful for the economy as it forces banks into premature liquidation of assets which disrupts the production process. This supports the Diamond and Dybvig (1983) argument. In addition, such a bank run may create a 'contagion' run which creates a system risk in the entire financial system (Freixas & Rochet, 2008). According to Freixas and Rochet (2008), there are four sources of 'contagion' in the banking industry which lead to systemic risk: (i) changes in expectation of investors, (ii) large-value payment systems, (iii) interbank markets and (iv) over-the-counter operation (mainly on derivatives). However, the critics of Freixas and Rochet (2008) view is, such a 'domino effect' analysis of contagion run has portrayed the passive pictures of the financial institutions who standby and do nothing in response to the sequence of default but in practice they act in reaction to contagion run and impending default (Geneva Report, 2009). To sum up, the actions of institutions can be defined as financial regulations which prevent systemic risk in the financial system. In the next sub-section, we discuss the institutions that are used to prevent systemic risk and bank runs.

Regulations Used to Prevent Systemic Risk and Bank Runs

Davis (1995) mentioned three lines of defense against systemic risk as well as bank run; these are: lender of last resort (LLR), deposit insurance, capital requirements. In addition, Santos (2001) mentioned narrow banking and suspension of convertibility can also be used to insulate banks from run. Some of these proposals are discussed below.

Narrow Banking

It refers a set of regulatory constraints on a bank's portfolio selection that would make them safe in any possible event (Freixas & Rochet, 2008, p. 223); that is, banks will invest in riskless investment opportunities. This approach is largely explained by several scholars (see Bryan, 1988; Gorton & Pennacchi, 1990; Kareken, 1986; Litan, 1987; Pierce, 1991). However, the idea of the narrow banking view is a kind of inefficient allocation of resources. For example, intermediaries may lose the potential gain that exists while taking long-term lending risks (Kashyap et al., 1999). New firms that will take on the banking role to fill the vacuum in the market might also trigger a bank run, and in fact, bank runs cannot be removed from the market by narrow banking (Diamond & Dybvig, 1986).

The Lender of Last Resort (LLR)

The concept of LLR is chiefly based on the argument presented by Bagehot (1873), wherein he argues the central bank has a responsibility to provide enough liquidity to the market to make it vibrant. Bagehot's (1873) argument is succinctly explained by Davis (1995) in the following way: as the central bank has the supreme power to print the currency note to support the financial institutions that face a liquidity problem, the central bank should be considered as LLR. The central bank's LLR role helps the problem bank to avoid fire sales of assets and delay insolvency of an institution and can operate either by injecting funds in the market directly or to provide fund to any individual bank (Davis, 1995). However, Bagehot (1873) put some restrictions while advocating for LLR such as these loans cannot be utilized for lending operations, they should be provided to the financial institutions who have good collateral; that is, LLR role in lending is to illiquid solvent financial institutions (Freixas & Rochet, 2008, p. 223). The LLR function still relevant in the modern banking system as the interbank money market will not provide enough liquidity to the solvent bank in the case of liquidity crisis because of the 'potential coordination problem' (Rochet & Vives, 2004). Davis

(1995) views that LLR operation can save the agency cost of monitoring provided by depositors because when the depositors are assured that any uncertainty faced by the banks can be backed up by the LLR function, depositors will not monitor banks' risk and in turn banks can run with less liquidity. In this case, the risk is, large banks will lose their incentive to monitor borrowers because of the existence of LLR and reduced monitoring by depositors (Davis, 1995). On the contrary, Goodhart (1995) argued that LLR cannot assure depositors because when a bank requires the assistance of the LLR, it signals as insolvent, and hence, depositors will run to the bank. In addition, as the residual risk of the bank will not be granted by LLR assistance, there is still a chance of a contagion run occurring (Davis, 1995).

Deposit insurance

Advocated by Diamond and Dybvig (1983), deposit insurance provides a guarantee that banks are completely protected from runs (Santos, 2001). In practice, deposit insurance covers a maximum ceiling[1] of bank liability which is convertible into cash when a bank becomes bankrupt; that is, under this system, small retail depositors are assured to receive their deposit. This way deposit insurance removes the incentive for 'runs' on solvent banks by uniformed depositors (Davis, 1995). In the US, deposit insurance premiums were instrumentalized by the Federal Reserve mainly to protect from banking panics and random withdrawal risks caused by the Great Depression in the 1930s (Calomiris & Gorton, 1991). The United States Federal Deposit Insurance Corporation (FDIC) was established in 1934 with an initial coverage amount of up to $2,500 (Schooner & Taylor, 2010) which is now $250,000 per depositor, per insured bank (FDIC, 2020). There are two views which are observed for bank panics when suggesting the introduction of the deposit insurance scheme in the US; one is the asymmetric information view and another is the withdrawn risk view (Schooner & Taylor, 2010). The main difference between both views is identifying the source of panic; however, both recommended deposit insurance as an optimal solution. There are debates on how deposit insurance could be offered, either private or public sector. In the case of the private insurance system, the potential advantage is

---

[1] In Bangladesh, the maximum insured deposit is BDT 200,000 (equivalent to USD 2,300) in the case of bankruptcies, under Deposit Insurance System & proposed Deposit Protection Act 2020 (*Amanat Surokka Aain 2020*) of Ministry of Finance.

competition provides incentives for information extraction and accurate pricing; however, the lack of creditability during systemic risk is a major drawback of the private system (Freixas & Rochet, 2008). In addition, Davis (1995) argued that public sector deposit insurance can only provide unconditional guarantees which private sector cannot, as the government has power to tax and to create money.

The critique on deposit insurance system can be raised from three perspectives: (i) moral hazard, (ii) pricing issue and (iii) incomplete information issue. Moral hazard raised from depositors in the sense that they lost the incentive to monitor the bank as their losses are already guaranteed by insurance (Dothan & Williams, 1980; Kareken & Wallace, 1978). From the bankers' perspective, when the insurance scheme charges the bank a flat rate premium, banks cannot internalize the full cost of risk, and therefore, banks have an incentive to take more risk which leads to moral hazard (Santos, 2001). However, flat or risk-based pricing of deposit insurance is another debatable issue in academic circles. A good amount of empirical research (see Buser et al., 1981; Marcus & Shaked, 1984; Pennacchi, 1987; Ronn & Verma, 1986) has been conducted on risk-based pricing of deposit insurance based on Merton's (1977, 1978) arbitrage pricing model; however, they found that arbitrage-based methods can only be possible under certain conditions—for example, if an insurance company is able to perfectly observe the banking risk (Freixas & Rochet, 2008). Besides, the existence of information asymmetry in the banking business makes it difficult (or inefficient) to charge banks a fair price for deposit insurance (Campbell et al., 1992; Santos, 2006). Their point is that undercapitalized banks will take more risk (a kind of adverse selection) due to time lag in the implementation stage of an insurance premium, i.e., as the bank managers and equity holders know that they will not be liable in the case of bank failure.

<u>Bailout and bank closure policy</u>
This policy garnered heavy attention in public policy and in academic debate after the financial crisis of 2007–2008. The debate is, at what point should the government bail out the banks and in what circumstances should the government leave the banks to die? Because bailouts require huge a transfer of tax payers' money to the financial institutions, by contrast, bankruptcies have a social cost such as households losing their savings and bankruptcies disrupt the payment systems as well as the production process. Acharya and Yorulmazer (2007) advocate for

a bank closure policy when a banks' failure is small, and they can be acquired by other surviving banks. Farhi and Tirole's (2009) view is that bailouts act as a kind of 'loss of reputation' by the central bank as it is evidence of the central bank's failure of supervision and monitoring. Bernard et al. (2018) analyze the network effect model to justify when the bailout option provides incentive to the market and conclude that bailout is effective when there is a high chance to develop systemic risk by a 'too important to fail' type of bank; otherwise, it creates the wrong incentive for market discipline. Lucchetta et al. (2018) also have a similar view. In fact, as discussed earlier, banks take deposits from households which actually provide an incentive to banks to monitor their borrowers less, in a sense that bad banks can use the depositors as a hostage during the financial crisis or 'bank closure policy' and go to the central bank for a bail out. However, in the case of bankruptcies, it makes sense to bail out the depositors to avoid the social cost of bank failure; however, it makes no sense to bail out the equity holders of the bank and the subordinate debt holders (who enjoy high risk premium) as they are responsible for bank management and performance. If equity holders and subordinated debt holders are bailed out along with other claimholders of the bank, at the end, the shareholders and bond holders are not bearing any risk at all. In nutshell, a bailout policy is a last line of defense to stop systemic risk; however, there are critics on the process of bailouts mainly from the viewpoint of the ultimate cost of taxpayers and there should be an optimal clear-cut bailout policy from the government in the case of financial crisis or to prevent systemic risk.

To sum up, although the tools we discussed so far have some advantages, the prime drawback of these tools (LLR, deposit insurance and bailout policy) is that all of them are vulnerable to excessive risk taking by banks which in turn impose heavy burdens on regulators (Davis, 1995). In other words, these tools cannot put any restriction on the bank owners and managers for taking more risk. From this perspective, next we discuss on capital regulation's (minimum capital adequacy) role on preventing systemic risk and bank run.

Capital regulation

The general theme of capital regulation is shifting the risk insured by regulators to the equity holder's shoulders to some extent. It is presumed that; shareholders have to bear the risk at first in case of bankruptcies. In addition, capital regulation dictates that banks must choose an optimal portfolio in a sense that banks have to choose risky projects in their portfolio at the cost of additional capital. There are various approaches such as the corporate finance perspective, portfolio perspective, principal-agent problem perspective and externalities perspective in the existing banking regulation literature to justify capital regulation, which are described below.

(a) Corporate finance theory approach

Modigliani and Millar's (MM) (1958) theory of capital structure in corporate finance assumes that the market value of a firm is independent from its capital structure—in other words, they hypothesized that the proportion of equity and debt in a firm's capital is irrelevant when analyzing the expected return of the firm. Schooner and Taylor (2010) mentioned that the MM theory strictly maintained the assumptions that there is no information asymmetry in the market and the market is frictionless (no transaction cost and taxes), but in the real world there are information asymmetries in the credit market which make it imperfect (Stiglitz & Wesis, 1981). This reality demonstrates that the MM theory is inapplicable to the banking industry. Hence, Schooner and Taylor (2010) advocate for considering the capital structure of banks when discussing banking regulation. In addition, while analyzing the capital structure of the banking firm, they consider two more issues (which we discussed earlier): (i) the safety net (deposit insurance) that exists in the banking sector cannot stop bank run of uninsured depositors, and (ii) even if the deposit insurance can be properly priced, bank has risk shifting incentives (toward depositors) due to bank owners' limited liability.

(b) Portfolio approach

Freixas and Rochet (2008) view that capital regulation for banks is required as the introduction of deposit insurance and LLR function cannot fully prevent systemic risk in the banking industry (since both instruments have their structural limitations such as deposit insurance has a moral hazard problem and LLR function has a huge social cost). They argued while discussing portfolio approach that if risks are correctly measured through risk-based weightages, then banks will behave as portfolio managers and in turn solvency regulation would be effective.

However, Suzuki (2011) views that this argument for capital regulation has two flaws: (i) there is a 'market-based' risk weight which suffers reliability problem and (ii) the correct measurement of risk is still debatable in capital regulation. In addition, Eichberger and Harper (1997, p. 238) view that the capital regulation can only prevent bank runs or systemic risk if the illiquid assets are riskless because the cost of this regulation for the bank owners depends on the opportunity cost of their funds. This means that if the bank owner's incentive will not be enhanced by injecting fresh capital, they will not inject capital in the bank which makes the capital regulation futile.

(c) Principal- Agent problem approach

The essence of capital regulation in the 1990s was argued from a principal-agent problem perspective. Scholars examined the capital regulation under principal-agent conflicts. For instance, Santos (1999) views that due to information asymmetries between banks and firms, banks use standard contracts with firms. However, as bank deposits are insured, banks can distort the contract and can lend the firms more than they deserve. He also argued that capital regulation can stop such distortion because if the cost of capital of the bank is higher, then the bank will execute the contract in a standard way to minimize the information asymmetries in the borrower's firm which prevents bank failure risk on individual bank-level. In addition, Besanko and Kanatas (1996) examined the principal-agent problem between bank owners and bank managers. They view that stringent capital regulation can minimize the conflicts between owners and managers because issuing equity may decline the stock price and dilute the ownership of bank and thereby reduce incentive for bank owners to take more risk. On the other hand, bank managers will also lose their incentive to take more risk as there is no way to issue new capital to maintain capital adequacy. However, the problem within this approach is there are other legal institutions, for example corporate governance code, banking companies act used to limit the conflicts of principal-agent in banking, and hence, it is difficult to precisely quantify the contribution of capital regulation for minimizing such conflicts.

(d) Externalities effect approach

Acharya (2009) and Gorton and Winton (1995) advocated the capital regulation from an externalities effect perspective. Acharya (2009) views that, in the case of portfolio diversification, individual banks can diversify the risk, and in turn, the risk of failure may be minimized. However, this risk diversification creates another probability of systemic risk as all banks are perfectly correlated in this state and can fail together which he called the negative externalities effect. He opined to avoid such systemic risk and negative externalities by prudential regulation such as capital regulation (hoping capital regulation can act as proxy of monitoring activities of regulators). Gorton and Winton (1995) opined that bank owners need to enhance a bank's charter value while issuing additional capital under capital regulation. They mainly stressed that as the cost of capital is higher in banking industry, shareholders have less incentive to raise capital which limits them from taking more risk, and this is the positive externalities effect of capital regulation in the industry. The limitation of both approaches (Acharya, 2009; Gorton & Winton, 1995) is they didn't consider the macroeconomic factor in the economy which contributed more to the externality's analysis. In our view, this is the major lacuna that exists in the capital regulation which needs to be addressed.

To sum up, the rationales for capital regulation we discussed above are tabulated in Table 3.1.

An academic debate on capital regulation vs. deposit insurance

The effectiveness of capital regulation and deposit insurance is examined from various perspectives in academic circles, and there is sharp debate on which one is more efficient to prevent systemic risk and bank run. For example, Kareken and Wallace (1978) and Sharpe (1978) examined the fixed deposit insurance premium and bank risk taking attitude under a perfect market and found that under a fixed premium rate, banks have an incentive to take more risk and shift the cost of bankruptcies to the central bank's shoulders. Their point is, if capital regulation is imposed along with deposit premium scheme, the risk shifting can be minimized; however, their analysis didn't make it clear why deposit insurance is required if the market is perfect and when there is no information asymmetry. In addition, when the deposit insurance is properly priced, then banks have no incentive to take more risk or shift the risk to regulators. On the other hand, Kim and Santomero (1988) study the effect of capital regulation

Table 3.1 Rationales for capital regulation

Sl	Approaches	Views	Critique
1	Corporate finance theory approach	Firm capital structure and bank capital structure are different in nature, hence capital matters in banking business	Fails to quantify the minimum capital requirements
2	Portfolio approach	Capital regulation is effective if risk is properly assigned to assets	Reliability on risk measurement
3	Principal-agent problem	Capital regulation can minimize the principal-agent problem	Other institutions like governance code can be used instead of capital regulation
4	Externalities effects	Capital regulation can prevent externalities effect	Ignore the macroeconomic factors for externalities

under an imperfect market scenario and information asymmetry. Their argument is that when banking assets are assigned a risk weightage, banks have no incentive to reshuffle their portfolio and hence reduce their risk appetite. In other words, they suggest that risk-based capital regulation reduces the probability of bank insolvency. In addition, Rochet (1992) suggests that minimum capital requirements along with the risk-weight-based regulation can prevent the systemic risk in the banking industry which arises from information asymmetry. Furlong and Keely (1989) test the marginal gains from increasing asset risk with higher capital requirements under imperfect market conditions and view that higher capital requirement can reduce the marginal gains of taking more risk (i.e., expanding the asset risk). The reason is that the marginal value of the deposit insurance option with respect to asset risk declines as leverage declines, and in turn, higher capital requirement reduces the bank's incentive to take more risk (Santos, 2001). More specifically, their view is that stringent capital can eliminate the incentive for banks to take more risk as marginal cost of capital will be higher when flat insurance premium is practiced in the market. However, they consider that banks can only issue new capital to respond the stringent capital regulation and they did not consider subordinated debt as an alternative source of regulatory capital. To sum up, there is mixed views on the effectiveness of capital regulation on risk taking behavior. For example, approach with the 'utility maximization' model, Kahane (1977), Koehn and Santomero (1980) claim that capital stringency can enhance the bank risk taking behavior, on the contrast, Furlong and Keely (1989), Keely and Furlong (1990) while approaching with the 'option model' claim that capital stringency can prevent risk taking behavior of the bank. However, the common in both sides is, deposit insurance premium (whether it is properly priced or mispriced) cannot alone stop bank insolvency and capital regulation can be an additional instrument for regulating banks.

Limitations of capital regulation and systemic risk

A contemporary debate among academic researchers is, can capital regulation prevent systemic risk, or an international bank run? In fact, it is difficult to answer this in a generalized way, as there are flaws in capital regulation on the one hand and there are other factors such macroeconomic issues which can trigger systemic risk on the other hand. However, below, we discuss some flaws in Basel-type capital regulation (Basel I, II & III) rather than other issues of systemic risk and bank run.

There were couple of limitations of Basel Accord I. For example, (i) the difference in tax and accounting rules across the globe was not taken into consideration while computing eligible capital (Matthews & Thompson, 2014, p. 218); (ii) the accord only considers credit risk of the bank and ignores the interest rate risk, liquidity risk, operational risk and currency risk (Matthews & Thompson, 2014); (iii) the distinction in lending OECD and non-OECD sovereign governments creates a political debate in the financial industry (Schooner & Taylor, 2010); and (iv) considering subordinated debt as regulatory capital without proper justification. The notable critique against Basel Accord II after the financial crisis in 2007–2008 was: (i) the accord was procyclical; that is, when the asset price increases, banks can maintain higher capital ratio and during recession or financial meltdown when the asset prices went down, banks capital adequacy cannot prevent bank insolvency (Goodhart, 2009), (ii) supervisory failure and failure of internal risk models were not addressed in Basel II (Freixas et al., 2015), (iii) the definition of regulatory capital was not modified from Basel I (Freixas et al., 2015) and (iv) credit rating agencies reporting proves inefficient and ineffective to bring market discipline (Freixas et al., 2015; Langohr & Langohr, 2008) and ECAIs prudence of rating in the case of bank loans (Abdelal, 2007). Finally, Basel Framework III was completely finalized in December 2017 which aims to overcome the limitations of Basel Accord II and ensure financial stability in the economic system and schedule to be fully implemented in 2022.[2] However, the question that remains is, can Basel III stop the next financial crisis? Freixas et al. (2015) argued that the financial crisis in 2007–2008 indicated that microprudential regulation like capital regulation and other safety nets to some extend can prevent individual bank failures; however, it cannot prevent the systemic risk in the banking industry as a whole. They proposed macroprudential policy measures such as liquidity requirement for individual banks, impose sectoral credit limits, quality of borrowers and monitor all levels of risk in the banking industry, the sources of those risk such as spillovers to financial markets, and bubble in assets to prevent systemic risk in the industry.

To wrap up the discussion, a fundamental problem of the Basel Accords is that they follow a 'backward approach' of banking regulation in a sense that after a financial crisis, the regulators can identify the loopholes of the existing regulation and then take initiative to amend the accord, which means that without a financial shock/crisis we cannot predict how effective the Basel-type capital regulation is. In fact, because of this fundamental loophole within the institution, it is difficult to prevent systemic risk (bank run) in the banking industry through capital regulation. Although it is true for formal institutions that the changes in institutions are incremental (North, 1990, 2005), the costs for such changes in the institutions, especially in the financial sector, are too high.

3.4 EXISTING DEBATE ON QUANTIFICATION OF CREDIT RISK IN BASEL REGULATION

There are two mechanisms advocated in Basel regulation while quantifying credit risk (detailed discussed in Chapter 4) and CRAs/ECAIs are assigned in this process for quantification of credit risk under standardized approach. In this section, we mainly discuss the existing academic debate on CRAs/ECAIs, their informational value and role in the Basel Accord. This theoretical discussion will aid our discussion in Chapter 5.

---

[2] It is noted that as on March 27, 2020, the implementation date of the Basel III standards that finalized in December 2017 has been deferred by one year to January 1, 2023, and transitional arrangements for output floor has also been deferred by one year to January 1, 2028, by BCBS to respond to COVID-19 global pandemic. See details at https://www.bis.org/press/p200327.htm.

Definition of Credit Rating and CRAs

There is no industry definition or standard to describe credit ratings and no trade association of credit rating agencies (CRAs), and during the 2003–2006 worldwide review of the credit rating industry, various regulatory bodies from around the globe offered their definition of credit rating (Langhor & Langhor, 2008, p. 23). In broad sense, the definition of credit rating and credit rating agency can be explained from two views: the academic and regulatory views. Credit rating agencies are experts in analyzing firm's information for a long period as they have access to the private information which is not publicly disclosed; investors are relying on CRAs' information, and thus, they reduce information asymmetries between issuer and investors (Boot et al., 2006; Cho & Choi, 2015; Kammoun & Louizi, 2015; Yang et al., 2017). The chief question here is, how trustworthy is the information that the credit rating agencies provide. Regarding the value of CRAs information, Coffee (2006, p. 288) mentioned CRA as 'reputational intermediaries' as the issuer discloses some confidential information to the CRA which they cannot disclose to an individual security analyst. This 'reputational capital' is the main strength of credit rating agencies. Some scholars noted CRAs as 'gatekeeper[s] of capital' (Rahim, 2010; Strier, 2008). It is a kind of gatekeeper that differs from other gatekeepers in three ways such as profitability, conflict of interest and structured finance (Partnoy, 2006). Wymeersch and Kruithof (2006) noted, credit rating agencies are private independent companies that evaluate the creditworthiness of financial instruments or issuers of such instruments and reflecting their credit rating opinion using classification system of gradation. The value of credit rating is the objective feedback that the credit rating agencies provide to all concerned about the long-term implications of the firm's current risk posture (Santomero, 2006). Therefore, from an academic point of view, CRAs eliminate the informational barriers between investors and issuers.

In contrast, the regulatory and legal definition of a CRA is a bit more descriptive, clear and wider than the definition used in the academic circle. According to the International Organization of Securities Commission (IOSCO), 'Credit rating' or 'rating' means an assessment regarding the creditworthiness of an entity or obligation, expressed using an established and defined ranking system and 'Credit rating agency' or 'CRA' means an entity that is in the business of issuing credit ratings (IOSCO, 2015, p. A-4). Below we mention few regulatory definitions of credit rating and CRA. 'A credit rating is defined as an opinion regarding the creditworthiness of an entity, a debt or financial obligation, debt security, preferred share or other financial instrument, or an issuer of such debt or financial obligation, debt security, preferred share or other financial instrument, issued using an established and defined ranking system of rating categories. A credit rating agency is defined as a legal person whose occupation includes the issuing of credit ratings on a professional basis' (EC, 2009). According to the US CRA regulatory program, 'a credit rating is defined as an assessment of the creditworthiness of an obligor as an entity or with respect to specific securities or money market instruments' and 'a credit rating agency is defined as a person that, among other things, is engaged in the business of issuing credit ratings on the Internet or through another readily accessible means, for free or a reasonable fee' (U.S. SEC, 2013). 'A credit rating is defined as a grade indicating the result of an assessment regarding the credit status (creditworthiness) of financial instruments or legal persons using symbols or figures, while a credit rating agency is defined as, among other things, a person whose occupation includes determining credit ratings and either providing them to someone or making them available to the public on a professional basis and who is registered with the Japan Financial Service' (FIE Act, 2006, Article 2 (36)). Whereas the Bangladeshi securities regulator defines, 'Credit Rating' means formal evaluation of credit and/or investment and capability of servicing obligations. 'Credit Rating Company' refers to an investment advisory company which intends to engage in or is so engaged primarily in the business of evaluation of credit or investment risk through a recognized and formal process of assigning rating to present or proposed loan obligations or equity of any business enterprise (BSEC, 1996). Therefore, according to the regulatory bodies' definition, we can simply define CRA as a formal entity for providing authentic information or judgments to market participants and CRAs act as 'gatekeeper[s] of capital' which ultimately protects public interest.

Existing Debate on the Role of CRA in Basel Accord

In academic circles, the role of CRAs is a debatable issue. Specifically, some are highly critiqued for regulatory uses of CRAs rating (Partnoy, 1999). Some scholars mentioned that CRAs are neither public nor any meaningful sense of private (Abdelal, 2007). Some argue (Coffee, 2011; Miglionico, 2014) that CRAs' existing regulation is based on 'input' (what the agencies do, how and how frequently) rather than 'output' (whether the agencies perform their task well) and this regulatory approach ultimately goes in favor of CRAs because of their regulatory designation and uses (Abdelal, 2007; White, 2010). While in the academic discussion, two rationales are put forward in favor to regulate the CRAs: (i) as an information provider (ii) the information is used as a regulatory tool for financial institution regulation. Theoretical analysis on CRAs' regulation is chiefly based on these two rationales. Hemraj (2015) summarized five CRAs regulation-related theories while advocating to regulate CRAs. These are: reputation theory, gatekeeper theory, yield hunt theory, agency theory and deterrence theory. To keep our discussion on track, the study does not attempt to discuss those. In fact, CRAs and their regulations play an important role in the financial industry. We presume that based on the historic roles played by CRAs in bond rating in early 1900s (see Appendix), the BIS has allowed rating bank exposure by CRA and its rating can be used in the Basel Accord. In the following we elaborate on this.

Expected role of ECAI in banking industry

CRAs' historical background (see Appendix for CRAs history in the US) shows that the *Raison d'être* of credit rating is that it serves the expectation of both lenders and borrowers. It is evident from Appendix that investors wish to ensure the expected return from their investment, whereas issuers badly need to access investors' funds, which is the main reason for bond rating by CRAs in the early 1900s in the US. CRAs assure the investors regarding the bonds' expected yield through rating notch. Hence, CRAs business depends on the perfection of its provided information. Scholars argue that CRA business depends on two critical factors such as its reliability in making predictions and its public acceptability (Miglionico, 2014). In addition, CRAs play an important role in the financial market, specifically the assessment of default debt instruments issued by corporations and other institutional players in the market (Miglionico, 2014). Rating plays an important role by reducing information asymmetry problems between investors and borrowers, and if rating is not playing that role, 'adverse selection' and 'moral hazard' would significantly contribute to an increase in cost of external financing (Langohr & Langhor, 2008). Besides, Darbellay (2013) mentioned that credit rating plays four roles in the modern financial market: information intermediaries, acting as regulatory tools, as a contracting tool and as a monitoring tool. Miglionico (2014) considered credit rating as a responsible 'public good' as it deals 'as an intermediary to manage financial information.' However, in academic circles, there is debate as to whether credit rating should be considered as a 'public good' or not. For example, Stiglitz (2009) considered 'information' as a public good and that good information is required for a well-functioning market economy. Based on this argument, Stiglitz (2009) is in favor of considering the rating information as a public good. Choi (2004) argued for 'protecting investors' and agrees credit rating should be a public good.

On the other hand, White (2013) argued, as CRAs' pay model (whether it is issuer pay or investors pay) is complicated when it is considered as public good, CRAs will lose incentives for prudent ratings. At this point, the question is, if the CRA pay model is complicated then why is ECAIs' credit information allowed to be used in Basel regulation? However, White (2013) did not answer the question but critiques that CRAs regulations in fact did not bring any solution at the end, at least from the Basel Accord perspective. We presume that if the BIS abandons the regulatory use of CRAs' rating, this will create incentives for banks, as bank managers can then solely rely on the IRB approach for credit risk quantification in which the methodologies can be tailored to take more risk and maximize managerial incentive. In turn, systemic risk cannot be protected. However, if we take the Stiglitz (2009) arguments that for a well-functioning financial market, the rating information should be free to all, then how we can judge/evaluate the quality of the information that is provided by CRAs to the market is not explored by Stiglitz (2009) argument. Besides, what is the guarantee that the market will be smooth functioning even if CRAs provided information mitigated the information asymmetries? Therefore, there is ongoing academic debate on a CRA's expected role in the Basel framework.

To wrap up the discussion, our view is that credit risk mitigation in the banking industry largely depends on the monitoring and screening skills of the professional bankers, as CRAs are rating the client's overall business, not the specific loan proposal under Basel Accord guidelines. In fact, bankers are the main players in this context who have access to identifying the real credit risk involved with the loan proposal and subsequent follow up in the utilization of the funds. Hence, bankers have incentives to hire CRAs or to use the standardized approach of the Basel Accords, as bankers can shift their obligation or responsibility of measuring the credit risk of the projects to the CRAs' shoulder to some extent. Therefore, we believe that, from the Basel Accord perspective, a CRA's/ECAI's role is to provide quality credit information of the borrower's business to banks which is expressed in a rating notch. Besides, as an ECAIs' rating is used for computation of the RWA of credit risk, it is essential to investigate the quality of credit information that ECAIs provide. We analyze the quality of Bangladeshi domestic ECAIs' credit information in detail in Chapter 5.

Wrap Up Comment on Existing Debate on CRA

To sum up, from this theoretical consideration of a CRA's role, the current view is that CRAs should play a role to reduce the information asymmetries between banks and borrowers. As reputation theory suggests that CRAs' business depends on reputation, the chief question is, is reputation enough to ensure ECAIs' rating quality which ultimately helps to prevent systemic risk and stabilize the banking system? Darbellay (2013) and Miglionico (2019) strongly oppose that reputation is not enough; rather, creating a 'liability regime' in the CRAs institutions ensures a CRAs' rating accuracy. As the Basel framework endorsed the CRAs/ECAIs rating for quantification of credit risk, the current study supports the theses of Darbellay (2013) and Miglionico (2019) that the anomalies that we observed in the Bangladeshi banking industry are the outcome of institutional loopholes in ECAIs' regulations. We briefly analyze the ECAIs' liability regime from institutional perspective in Chapter 4.

3.5   EXISTING DEBATE ON ROLE OF SUB-DEBT IN THE BASEL ACCORDS

As was mentioned earlier, sub-debt is considered as regulatory capital under the Basel Accords since 1988. There is an existing academic debate on the role of sub-debt in the Basel framework and this debate is based on two key issues (i) how well sub-debt brings market discipline (ii) does sub-debt act to 'leverage' with equity? In this sub-section, we discuss those issues which will aid our discussion regarding sub-debt in Chapters 6 and 7.

Sub-debt and Market Discipline

The first use of sub-debt as a capital component (maximum one-half of bank equity) in the US banking system was acknowledged by the Office of the Comptroller of the Currency (OCC) in 1962 as the US commercial banks ratio of 'capital to risk assets' fell steeply in 1961 due to financial disintermediation and overseas expansion of the large US banks (Goodhart, 2011). The facts for widely used sub-debt by American bankers include more accessibility of funds than equity, lower cost than equity, interest expenses are tax deductible (but dividend are not), and issuance of debt can avoid dilution of earnings per share (EPS) (Goodhart, 2011). On the other hand, when risk-based capital requirements were introduced in 1988, sub-debt was considered as a capital component chiefly to bring market discipline in banks' risk-taking behavior hoping that a bank run would not occur (Evanoff, 1994, p. 514; Evanoff & Wall, 2000, 2001, 2002; Evanoff et al., 2011). However, the BIS (1988), while considering sub-debt as capital component, commented cautiously and stated that 'subordinated term debt instruments have significant deficiencies as constituents of capital in view of their fixed maturity and inability to absorb losses except in a liquidation.' However, later sub-debt was considered as supplementary capital by central banks globally hoping that sub-debt would be used as an instrument to cushion the deposit insurance fund and reduce the burden of taxpayers in case of bankruptcy cost. It is presumed that debt holders are risk sensitive, having more information than individual depositors, thus debt holders seek higher interest rates (kind of risk premium) from the risky bank and thus behavior of banks can be effectively controlled by market force which could bring market discipline at the end (Garten, 1986). In addition, this behavior of debt holders may give a signal for national supervisors for on-site and off-site supervisions of problem banks (Ahmed, 2009). Hence, subordinate debt proposal is considered a superior alternative in the early 1990s, when Basel Accord I was supposed to be reformed. Therefore, the main objectives of sub-debt in the Basel framework are twofold: one is direct market discipline, and another is indirect market discipline. Direct discipline in the sense that, 'increased cost of raising new debt in the primary capital markets could exert direct market discipline on banks i.e. the anticipation of higher re-financing cost may constrain banks' risk-taking. This could complement the activities by supervisory authorities in constraining banks' risk-taking attitude' (BCBS, 2003). Indirect discipline in the sense that, 'the prices of banks' outstanding securities (bond yield-spreads and share prices) could provide a signal of the bank's financial condition and risk outlook (i.e. default risk). Therefore, spreads and share prices could provide inputs to the monitoring exercised by private investors, supervisors and central banks. The monitoring and potential corrective actions by market participants and authorities have been labeled as indirect market discipline' (BCBS, 2003).

The crucial question is, was sub-debt successful in bringing market discipline? It is difficult to answer as there are mixed empirical results dating back to its inception. For example, Chen and Hasan (2011), DeYoung (1988), Flannery and Sorescu (1996), Jagtiani et al. (2000), Jagtiani and Lemieux (2001), Morgan and Stiroh (2000, 2001) argue from empirical evidence that sub-debt coupon rates can enhance market discipline. In contrast, Ferguson (1999), Greenspan (2000), Meyer (1999), Moskow (1998) argued not to depend on subordinated debt coupon rates for monitoring the banks. Birchler and Hancock (2003) from theoretical and empirical analysis note that 'the subordinated yield spread does not reflect the best available information on a banking organizations' risk.' In addition, after financial crisis, both academics and practitioners (governors of the central bank) don't believe that sub-debt can bring market discipline (Brown et al., 2017; Götz & Tröger, 2016; Rixtel et al., 2015; Tucker, 2013, 2014) and some scholars argue that sub-debt yield fails to provide strong signal to the national supervisor regarding banks' distress (Miller et al., 2015).

Sub-debt and Leveraging

When a bank accumulates NPL, there are two significant factors for the banks: they must maintain provisioning (a system to keep the money against the non-performing assets) against their NPL or defaulted loans, and consequently, it directly affects their net profit as well as shrinking their ROE (Ahmed et al., 2017; Bony & Moniruzzaman, 2017; Dey, 2019). Secondly, raising NPL causes an increase in RWA under the Basel Accords and it lowers the CRAR of the bank (discussed in Chapter 1). In fact, this is the essence of the capital adequacy ratio that it acts as leverage to the risk-taking behavior of the banks, in so far as banks' risk appetite is controlled by CRAR. However, Suzuki (2011) succinctly summarized the essence of capital adequacy ratio in another theoretical approach and it is worth quoting this, 'a historical perspective shows that capital adequacy requirements (the level of equity capital to total assets) was conceptualized by US regulators as a mechanism for preventing banks from over-lending to risker projects' (Miyoda, 1994). In the US, Return on Equity (ROE) had long been used as an important indicator for measuring business management performance. If operating cost remains unchanged, there were two major ways for bank managers to raise ROE. One was to expand the loan assets by leveraging. This involved borrowing funds and increasing the weight of debts for lending in order to earn profits for equity capital. The other was to pursue higher Returns on Assets (ROA). ROA is a ratio of profits to total assets [ROA = Profits/Total Assets], while ROE is a ratio of profits to equity capital [ROE = Profits/Equity Capital]. Thus, we could say that the capital adequacy ratio is a ratio of ROA to ROE (ROA/ROE = Profits/Total Assets ÷ Profits/Equity Capital = Equity Capital / Total Assets = capital adequacy ratio. In other words, ROE is a ratio of ROA to capital adequacy ratio. Therefore, the capital adequacy requirement aimed to prevent banks from expanding loan assets by leveraging and thereby promoted safety and soundness in the banking system by getting banks to maintain an adequate capital buffer against unexpected credit losses' (Suzuki, 2011, p. 54). Posner (2015) while analyzing the history of adopting capital adequacy requirements in the US has mentioned that one of the objectives of the Fed adopting capital adequacy ratio was to limit the incentives of banks which support Suzuki's (2011) explanation. From the theoretical approach explained by Suzuki (2011), we can say that when banks experience defaulted loans in their portfolio, CRAR can be maintained by either (i) enhancing ROA or (ii) leveraging the equity (which will enhance the ROE). In fact, the main point of this unconventional thesis that Suzuki (2011) made, that the chief objective of CRAR is to refrain the bank managers to higher ROE. The study empirically investigates this thesis and the relationship between sub-debt and ROE in Chapter 6.

Wrap Up Comment on Existing Debate on Role of Sub-debt in the Basel Framework

In conclusion, from this theoretical discussion on sub-debt, we show that one of the objectives of sub-debt is to ensure 'market discipline' (Evanoff, 1994; Evanoff & Wall, 2000, 2001, 2002; Evanoff et al., 2011; Goodhart, 2011, pp. 197–205). The logic is, if the yield of sub-debt indicates the bank performance, then the weak banks have to subscribe their issued bond with high yield (as a risk premium) which in turn helps to reign in the banks' risk appetite and in this way sub-debt is expected to bring market discipline. Based on this argument, sub-debt is widely accepted as a regulatory capital component by US regulators (Federal Reserve) in 1970s and later by BCBS in Basel Accords I, II and III. However, the puzzle is the reality of the banking sector that is not endorsing the role of sub-debt (as expected by theorists) to bring 'market discipline' in Bangladesh. For example, the amount of issuance of sub-debt by commercial banks has tremendously increased since 2009 to 2018 as a Tier 2 capital under the Basel Accords; however, the industry performance deteriorated significantly during the same period (see discussion in Chapter 1). We have also discussed another role of sub-debt, i.e., the 'leveraging' strategy theoretically in this chapter. In the case of Bangladesh, subordinated debt was proposed to be considered as Tier 2 capital to mitigate the capital adequacy problem and implementation of Basel II (Ahmed, 2009). However, all debts (except one) that are issued for capital adequacy purposes are not traded in the market, and as a result, it is quite difficult to judge the role of sub-debt from a 'direct market discipline' thesis from the Bangladeshi perspective. Therefore, to examine the role of sub-debt in the Basel Accords, this study extends the thesis of Suzuki (2011) in such a way that sub-debt could be used to leverage equity which finally increases bank ROE. To conclude, in our view, though the capital adequacy ratio of the industry has slightly been improved with sub-debt, it creates two serious systemic problems such as (i) ill-incentives for 'leveraging' and thereby to expand loan exposure (ii) funding pattern of sub-debts which create a systemic risk on the financial stability of the country (see details in Chapter 6).

3.6   Concluding Remarks

In this chapter, we briefly discussed the banking business model with two contemporary theories and explain the limitations of banking business model. Then, we discussed the banking role and business models with portfolio theory and monitoring theory and extend our argument for banking regulation from depositors' representative approach and systemic risk approaches. These theories explain the basic systemic risk that exists in the banking industry and how systemic risk is managed through banking regulations. We also discussed capital regulation and analyzed its rationale from various perspectives. We have pointed out that the philosophy of the capital regulations is to stop bank run and systemic risk and in turn ensure financial stability. Then, we turned our focus on the existing debate on CRAs' roles in the Basel framework. It will aid our discussion on ECAIs and their rating quality associated discussion in Chapters 4 and 5. We also discussed the academic debate on sub-debt from the 'market discipline' and 'leveraging' perspective which will help to understand our discussion in Chapter 6.

REFERENCES

Abdelal, R. (2007). *Capital rules: The construction of global finance.* Harvard University Press.

Acharya, V. V. (2009). A theory of systemic risk and design of prudential bank regulation. *Journal of Financial Stability, 5,* 224–225.

Acharya, V. V., & Yorulmazer, T. (2007). Too many to fail- An analysis of time-consistency in bank closure policies. *Journal of Financial Intermediation, 16,* 1–31.

Ahmed, M. K. (2009). The role of an explicit subordinated debt policy in the smooth transition to Basel II: Developing economy perspective. *Journal of Banking Regulation, 10*(3), 221–233.

Ahmed, M. N., Pandit, A. C., Hossain, M. Z., Banu, R., & Siddiqui, M. S. (2017). *Research report on impact of adopting Basel accords in the banking sector of Bangladesh.* Bangladesh Institute of bank Management.

Bagehot. (1873). *Lombard street: A description of the money market.* Charles Scribner's Sons.

Baltensperger, A. (1980). Alternative approaches to the theory of banking firm. *Journal of Monetary Economics, 6,* 1–37.

Bangladesh Securities and Exchange Commission (BSEC). (1996). *Credit rating companies rules 1996.* BSEC. https://www.sec.gov.bd/home/lbook.

Bank for International Settlements (BIS). (1988). *International convergence of capital measurement and capital standards.* BCBS, Bank for International Settlements.

Basel Committee on Banking Supervision (BCBS). (2003). *Markets for bank subordinated debt and equity in basel committee member countries.* Bank for International Settlements.

Benston, G. J. (1964). Interest payments on demand deposits and bank investment behavior. *Journal of Political Economy, 72*(5), 431–449.

Bernard, B., Capponi, A., & Stiglitz, J. E. (2018). *Bail-ins and bails-outs: Incentives, connectivity, and systemic stability* (NBER Working Paper 23747). National Bureau of Economic Research.

Besanko, D., & Kanatas, G. (1996). The regulation of bank capital: Do capital standards promote bank safety? *Journal of Financial Intermediation, 5,* 160–183.

Bhattacharya, S., & Gale, D. (1987). Preference shocks, liquidity, and central bank policy. In W. A. Barnett & K. J. Singleton (Eds.), *New approaches to monetary economics* (pp. 69–88). Cambridge University Press.

Birchler, U. W., & Hancock, D. (2003). What does the yield on subordinated bank debt measure? *Review of Financial Studies, 13*(3), 813–840.

Bony, S. Z., & Moniruzzaman, M. (2017). A comparative analysis between commercial banks and insurance companies in Bangladesh on the basis of capital structure. *International Journal of Business and Social Research, 7*(8).

Boot, A. W. A., Milbourn, T. T., & Schmeits, A. (2006). Credit ratings as coordination mechanisms. *Review of Financial Studies, 19*(1), 81–118.

Brown, M., Evangelou, I., & Stix, H. (2017). *Banking crises, bail-ins and money holdings* (Working Paper No. 2017-2). Central Bank of Cyprus. https://www.centralbank.cy/en/publications/working-papers.

Bryan, L. L. (1988). *Breaking up the bank: Rethinking on industry under Siege.* Dow Jones-Irwin.

Bryant, J. (1980). A model of reserves, bank runs, and deposit insurance. *Journal of Banking and Finance, 4,* 335–344.

Buser, S., Chen, A., & Kane, E. (1981). Federal deposit insurance, regulatory policy and optimal bank capital. *Journal of Finance, 26*(1), 51–60.

Calomiris, C. W., & Gorton, G. (1991). The origins of banking panics: Models, facts, and bank regulation. In R. G. Hubbard (Ed.), *Financial markets and financial crises* (pp. 109–174). University of Chicago Press.

Campbell, T. S., Chan, Y., & Marino, A. M. (1992). An incentive-based theory of bank regulation. *Journal of Financial Intermediation, 2*(3), 255–276.

Carapeto, M., Moeller, S., Faelten, A., Vitkova, V., & Bortolotto, L. (2010). *Distress classification measures in the banking sector.* City University of London.

Chen, Y., & Hasan, I. (2011). Subordinated debt, market discipline, and bank risk. *Journal of Money, Credit and Banking, 43*(6), 1043–1072.

Choi, H., & Choi, S. (2015). What drives credit rating changes? A return decomposition approach. *Asia-Pacific Journal of Financial Studies, 44,* 899–931. https://doi.org/10.1111/ajfs.12118.

Choi, S. J. (2004). A framework for the regulation of securities market intermediaries. *Berkeley Business Law Journal, 1*(1), 48–81.

Coffee, J. C. (2006). *Gatekeepers: The professions and corporate governance.* Oxford University Press.

Coffee, J. C. (2011). Rating reforms: The good, the bad and the ugly. *Harvard Business Law Review, 1,* 231–278.

Cooper, R., & Ross, T. W. (2002). Bank runs: Deposit insurance and capital requirements. *International Economic Review, 43*(1), 55–72. https://doi.org/10.1111/1468-2354.t01-1-00003.

Darbellay, A. (2013). *Regulating credit rating agencies.* Edward Elgar.

Davis, E. P. (1995). *Debt financial fragility and systemic risk.* Oxford University Press.

Dewatripont, M., & Tirole, J. (1994). *The prudential regulations of banks.* MIT Press.

Dey, B. K. (2019). *Managing nonperforming loans in Bangladesh: ADB Briefs, no 116, November, 2019.* Asian Development Bank. https://www.adb.org/publications/papers. https://doi.org/10.22617/BRF190507-2.

DeYoung, R. (1988). The efficiency of financial institutions: How does regulation matter? *Journal of Economics and Business, 50,* 79–234.

Diamond, D. W. (1984). Financial intermediation and delegated monitoring. *The Review of Economic Studies, 51*(3), 393–414.

Diamond, D. W. (1996). Financial intermediation as delegated monitoring: A simple example. *Federal Reserve Bank of Richmond Economic Quarterly, 82*(3), 51–66.

Diamond, D. W., & Dybvig, P. H. (1983). Bank runs, deposit insurance, and liquidity. *The Journal of Political Economy, 91*(3), 401–419.

Diamond, D. W., & Dybvig, P. H. (1986). Banking theory, deposit insurance, and bank regulation. *The Journal of Business, 59*(1), 55–68.

Diamond, D. W., & Rajan, R. G. (2000). A theory of bank capital. *Journal of Finance, LV*(6), 2431–2465.

Dothan, U., & Williams, J. (1980). Banks, bankruptcy, and public regulation. *Journal of Banking and Finance, 4,* 65–88.

Eichberger, J., & Harper, I. R. (1997). *Financial economics.* Oxford University Press.

Elyasiani, E. (1983). The two-product banking firm under uncertainty. *Southern Economic Journal,* 1002–1017.

European Commission (EC). (2009). *Regulation (EC) No 1060/2009 Of the European parliament and of the council of 16 September 2009 on credit rating agencies.* European Commission. https://eur-lex.europa.eu/legal-content/EN/TXT/PDF/?uri=CELEX:02009R1060-20150621&from=EN.

Evanoff, D. D. (1994). Capital requirements and bank regulatory reforms. In C. A. Stone & A. Zissu (Eds.), *Global risk based capital regulation Volume 1: Capital adequacy.* Irwin Professional Publishing.

Evanoff, D. D., & Wall, L. D. (2000). *Subordinated debt as bank capital: A proposal for regulatory reform* (WP 2000-07). Federal Reserve Bank of Chicago.

Evanoff, D. D., & Wall, L. D. (2001). Sub-debt yields spreads as bank risk measures. Subordinated debt as bank capital: A proposal for regulatory reform. *Journal of Financial Services Research, 20*(2/3), 121–145.

Evanoff, D. D., Jagtiani, J. A., & Nakata, T. (2011). Enhancing market discipline in banking: The role of subordinated debt in financial regulatory reform. *Journal of Economics and Business, 63*, 1–22.

Evanoff, D. D., & Wall, L. D. (2002). Measures of the riskiness of banking organizations: Subordinated debt yields, risk-based capital, and examination ratings. *Journal of Banking & Finance, 26*, 989–1009.

Farhi, E. & Tirole, J. (2009). *Collective moral hazard, maturity mismatch and systemic bailouts* (NBER Working Paper No. 15138). National Bureau of Economic Research.

Federal Deposit Insurance Corporation (FDIC). (2020). *2019 Annual Report*. FDIC.

Ferguson, R. W. (1999). Evolution of financial institutions and markets: implications for public and private policies and practices. *Speech delivered at the Money Marketers of New York University, New York.* Board of Governors of the Federal Reserve System. https://www.federalreserve.gov/boarddocs/spe eches/1999/199902252.htm.

Financial Instrument and Exchange (FIE) Act. (2006). *The Act for the Amendment of the Securities and Exchange Act, etc. (Act No. 65 of 2006) and the Act for the Development, etc. of Relevant Acts for Enforcement of the Act for the Amendment of the Securities and Exchange Act, etc. (2006 Act No. 66).* Financial Services Agency. https://www.fsa.go.jp/common/law/fie01.pdf.

Flannery, M. J. (1996). Financial crises, payment systems problems, and discount window lending. *Journal of Money Credit and Banking, 28*(4), 804–824.

Flannery, M., & Sorescu, S. M. (1996). Evidence of bank market discipline in subordinated debenture yields: 1983–1991. *Journal of Finance, 51*(4), 1347–1377.

Flori, A., Giansante, S., Girardone, C., & Pammolli, F. (2019). Banks' business strategies on the edge of distress. *Annals of Operations Research.* https://doi.org/10.1007/s10479-019-03383-z.

Freixas, X., & Rochet, J.-C. (1997). *Microeconomics of banking*. The MIT Press.

Freixas, X., & Rochet, J.-C. (2008). *Microeconomics of Banking* (2nd ed.). The MIT Press.

Freixas, X., Leven, L., & Peydro, J. (2015). *Systemic risk, crises, and macroprudential regulation*. The MIT Press.

Furlong, F. T., & Keeley, M. C. (1989). Capital regulation and bank risk-taking: A note. *Journal of Banking and Finance, 13*, 883–891.

Garten, H. A. (1986). Banking on the market: Relying on depositors to control bank Risks. *Yale Journal on Regulation, 4*(1), 129–172.

Geneva Report. (2009). *The fundamental principles of financial regulation: Geneva reports on the world economy 11*. Centre for Economic Policy Research (CEPR).

Goodhart, C. (1989). *Money, information and uncertainty* (2nd ed.). Macmillan.

Goodhart, C. (1995). *The central bank and the financial system*. Palgrave Macmillan.

Goodhart, C. (2009). *The regulatory response to the financial crisis*. Edward Elgar.

Goodhart, C. (2011). *The Basel Committee on banking Supervision: A history of the early years 1974–1997*. Central Bank and the Financial System. Cambridge University Press.

Gorton, G., & Pennacchi, G. (1990). Financial intermediaries and liquidity creation. *The Journal of Finance, 45*(1), 49–71.

Gorton, G., & Winton, A. (1995). *Bank capital regulation in general equilibrium*. (NBER Working Paper No. 5244). National Bureau of Economic Research.

Götz, M. R., & Tröger, T. H. (2016). *Should the marketing of subordinated debt be restricted/different in one way or the other? What to do in the case of mis-selling?* Economic and Monetary Affairs Committee, European Union.

Greenspan, A. (2000). Banking evolution. In *Proceedings of a Conference on Bank Structure and Competition*. Federal Reserve Bank of Chicago.

Hart, O. D., & Jafee, D. M. (1974). On the application of portfolio theory to depository finance intermediaries. *Review of Economic Studies, 41*, 129–147.

Hemraj, M. (2015). *Credit rating agencies self-regulation, statutory regulation and case law regulation in the United States and European Union*. Springer International Publishing.

International Organization of Securities commissions (IOSCO). (2015). *Code of conduct fundamentals for credit rating agencies: Final report* (FR05/2015). IOSCO. https://www.iosco.org/library/pubdocs/pdf/IOSCOPD482.pdf.

Jacklin, C., & Bhattacharya, S. (1988). Distinguishing panics and information based bank runs: Welfare and policy implications. *Journal of Political Economy, 96*, 568–592.

Jagtiani, J., & Lemieux, C. M. (2001). Market discipline prior to bank failure. *Journal of Economics and Business, 53*(2–3), 313–324.

Jagtiani, J., Kolari, J. W., Lemieux, C. M., & Shin, G. H. (2000). *Predicting inadequate capitalization: Early warning system for bank supervision* (S&R-2000-10R). Supervision and Regulation Department, Federal Reserve Bank of Chicago.

Kahane, Y. (1977). Capital adequacy and the regulation of financial intermediaries. *Journal of Banking and Finance, 1*, 207–218.

Kammoun, R., & Louizi, A. (2015). Credit rating agencies: Development and analysis of business models. *Journal of Contemporary Management, 3*(2), 53–66.

68 A K M K. HASAN AND Y. SUZUKI

Kareken, J. H. (1986). Federal bank regulatory policy: A description and some observations. *Journal of Business, 59*, 3–48.

Kareken, J. H., & Wallace, N. (1978). Deposit insurance and bank regulation: A partial-equilibrium exposition. *Journal of Business, 51*, 413–438.

Kashyap, A. K., Rajan, R. G., & Stein, J. C. (1999). *Banks as liquidity providers: An explanation for the co-existence of lending and deposit-taking* (NBER Working Paper 6962). National Bureau of Economic Research

Keeley, M. C., & Furlong, F. T. (1990). A re-examination of the mean-variance analysis of bank capital regulation. *Journal of Banking and Finance, 14*, 69–84.

Keynes, J. M. (1930). *A treatise on money* (Vol. 1). Macmillan.

Kim, D., & Santomero, A. M. (1988). Risk in banking and capital regulation. *The Journal of Finance, 43*(5), 1219–1233.

Koehn, M., & Santomero, A. M. (1980). Regulation of bank capital and portfolio risk. *Journal of Finance, 43*(5), 1235–1244.

Langhor, H. M., & Langhor, P. T. (2008). *The Rating agencies and their credit ratings What they are, how they work and why they are relevant*. Wiley.

Litan, R. E. (1987). *What should banks do?* Brookings Institution Press.

Lucchetta, M., Moretto, M., & Parigi, B. M. (2018). *Systemic risk, bank moral hazard, and bailouts* (CESifo Working Paper Series 6878). CESifo Group.

Marcus, A. J., & Shaked, I. (1984). The valuation of FDIC deposit insurance using option-pricing estimates. *Journal of Money Credit and Banking, 16*(4), 446–460.

Markowitz, M. H. (1952). *Portfolio selection efficient diversification of investment* (Cowles Foundation Monograph, No. 16). Cowles Foundation.

Matthews, K., & Thompson, J. (2014). *The economics of banking*. Wiley.

Merton, R. C. (1977). An analytic derivation of the cost of deposit insurance and loan guarantees. *Journal of Banking and Finance, 1*, 512–520.

Merton, R. C. (1978). On the cost of deposit insurance when there are surveillance costs. *Journal of Business, 51*, 439–452.

Meyer, L. H. (1999). Market discipline as a complement to bank supervision and regulation. *Speech before the Conference on Reforming Bank Capital Standards*. Council on Foreign Relations. https://www.federalreserve.gov/boarddocs/speeches/1999/19990614.htm.

Miglionico, A. (2014). *Recasting credit rating agencies' responsibility: Suggestions for Reform* (Doctoral Dissertation, University of London, London, UK). https://qmro.qmul.ac.uk/xmlui/bitstream/handle/123456789/12986/Miglionico_Andrea_PhD_Final_260216.pdf?sequence=1.

Miglionico, A. (2019). *The governance of credit rating agencies regulatory regime and liability issues*. Edward Elgar.

Millers, S., Olson, E., & Yeager, T. J. (2015). The relative contributions of equity and subordinated debt signals as predictors of bank distress during the financial crisis. *Journal of Financial Stability, 16*, 118–137.

Miyoda, M. (1994). *Revival of US Banks-Merchant Bank, Investment Bank, Money-center Bank, Super-regional Bank.* Nihon Keizai Shinbun Sha.

Modigliani, F., & Miller, M. (MM). (1958). The cost of capital, corporation finance and the theory of investment. *American Economic Review, 48*(3), 261–297.

Morgan, D. P., & Stiroh, K. J. (2000). *Bond market discipline of banks: Is the market tough enough?* (Federal Reserve Bank of New York Staff Report, No. 95). Federal Reserve Bank of New York. https://www.newyorkfed.org/research/economists/medialibrary/media/research/staff_reports/sr95.pdf#search='Bond+market+discipline+of+banks%3A+Is+the+market+tough+enough%3F.

Morgan, D. P., & Stiroh, K. J. (2001). Market discipline of banks: The asset test. *Journal of Financial Services Research, 20*, 195–208.

Moskow, M. H. (1998). Regulatory efforts to prevent banking crises. In G. Caprio, W. C. Hunter, G. G. Kaufman, & D. M. Leipziger (Eds.), *Preventing bank crises: Lessons from recent global bank failures* (pp. 13–26). World Bank.

North, D. C. (1990). *Institutions, institutional change and economic performance.* Cambridge University Press.

North, D. C. (2005). *Understanding the process of economic change.* Princeton University Press.

Partnoy, F. (1999). The Siskel and Ebert of financial markets? Two thumbs down for the credit rating agencies. *Washington University Law Quarterly, 77*(3), 619–713.

Partnoy, F. (2006). *How and why credit rating agencies are not like other gatekeepers* (University of San Diego Legal Studies Research Paper Series No. 07-46). In Y. Fuchita & R. E. Litan (Eds.), *Financial gatekeepers: Can they protect investors?* Brookings Institution Press & the Nomura Institute of Capital Markets Research.

Pennacchi, G. (1987). Alternative form of deposit insurance, pricing and bank incentive issues. *Journal of Banking and Finance, 11*(2), 291–312.

Pierce, J. (1991). *The future of banking.* Yale University Press.

Porter, R. C. (1961). A model of bank portfolio selection. *Yale Economic Essays, 1*(2), 323–359.

Posner, E. A. (2015). How do bank regulators determine capital-adequacy requirements? *University of Chicago Law Review, 82*, 1853–1895.

Rahim, M. M. (2010). Credit rating agencies' roles have to be reassessed. *Law and Financial Markets Review, 4*(4), 433–438.

Rajan, R. G. (1992). Insiders and outsiders: The Choice between informed and arm's length debt. *The Journal of Finance, 47*(4), 1367–1400.

Rixtel, A. V., González, L. R., & Yang, J. (2015). *The determinants of long-term debt issuance by European banks: Evidence of two crises* (BIS Working Papers No. 513). Bank for International Settlements.

Rochet, J. C. (1992). Capital requirements and the behavior of commercial banks. *European Economic Review, 36*, 1137–1178.

Rochet, J.-C., & Vives, X. (2004). Coordination failures and the lender of last resort: Was Baghehot right after all? *Journal of the European Economic Association, 2*(6), 1116–1147.

Ronn, E. I., & Verma, A. (1986). Pricing risk-adjusted deposit insurance: An option-based model. *Journal of Finance, 41*(4), 871–895.

Santomero, A. M. (1984). Modeling the banking firm: A survey. *Journal of Money, Credit and Banking, 16*(4), 576–602.

Santomero, A. M. (2006). Forward. In H. Langhor & P. Langhor (Eds.), *The rating agencies and their credit ratings what they are, how they work and why they are relevant* (p. x). Wiley.

Santos, J. A. C. (1999). Bank capital and equity investment regulations. *Journal of Banking and Finance, 23*, 1095–1120.

Santos, J. A. C. (2001). Bank capital regulation in contemporary banking theory: A review of the literature. *Financial Markets, Institutions & Instruments, 10*(2), 41–84. https://doi.org/10.1111/1468-0416.00042.

Santos, J. A. C. (2006). Insuring banks against liquidity shocks: The role of deposit insurance and lending of last resort. *Journal of Economic Surveys, 20*(3), 459–482.

Schooner, H. M., & Taylor, M. W. (2010). *Global bank regulation principles and policies*. Elsevier.

Sharpe, W. F. (1978). Bank capital adequacy, deposit insurance and security values. *Journal of Financial and Quantitative Analysis, 13*, 701–718.

Stigler, G. T. (1971). The theory of economic regulation. *The Bell Journal of Economics and Management Science, 2*(1), 3–21.

Stiglitz, J. E. (2009). *Report of the commission of experts of the president of the United Nations general assembly on reforms of the international monetary and financial system*. United Nations.

Stiglitz, J., & Greenwald, B. (2003). *Towards a new paradigm in monetary economics*. Cambridge University Press.

Stiglitz, J. E., & Weiss, A. (1981). Credit rationing in markets with imperfect information. *American Economic Review, 71*(3), 393–410.

Strier, F. (2008). Rating the raters: Conflicts of interest in the credit rating firms. *Business and Society Review, 113*(4), 533–553.

Suzuki, Y. (2011). *Japan's Financial Slump: Collapse of the monitoring system under institutional and transitional failures*. Palgrave Macmillan.

Tobin, J. (1958). Liquidity preference as Behavior towards bank risk. *Review of Economic Studies, 25*, 65–67.

Tobin, T. (1965). Money and economic growth. *Econometrica, 33*(4), 671–684.
Tucker, P. (2013). Resolution and future of finance. *Speech at the INSOL International World Congress, The Hague, Netherlands*. https://www.bis.org/review/r130606a.pdf#search='Paul+Tucker%3A+Resolution+and+future+of+finance.
Tucker, P. (2014). Banking reform and macroprudential regulation: Implications for banks' capital structure and credit conditions. In E. Jokivuolle & J. Vilmunen (Eds.), *Banking after regulatory reforms-business as usual?* (pp. 65–77). A Joint publication of SUERF—The European Money and Finance Forum & Bank of Finland. https://www.suerf.org/studies/4139/banking-after-regulatory-reforms-business-as-usual.
U.S. Securities and Exchange Commission (U.S. SEC). (2013). *Report to congress credit rating agency independence study*. U.S. Securities and Exchange Commission.
White, L. J. (2010). The credit rating agencies. *Journal of Economic Perspective, 24*(2), 211–226.
White, L. J. (2013). Credit rating agencies: An overview. *Annual Review of Financial Economics, 5*, 93–122. https://doi.org/10.1146/annurev-financial-110112-120942.
Wymeersch, E. O., & Kruithof, M. (2006). *Regulation and liability of credit rating agencies under Belgian law* (Ghent University Financial Law Institute Working Paper No. 2006-05). Ghent University. http://www.law.ugent.be/fli/wps/archive.php#2006. https://doi.org/10.2139/ssrn.894820.
Yang, H., Ahn, H. K., Maria, H., & Ryu, D. (2017). Information asymmetry and investor trading behavior around bond rating change announcements. *Emerging Markets Review, 32*, 38–51.

CHAPTER 4

Basel Accord Associated Institutions in Bangladesh

4.1 Introduction

In Chapter 2, we have discussed that how BIS has adopted Basel Accord as a capital regulation for internationally active banks. The acceptance of Basel Accord by G 10 countries made it as an acceptable prudential regulation by the central banks around the globe and adopted it taking into consideration of local context. Following this trend, Bangladesh Bank (BB) has adopted Basel Accord in a customized way considering the country's banking sector context and initiated several institutions to implement the Basel Accord. As the study emphasizes on the discussion on Basel Accord with reference to Bangladesh, we focus on those institutions in depth and analyze the key features of all institutions. Readers might recall that we hypothesized in Chapter 1 that homogenization of credit risk screening under standardized approach (SA) fails to capture the real credit risk in case of Bangladesh. To discuss on this issue in depth, we will critically analyze the regulations related with SA from an institutional perspective in this chapter. In addition, we analyze how credit risk quantification is conducted in the Basel framework and how the homogenization of credit risk screening works in Bangladesh, as well as the institutional cost/transaction cost involved in the issuance of sub-debt. Before moving to our core discussion, we reviewed neo-institutional economists' views on the role of regulations. The outline of this chapter is as follows. Section 4.2 analyzes the institutional economists view on regulations. Section 4.3 presents the brief discussions on credit risk quantification approaches under Basel Framework. Section 4.4 reviews the institutions of ECAI in Bangladesh from institutional perspectives. Sub-debt-related institutions are discussed in Sect. 4.5. Section 4.6 is concluding remarks.

4.2   NEO-INSTITUTIONAL ECONOMISTS VIEW ON REGULATION

The economic theory of regulation can be categorized from two perspectives: public interest view and private interest view (Peláez & Peláez, 2009). According to Peláez and Peláez (2009), a public interest view argues that governments should interfere in the market regulation for the greater welfare of society whereas a private interest view raises doubts about the effectiveness of such initiatives on market power. Some researchers advocate for regulation to reduce the effect of externalities (Coase, 1960). Some favored reducing 'information asymmetries' in the market. For instance, 'market for lemon' (Akerlof, 1970) and 'credit rationing' (Stiglitz & Weiss, 1981) are widely used terms to explain information asymmetries in the credit market. The important question at this point is what are the key factors that should be consider while making a regulation? Scholars point out that three important disciplines underpin the regulation such as (i) a well-designed institution which promotes responsibility and accountability, (ii) a fiduciary legal system and (iii) behavioral aspects of economic systems (Davis et al., 2016). However, neo-institutional economists view on regulation are quite comprehensive and slightly different. Langlois (1986a, 1986b) summarized the contributions of neo-institutional economics on regulations into three main points: (i) transaction cost and property rights, inspired by Coase (1937) and further extended by Williamson (1979, 1985); North (1990) (ii) shed lights on commons, based on Hayek (1948) and further explained by Ostrom (2005) (iii) analyzing innovation (Schumpeter, 1926, 1934, 1942) and economic agent (Alchian, 1950) which is extended as evolutionary theory by Nelson and Winter (1982). Besides, Scott (2014) mentioned four influential neo-institutional economic theories that contributed more to the conceptualization of institutions in economics such as (i) transaction cost economics, (ii) game-theoretic approaches, (iii) evolutionary economics theory and finally, (iv) resource-based theory. He, however, mentioned three pillars of institutions, namely the regulative pillar, the normative pillar and the cultural-cognitive pillar, and put institutional economists views of institutions on the 'regulatory pillar' (Scott, 2014, p. 60). It is not possible here to discuss all the theories and approaches of neo-institutional economics, but we will focus on Douglass North's view (as he analyzes the institutions and institutional change in more coherent ways) in detail to facilitate our analysis of Basel regulation.

Douglass North's View on Institutions:

Prominent institutional economist and Noble laureate Douglass North stressed rules as systems and enforcement mechanisms in his analysis (Scott, 2014). It is worth to quote, "institutions are set of rules, compliance procedures, and moral and ethical behavioral norms designed to constrain the behavior of individuals in the interests of maximizing the wealth or utility of principals" (North, 1981, pp. 201–202). Terming institutions as "the rules of the game in a society" (North, 1990, p. 3), he specified that institutions provide the structure of cost of production which is the combination of transformation cost (typically land, labor and capital) and transaction cost (cost of property rights). Here he elaborates on the concept of transaction cost as used by Williamson (1985). North (1990) further argued that institutions are made up of formal rules (e.g., political and judicial rules, economic rules and contracts) and informal rules (e.g., codes of conduct, norms of behavior and conventions). Any changes in the formal rules should be compatible with the informal rules which exist in the society or organization, and the incentives provided to enforce rules are essential to make an efficient institution (North, 1990). He argued that, in the absence of such 'incentives for institutions,' the outcome of implementing any rules in a society is insignificant. In fact, North focused on two issues such as: (i) institutional structure should be aligned with formal and informal rules of the society and (ii) institutions should offer incentives to each player in the society. As an economic historian, North (1981, 2005) elaborated on the above-mentioned theoretical analysis on the substance of institutions from world economic development history. For instance, he compared North American and Latin American economic development history from an institutional point of view and argued that the former region was able to establish stable institutions and the latter one had and still has unstable and fragile institutions which dictate their economic development outcomes (North, 2005). He succinctly documents that the structure of the institutions in North

American societies (such as federalism, democracy, limited government and thriving markets) was different from that of Latino societies, especially Spanish and Mexican (which suffered from instability and turmoil, personal exchange/extreme rent seeking and authoritarian polity) which was the prime reason behind this difference. Hence without developing such institutions, nor the existence of an adaptive society, the regulation became ineffective. Rather, it makes the existing problems worse if the institutional structure is not aligned with the existing regulations. That is, 'institutional structure' is the prerequisite for the optimum efficiency from institutions as North (2005) viewed.

What is more, he considered 'appropriate incentives' to bring any change in existing institutions or organizations and refers to institutions as a 'set of rules' and to organizations as a 'group of individuals bound together by some common objectives' (North, 2005, p. 59). While discussing the history of the rise of the western world in the eighteenth century and the fall of Soviet Union in the 1990s, the key point, from North's point of view, was the existence of an 'appropriate incentive' between institutions and economic policy; the western world has successfully provided incentives to institutions which enhance economic growth, while on the other hand, the Soviet Union held on to an inflexible institutional framework and failed to provide incentives for the acceleration of economic growth (North, 2005). Besides, while discussing reasons for the fall of the Roman empire in the fifth century and the decline of feudalism in the middle ages, he argued a similar 'incentive' approach between institutions and states (North, 2005). North's view is compatible with the views of Ostrom et al. (1993) on the role of incentives on sustainability of public infrastructure in developing countries. Ostrom (1993), herself also a Noble laureate in economics in 2009, mentioned that the institutional arrangements and incentives can limit the rent seeking behavior of civil servants and large landowners in host countries. It means that institutions should provide incentives to the implementing agencies while adopting new institutions, and when such incentives are sufficient and appropriate, then sustainable development can be achieved from infrastructure, especially in developing countries.

However, North's approach has some weaknesses and is criticized by contemporary economists. Suzuki (2011), while referring to the Knight (1992) discussion on 'cost minimization standard' in the transaction cost theory, mentioned that such a style of institutional analysis is often misleading and raises at least three factors as exceptions to the standards: (i) hidden benefits that are not readily apparent; (ii) formal external constraints (i.e., the interest of the state); and (iii) uncertainty as a result of which economic agents may not create the least costly rules because they lack either the capacity or the knowledge to establish them (p. 45). In addition, Suzuki (2011) argued that North's functionalist's view of institutional change is drifting from real-world scenarios as North argued that the institutional change occurred under negotiation and compensation; however, when one party is stronger than another, the stronger one does not need to negotiate and compensate its counterpart in every case. In addition, 'Regulatory Capture Theory' pioneered by Stigler (1971) which is further extended by Boot and Thakor (1993); Laffont and Tirole (1991) and Posner (2013) argued that institutions can be affected by conflicts between regulators and the regulated. In fact, regulatory capture is the control of regulation by those who are regulated, and it is argued that industry captures the regulatory process as well as institutions (Carrigan & Coglianese, 2015). If we consider regulatory capture theory in banking regulations, it has two effects: (i) it influences the regulatory policymaking process and (ii) it uses government regulation to maximize the bank's incentive or interests of the bank owners and managers (Mourlon-Drulo, 2015). However, in the case of Basel Accord implementation in Bangladesh, the role of institutions and organizations under regulatory capture theory might need separate discussion and will be kept for future research.

In summary, neo-institutional economic theory (according to North) held that institutional efficiency depends on 'institutional structure' and 'appropriate incentives' for institutions and organizations. When introducing institutions into the economic organization, we should take into consideration the 'institutional structure' and 'institutional incentives,' otherwise the expected result might not be obtained from the institutional change. While examining the Basel-related institutions that initiated by BB, we focus on these two issues that how the Basel Accords associated institutions are made up with and what kind of incentives or disincentives are offered in the regulations to the concerned players.

4.3   QUANTIFICATION OF CREDIT RISK UNDER BASEL FRAMEWORK[1]

We discussed earlier that several risk factors in the banking industry such as credit risk, market risk and operational risk are included while computing total RWA under pillar I of Basel Accord II and III. In this study we solely focused on credit risk (specially credit risk derives from the balance sheet exposures) as it is largely dominated in the total RWA of the country's banking system (see BB, 2018, p. 52). Two approaches are acknowledged to quantify the credit risk under Basel Accords II and III, one is internal rating-based approach (IRB), and the other is the standardized approach (SA). Adopting either of the two approaches, the credit risk of the banks is expected to be identified and assigned weights to explain the riskiness of various types of exposure which can be termed as 'quantification of credit risk' (see Fig. 4.1). We summarize the two approaches below.

Internal ratings-based Approach (IRB)

"The IRB approach for credit risk allows banks, under certain conditions to use their internal model to estimate credit risk and therefore RWAs" (BCBS, 2017). It refers to two approaches for computing credit risk under IRB, namely Foundation IRB (F-IRB) and Advanced IRB (A-IRB) and explains in detail the operational treatment of each asset category (Bank balance sheet wise such as claims on financial institutions, investment in shares and securities, corporate exposure, retail exposure, SME and so on) at a risk category to quantify the risk components including estimation of probability of default (PD), loss given default (LGD), the exposure at default (ED) and effective maturity (EM) (BCBS, 2017). Then banks must determine their own minimum capital requirement to comply with the Basel framework. The mapping process is comprehensively described in the Basel framework under twelve (12) separate sections and then based on this comprehensive computation bank compute the RWA. In a word, under the IRB approach, the prime responsibility is to quantify the credit risk of a bank's own in-house methodologies based on the guidelines provided in the latest version of the accord. Hence the risk management and responsibility to keep

---

[1] See the full and latest version of the Basel framework initiated by BCBS, BIS. https://www.bis.org/basel_framework/index.htm?m=3%7C14%7C697.

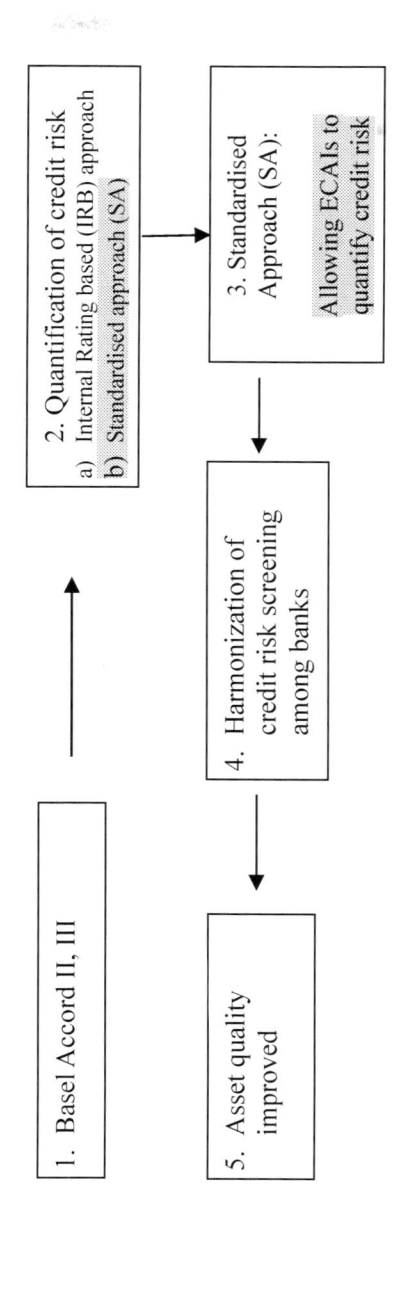

Fig. 4.1 Objectives of ECAIs rating in Basel framework

minimum capital requirements lies on the individual banks shoulders while regulators are simply vetting the methodologies in due course. However, the major limitation of the IRB approach is that banks are to independently quantify the risk, that may raise two concerns. Firstly, banks have a greater incentive to follow the IRB approach, as bank management has short-term incentives to underestimate the actual risk involved in each class of assets which require less minimum capital charge. Another is national supervisors (mainly central banks) have less incentives to adopt the IRB approach. This is due to it being quite difficult for national supervisors to quantify the overall actual industry risk as each bank follows its own methodologies and jurisdiction and therefore requires more effort to monitor each bank's rating methodologies. As a result, the harmonization of credit risk flows can be interrupted under an implementation of IRB approach. Scholars mentioned it as a 'failure of internal risk model' (Freixas & Leven, 2015).

Standardized approach (SA)

"Under this approach supervisors set the risk weights that banks apply to their exposures to determine RWAs" (BCBS, 2017). To determine the risk weights in the SA "for certain exposure classes, in jurisdictions that allow the use of external ratings for regulatory purposes, banks may, as a starting point, use assessments by external credit assessment institutions that are recognized as eligible for capital purposes by national supervisors" (BCBS, 2017). Therefore, under the SA, the risk-weighted assets (RWA) are determined with ECAIs rating parameter of a particular exposure and bank capital charges/requirements are determined based on the total RWA computed through the ECAIs rating notch. However, banks are allowed to use some specific collaterals such as cash, gold, debt securities (rated by recognized ECAIs) and so on to obtain capital relief by using credit risk mitigation (CRM) techniques under the SA, which is technically referred to as a 'Haircut' (BCBS, 2017, p. 33). In short, ECAIs play a key role in determining the risk weight of an exposure in the SA method and credit rating agencies (CRAs) are recognized as ECAIs by BIS while assessment of credit risk under the SA (BCBS, 2006, 2017). The important question at this point is what are the recognition process of ECAIs are prescribed under SA? what are the objectives of allowing the ECAIs rating in SA?

BCBS (2017) solely put the responsibility to recognize the ECAIs on national supervisors under some jurisdictions and it highly recommends following the International Organization of Securities Commissions (IOSCO) 'Code of Conduct Fundamentals for Credit Rating Agencies'. It mentioned eight criteria which ECAI must satisfy. These are: Objectivity, Independence, International access/transparency, Disclosure, Resources, Credibility, No abuse of unsolicited rating, Co-operation with the supervisor (BCBS, 2017). The mapping process should be monitored by national supervisors as BCBS recommended and expect that banks should not use ECAIs rating as per their incentive. That is to say that banks should not pick the higher rating which requires less capital charge rather than use the higher risk weight if a particular claim that has multiple ratings (BCBS, 2017). The related main clause is as follows: 'Banks must use the chosen ECAIs and their ratings consistently for all types of claim where they have been recognized by their supervisor as an eligible ECAI, for both risk-weighting and risk management purposes. Banks will not be allowed to "cherry-pick" the ratings provided by different ECAIs and to arbitrarily change the use of ECAIs' (p. 30). Therefore, the principles of ECAIs recognition process are clearly prescribed in the Basel Accord guidelines whereas the implementation is handed over to the national regulators.

Regarding the second query, the objective to mandate ECAIs rating under SA is not rationalized in the main Basel Accord text. We presume that ECAIs role in the assessment of credit risk of exposure in favor of national regulators which hopes to bring harmonization of credit risk among banks and finally the asset quality of the banking industry will be improved. If so, ECAIs play the role of 'quasi regulator' while rating an entity/loan exposure of a bank, as the central bank has authorized ECAIs for exposure rating which is used for calculating a bank's overall RWA under the SA. In other words, national regulators allowed the banks to use ECAIs rating on bank exposure for assigning risk weights under the standardized approach mainly to quantifying credit risk in a common methodology rather than individual methodologies adopted by each bank (under IRB), and wish to quantify the entire banking sector credit risk in a harmonized way. Figure 4.1 presents the objectives of allowing ECAIs rating under the SA in the Basel framework.

4.4   Regulations of ECAIs in Bangladesh and a Critical View

In line with the implementation of Basel Accord II, BB has recognized ECAI ratings since 2009 (BB, 2010), and subsequently in the 'Revised regulatory capital framework for banks in line with Basel III' in 2014[2] (BB, 2014). In the revised framework, BB has clearly mentioned that 'the capital requirement for credit risk is based on the risk assessment made by External Credit Assessment Institutions (ECAIs) recognized by BB for capital adequacy purposes' and has recognized eight credit rating agencies (CRAs) to act as ECAIs (BB, 2014, p. 20). It is mentionable here that the CRAs license should be obtained from Bangladesh Securities and Exchange Commission (BSEC). Following the BCBS guidelines, BB has recognized ECAIs credit rating categories with a BB rating (see Tables 4.1 and 4.2 in Annexure) for computing capital requirements for credit risk under Basel Accords (BB, 2010, 2014). Regarding the ECAIs monitoring and supervision, BB is responsible for monitoring the ECAIs on a continuous basis for ensuring six criteria such as Objectivity, Independence, International access/Transparency, Disclosure, Resources, Credibility (BB, 2014). Therefore, while regulating the CRAs in Bangladesh, there are two legal institutions involved, namely CRC rule 1996[3] and 'Guidelines for Recognition of Eligible ECAIs-2008'. In the next sub-sections, we will briefly discuss the various attributes of these two institutions.

Credit Rating Companies (CRC) Rules—1996

CRC rules initiated by BSEC in 1996 and all CRAs need to get license from the BSEC under this regulation. It consists of 16 Articles within the four chapters and we will focus on the key points of these rules which are related to the computation of Risk Based Capital Adequacy (RBCA) framework (Basel Accords guidelines) to keep our discussion relevant and on track. Chapter I describes the definition of the terms used in the rule and the date of adopting the rules. According to the

---

[2] See the full version of Basel Accord II & III guidelines and its related circulars issued by BB from time to time. https://www.bb.org.bd/mediaroom/baselii/baselII.php.

[3] See the main text in the BSEC web portal. https://www.sec.gov.bd/home/lbook or https://www.sec.gov.bd/lbook/F-03_2015.pdf.

rules, '"Credit Rating Company" means an investment advisor company which intends to engage in or is so engaged primarily in the business of evaluation of credit or investment risk through a recognized and formal process of assigning rating to present or proposed loan obligations or equity of any business enterprise' (BSEC, 1996, Article 2(d)). Chapter II presents the regulations of business. To be able to register as a Credit Rating Company (CRC), the core requirements are:

(a) Paid-up capital: To be incorporated as a public limited company under the Companies Act, 1994 and must have a paid-up capital of at least five million (Article 4(b)).
(b) Competence: The CRC has to be a joint venture technical collaboration with a reputed credit rating company (Article 4(c)). However, detailed scope of business for such collaboration is not specified in the institutions which makes the article pointless. The minimum requirement of professional staff in a CRC is two with two years professional experience in credit rating or investment advisory activities (Article 4(f)).
(c) Compliance: BSEC reserves the right to cancel or suspend or impose any directions on the CRC with the considerations of public interest or the interest of the capital market in mind. The CRC must submit a quarterly report of credit ratings to the BSEC (Article 6). However, Article 6 of the rules did not define any 'duty of care' issue in terms of civil liability of CRC, which is a major drawback in the regulation. We will discuss this issue further in later parts of the study.

Chapter III, Article 9, describes the detailed operational procedures of CRC. There are eight broad codes of conduct which are described in the said clause, and the CRC are asked to adopt, publish and follow these codes. We summarized the key points of each code in Table 4.1 for our further discussion in the rest of the chapter.

Finally, Chapter IV describes the inspection and investigation of CRC by BSEC if deemed necessary. The main lacuna is, the rules do not explain the specific punitive measures against CRC, rather, Article 16 states that under the SEC ordinance, 1969, the commission can take appropriate action based on the inspection or investigation report. The term 'appropriate' is arbitrary.

Table 4.1 Key points of Article 9 that is relevance with Basel Accord

Sl. no	Code of conduct	Relevant sub-clause
1	Quality of rating process	• Establish a rating methodology for each industry or each type of instrument and disclose it to the public Web site. Review of the methodologies and model at least once a year by rating committee of CRC • There should be a rating committee (RC) of each CRC with five members including two senior analysts. RC has the authority to announce the final rating • The Internal Review Committee (IRC) shall double check the documents and information on which the rating team made their rating. The rating team consists of at least two analysts
2	Monitoring and updating	• There are two types of rating—initial rating and surveillance rating. For entity rating the surveillance rating must be for at least the next three years after the initial rating and for issuance of instrument rating the surveillance rating must be for the lifetime of the instrument after the initial rating. However, if any part (either CRC or client) wants to terminate the contract, they need to get permission from the BSEC
3	Integrity of rating process	• CRC should establish an ethical standard and code of conduct for its employees and disclose it on their Web site

Sl. no	Code of conduct	Relevant sub-clause
4	CRC independence and avoidance of conflict of interest	• Directors and shareholders should not interfere with the activities and decisions of RC • CRC cannot rate any entity which has any relation with CRC or its director • There is a required declaration by the directors of CRC and CEO and affidavit by employees of CRC to avoid any conflict of interest and ensure independence
5	CRC procedures and policies	• If any CRCs receive 10% or more of its annual revenue from a single entity or group, it should be publicly disclosed
6	CRC analysts and employee independence	• Employees remuneration cannot be linked with the clients whose analysts' rate or CRCs shall not share any revenue with analyst except service benefits. Analysts are also prohibited from doing marketing, or negotiation fees • Any CRC or its employee cannot buy or sell or engage in any transaction with listed securities
7	CRC responsibility to the investing public and issuers	• CRC shall publish the list of updated ratings on its Web site • It should publish the historical default rate
8	Disclosures of these rules	• CEO of the CRC should submit a declaration after every rating report that it has rated the entity while complying with all rules described in CRC rules 1996

BSEC (1996, Article 9)

Guidelines for Recognition of Eligible ECAIs 2008[4] *(BB, 2008)*

BB refers to the CRC as 'External Credit Assessment Institutions' (ECAIs) and the Banking Regulation and Policy Department (BRPD) issued its first circular on September 23, 2008 regarding 'Guidelines for recognition of eligible External Credit Assessment Institutions (ECAIs)' which came into effect in January 2009. It should be noted that the guidelines are the only authenticating text recognizing ECAIs and their monitoring and supervision from a Basel Accord perspective. The guidelines (BB, 2008) have six general clauses while recognizing ECAIs, and these are: (i) recognition criteria, (ii) mapping process, (iii) application process, (iv) ongoing recognition, (v) guidelines to banks regarding nomination of ECAIs and (vi) general instruction. We briefly discuss the contents of said guidelines below.

(i) Recognition criteria

The guideline mentioned six major criteria: objectivity, independence, international access/transparency, disclosure, resources, and credibility for determining the recognition of ECAIs. Each criterion is more explicitly laid out through its respective sub-content, as shown in Table 4.2.

Interestingly, the guidelines have mentioned criteria for recognition but do not put any ceiling on the minimum or disclose any standard against these criteria. For example, regarding the ECAIs internal process, the rules mentioned that ECAIs must disclose their analysis team, rating committee and internal verification system while filing for recognition, but not disclose the minimum requirement or any benchmark regarding those yardsticks. Although the 'transparency' and 'disclosure' parts are significant issues for ECAIs, the mentioned rules hold no specific instructions which create room for ECAIs to escape these key issues. The authors, while checking the Web sites of the eight credit rating agencies of the country at the time of writing, found there is little disclosure on default rating and transition matrix. Besides, in the 'Resources' and 'Credibility' sections some description is required regarding each sub-section by ECAIs but there are no specific requirements or standard requirement

---

[4] See the full text at https://www.bb.org.bd/mediaroom/baselii/baselII.php.

Table 4.2 List of criteria for recognition as ECAI

Sl. no	Criteria	Sub-content of the criteria
1	Objectivity	(a) Manuscript of methodology
		(b) Internal process
		(c) Rating scale and their sensitivity
		(d) Validation system
		(e) Ongoing review
		(f) Database management
		(g) System back testing
2	Independence	(a) Registration system with SEC
		(b) Ownership quality
		(c) Procedure to ensure independence
		(d) Board members influence on rating activities
		(e) Solvency of the company
		(f) Schedule of credit assessment fees
3	Transparency/International access	(a) International exposure
		(b) Accessibility of the ECAIs rating
		(c) Availability of assessment methodology
		(d) Nature of rating
4	Disclosure	(a) Definition of default rating category
		(b) Actual transition rate toward default rating
		(c) Disclosure of transition matrix
		(d) Code of conduct
5	Resources	(a) Capital structure and net worth
		(b) Hard and soft infrastructure
		(c) Number of professional staffs
		(d) Personal policy
		(e) Internal work relationship
		(f) Data warehousing
6	Credibility	(a) Degree of acceptance by the client
		(b) Market share of ECAI
		(c) Handling conflict of interest
		(d) Market penetration approach

BB (2008)

prescribed by BB. As a result, whatever is written in the rules, the recognition process seems unclear and ambiguous to both the general public and academics.

(ii) Mapping process

BB will evaluate and bring harmony to the ECAIs rating notch through numerals 1 to 6 Cumulative Default Rate (CDR) and the short-term rating is used for short-term lending whereas the long-term rating is used for long-term lending (BB, 2008). BB considers CDR as a quantitative factor to evaluate an ECAIs rating category. The transition of an individual notch toward the default category observed in a particular ECAI category will be compared to the standards available domestically/regionally/internationally (BB, 2008). On the other hand, the qualitative factors are not disclosed in the guidelines and it is stated that it will be set by BB's working group.

(iii) Application process

To become eligible ECAI, the CRC must be registered under CRC Rule, 1996 of BSEC. This means that any credit rating company either domestic or international must get license from BSEC.

(iv) Ongoing recognition

This clause mentioned that BB is responsible for the monitoring and supervision of ECAIs. The recognition from BB will be reviewed annually, and BB can derecognize any ECAI if it seems necessary. However, from BSEC and BB notifications, we confirmed that so far, no ECAI has been derecognized by BB during the period reviewed.

(v) Guidelines to Banks

Banks can nominate the ECAIs for credit rating of banking book exposures and notify BB regarding their nomination of ECAIs and banks can use the ratings of nominated ECAIs for a reasonable period (p. 5).

(vi) Compliance instruction to ECAIs

Three general compliance instructions are referred to in the guidelines for the ECAIs. These are: (a) ECAIs should submit their quarterly rating report to BB, (b) there should be unique a pricing system among ECAIs and (c) all ECAIs will follow the IOSCO/BSEC code of conduct for CRC (p. 5).

Therefore, in Bangladesh, CRAs are regulated by two national statutory regulators such as BSEC and BB. Based on the above discussion of the two regulations, we have critically analyzed some issues in the next sub-section from an institutional perspective.

Critical Views on Regulations of ECAIs in Bangladesh

We critically assess the aforementioned ECAIs regulations from two perspectives (i) liability of ECAI for exposure rating and (ii) disclosure of ECAI. We attempt to examine what the ECAIs liability regime for mis-rating/inaccurate credit information is, and how its public disclosure helps to understand rating quality. The discussions will aid the readers to understand the existing institutional loopholes in the regulations of ECAIs.

(i) Liability of ECAI for Exposure Rating

First, in both regulations for the ECAIs, the liability position is not clear. For example, according to CRC rules 1996 (Article 9 (2), (b)), an entity rating should be the initial rating and next three years of surveillance rating, i.e., a consecutive four years rating by the same ECAI. However, there is no such obligation or instruction by the regulators to banks regarding this condition. As a result, banks' exposure rating is conducted for a short term, i.e., one year, and the banks' client seldom perform the surveillance rating. The fact is, once the loan has approved by the bank, the client need not be bothered about the surveillance rating. On the other hand, if the exposure turns out to be non-performing in the following year, the bank needs to maintain provisions against the exposure as per existing banking norms which means that the bank loses its incentive to repeat the client for surveillance rating. This 'omission' creates a liability gap for ECAIs while measuring their default rate or calculating the transition matrix, even though the number of rated exposures is increasing significantly. The ultimate impact is that the quality/objectivity of the rating is not being achieved and the ECAI's analyst or the RC members of the ECAI cannot be held liable for the rating assigned to an exposure and its quality or subsequent effect on a non-performing loan.

To make it clear-cut, another evidence could be forward in favor of this claim. For instance, the percentage of banking sector exposures rating increased significantly when BB adopted Basel II and Basel III with the standardized approach. The country's overall banking sector's corporate exposures stood at BDT 5,729.3 billion in 2018 of which 81.8% were rated exposure (BB, 2008). Figure 4.2 shows the trend of corporate exposure ratings in the Bangladeshi banking sector and total non-performing loans (NPL) of the banking sector for the period 2010–2018. The trend shows that the percentage of corporate exposure rating was 16.4% in 2010 which increased to 81.8% at the end of 2018. This trend shows how rapidly ECAI businesses grew over the years. On the other hand, overall NPL of the banking sector simultaneously increased during the same period (in 2010 banking sector total NPL was BDT 227.1 billion and in 2018 it stood at BDT 939.1 billion).

The reason for the increase in the corporate exposure rating in banking system can be explained as follows: banks are encouraged by their corporate clients to be rated by ECAIs, which ultimately provide banks an incentive in calculation of capital charges (since high rated corporate exposure carries low RWA under the SA) and this motivation multiplies the ECAIs number of clients and business volume. It is expected that the credit risk of the bank's clients is accurately assessed by respective ECAIs and the asset quality of the banks is supposed to improve. However, the result seems that it reflects the reverse of the expectation as the percentage of rated exposure increased on the one hand and NPL climbed on the

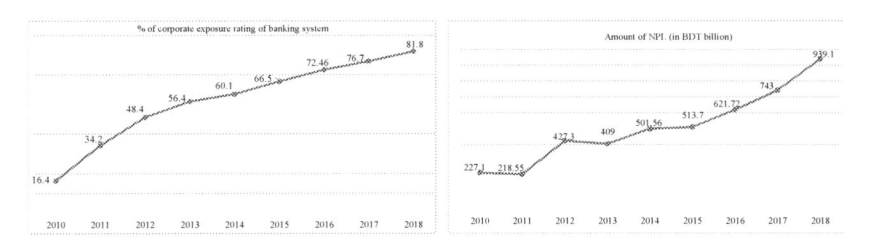

Fig. 4.2 Trend of corporate exposure rating and total NPL during 2010–2018 (prepared by authors from the Financial Stability Report, 2010–2018)

other. To solve this puzzle, one simple solution is to go to the ECAIs transition matrix to check its rating accuracy and the cumulative default rate (CDR). ECAIs transition matrix which was published in the Financial Stability Reports reflected that only 636 entities/exposures are enlisted in the transition matrix 2017–2018 (the percentage of corporate exposure rating was 76.7% in 2017); 612 entities/exposures are enlisted in the transition matrix 2016–2017 (the percentage of corporate exposure rating was 72.46% in 2016); 389 entities/exposures are enlisted in the transition matrix 2015–2016 (the percentage of corporate exposure rating was 66.5% in 2015); 320 entities/exposures are enlisted in the transition matrix 2014–2015 (the percentage of corporate exposure rating was 60.1% in 2014) for long-term rating under the surveillance category. This statistics documents that the all the clients who were rated in 2017 did not conduct the surveillance rating in 2018 and the same situation happened in previous years. This means that suppose an exposure that was rated in the previous year does not continue a surveillance rating in the current year if it would have already become non-performing by this time. Because banks have no incentive to follow up surveillance rating as banks already maintain loan loss provision against that exposure due to non-performing and thus no lower capital charge applies this time for this specific entity/exposure. We shall note that if an exposure became unrated it has 125% risk weight whereas the risk weight for B1 or below notch is 150%. As a result, the exposure became unrated after the initial rating (first year rating) if it became non-performing. However, this institutional gap/legal facility of 'avoidance of surveillance rating' (although client and ECAI have agreement to conduct surveillance rating) creates an opportunity (a kind of tax 'avoidance' and 'evasion' in auditing and taxation literature) to capitalize on the incentives of 'initial rating' for both banks and ECAIs. Because banks charge low capital from the initially rated exposure whereas ECAIs are rating the exposure with higher a rating notch without taking any responsibility for future downgrading risk. BB has also confessed this ill incentive embedded in the existing institutions, 'very few entities were found in low rating categories (i.e., 4, 5 and 6) suggesting the possible tendency of entities/exposures to remain unrated rather than rated with a poor score. This may help the entities to maintain the required capital adequacy since lower risk weight is assigned to unrated entities/exposures' (BB, 2018, p. 57). In fact, according to the regulation it is the supervisor's responsibility to follow up on the surveillance rating to reflect the ECAIs rating accuracy on CDR and transition matrix; however, both the regulators have failed to comply with their own initiated regulations which in our view is a kind of failure of 'omission' by the national supervisors of Bangladesh. In fact, this supervisory omission creates a legal indemnity from taking any civil liability for irresponsible/misrating/inflated rating by ECAIs. As a result, there are no incentives for ECAIs to allocate their resources to quantify the real credit risk of the exposure, rather they have incentives to produce the number of rating reports, which increases their revenue.

(ii) Disclosure of ECAI

Secondly, in our view, the disclosure requirement that is obligatory in the ECAIs regulation is not sufficient to protect public interest or protect systemic risk. Under CRC Rules 1996, there are few disclosures that a CRC must disclose. One is a disclosure within the rating deed (between CRC and firm) and another is a public disclosure of rating on their Web site. In order to make the rating agreement free from potential biases, the rules suggest disclosing the compensation arrangement with rating clients (BSEC, 1996, Article 9, (5) (b), p. 113). In the case of a public disclosure the CRC shall disclose the entity or group identity if it receives a significant percentage (10% or more) of revenue from a single group/entity and in addition, its director's shareholding position of listed securities on a half yearly basis (Article 9). The rules also made it compulsory to publish the updated rating of entities and the methodologies of the rating, as well as the historical default rating. At the time of writing (October 2020), we checked on all the ECAIs official web portal regarding this public disclosure, we did not find the public disclosures in full as these rules prescribed. As BSEC provides the license to CRAs for public interest (BSEC, 1996), it is the responsibility of BSEC to monitor the CRAs compliance to protect public interest. Whereas in BB guidelines, only the pricing system of ECAIs needs to be disclosed to the public and, the minimum methodology for rating corporate clients is described with five risk and sub-risk categories such as financial risk, business/industry risk, management risk, security risk and relationship risk. But there is no specific weight on each risk assigned by central bank guidelines. As a result, there is no disclosure from ECAIs regarding how they assigned the rating to a specific exposure based on this risk. Therefore, both general investors and banks simply know the rating notch of an exposure without its full disclosure.

Therefore, it is evident that the existing regulations for ECAIs in Bangladesh are providing some legal scope to skip the material disclosure. Readers can presume that such insufficient disclosure creates gray zone for banks, researchers and all other stakeholders to put trust in ECAI's exposure rating and it is urgent to clear such gray zones from the ECAI's disclosure. To wrap up, in our view, the legal institutions of ECAIs in Bangladesh failed to address the governance and objectivity of rating (which would normally be achieved via the civil liability of CRAs for irresponsible or inaccurate ratings) and meaningful public disclosures which are the main drawbacks of the institutions within.

Wrap-Up Comments on Regulations of ECAIs in Bangladesh

In this section, we investigated regulatory reliance on ECAIs and the role of ECAIs in this regard. As we mentioned earlier, ECAIs are duly recognized by BB to quantify the credit risk of exposure and based on ECAIs rating banks are computing their risk-weighted assets (RWA) and subsequently capital requirement. Our discussion on the Bangladeshi banking industry performance in Chapter 1 has create a puzzle, that despite credit risk being quantified by ECAI, NPLs soared rapidly in last decade in other words, why has the Basel Accord had a positive impact on loan growth. We presume that due to some specific reasons, an ECAIs rating fails to capture the actual credit risk of the associated bank exposure, and in turn, the entire banking industry has been deprived of the potential benefits of the Basel Accord. Besides, the regulator naïvely relies on ECAIs for homogenization of credit risk which creates an (ill) incentive to the bank managers. We critically examined the quantification of credit risk in Basel framework and critically reviewed the ECAIs regulation from an institutional perspective. We have found that the standardized approach has adopted while quantifying credit risk which creates a reliance on credit information based on ECAI's rating and bank managers therefore have an incentive to follow the SA as they just free ride on ECAIs rating notch. In contrast, due to the absence of any liability regime and insufficient disclosure requirements in the existing institutions, ECAIs easily skip their responsibility for providing accurate credit information. We can say that such naïve reliance on ECAIs credit information has a positive impact on loan growth.

4.5   REGULATIONS OF SUB-DEBT IN BANGLADESH AND A CRITICAL VIEW

Sub-debt (when issued for bank capital adequacy purposes) is issued to institutional investors like financial institutions, insurance companies, corporate firms and high net worth individuals and, the debt in nature is non-convertible, fully redeemable, unsecured, unlisted and either coupon bearing or floating rate interest (BSEC, 2012). There are two legal documents in Bangladesh that banks need to follow while issuing sub-debt as Tier 2 capital under Basel framework. These are (i) Guidelines on Subordinated Debt (BRPD circular no. 13, dated October 14, 2009) and (ii) Securities and Exchange Commission (Private Placement of Debt Securities) Rules, 2012 (SEC notification October 29, 2012). Below we summarize the key issues of both legal documents for our further discussion.

BB's Guidelines on Sub-debt 2009 (BB, 2009)

BB recognized sub-debt as a Tier 2 and Tier 3 capital component (BB, 2002, 2009, 2010) in Basel Accord I and II guidelines whereas it is considered as a Tier 2 capital component under Basel III guidelines (BB, 2014) and some amendments made in the existing guidelines on subordinated debt 2009. To keep updated, our analysis on sub-debt regulation is based on the guidelines that referred by BB (2014). The regulation refers that. 'A debt instrument which has no maturity date and redemption period (i.e. perpetual subordinated debt), is considered to be Additional Tier 1 (AT 1) and which has fixed maturity date and redemption period (i.e. not perpetual in nature) is considered as Tier 2 capital' (BB, 2014). As of December 2018, there is only few debt instruments which have been considered as AT 1 among all sub-debts issued by banks and in this study subordinated debt (sub-debt) refers to the debt instruments which are considered as Tier 2 capital under Basel Accord III guideline. We shall note that when issuing sub-debt, banks firstly need BSEC consent, then the application documents along with the consent of BSEC have to be submitted to BB for final consent. The key features of the guidelines for sub-debt are as follows.

(a) 'Subordinated debt will be referred to the debt instrument which will be subordinated to deposits and other liabilities of the bank.

It implies that the claims of the subordinated debt holders will be junior to the claims of the depositors and the other creditors' (BB, 2014, p. 88). 'In the event of liquidation or winding up of the issuers business and distribution of return on investment, the bondholders will ranked after claims of the depositors and other creditors i.e. it will be ranked immediately ahead of ordinary shareholders' (BB, 2014, p. 89).

(b) The tenure of the debt is at least 5 years and the amortization of the debt will be 20% annually during the last five years of the bond's life. In general majority of sub-debt is 7 years life.

(c) As it is not a deposit in nature and hence not include in the deposit insurance scheme.

(d) Sub-debt will be unsecured but supported by 'agreement of trust'/trust deed.

(e) The maximum ceiling of subordinate debt was 30% of the amount of Tier 1 capital (BB, 2009), however again stated that Tier 2 capital should be 4% of the total RWA or 88.89% of CET 1, whichever is higher (BB, 2014).

(f) The amortization of the debt will be 20% annually during the last five years.

(g) There should be an agreement with manager to the issue/lead arranger and underwriter of the issue (BB, 2014, p. 90).

(h) While application for issuing the debt, banks should submit a copy of subordinated note format and agreement and amortization schedule along with all salient features of the debt.

Securities and Exchange Commission (Private Placement of Debt Securities) Rules, 2012[5] (BSEC, 2012)

BSEC has adopted the rules in 2012 for the interest of the capital market and it applies for issuance of debt securities through private placement. As the sub-debt is offered through private placement, the rules are considered as the Bible for issuance of sub-debt. We summarize below the key points of the rules that are related to subordinated debt.

---

[5] Full text available at https://www.sec.gov.bd/home/laws.

(a) Definition: BB (2009) mentioned that subordinated debt would be 'unsecured' and the term is explained by the rules in the following way, 'unsecured debt instrument means debt securities, in which the issuer owes the holders an indebtedness and which is secured by claims over all present and future assets of the issuer subsequent to all secured lenders/eligible investors' (Article 1(t)).

(b) Role of CRC: The issue needs to be rated initially by any credit rating company (CRC) and its periodical surveillance rating shall be done by the said rating company till the full and final redemption or conversion of the debt instrument (Article 3(3)).

(c) Role of Trustee: Article 9 of the regulation provides that there should be a trustee (registered trustee by BSEC) of the issue which appointed by the issuer and a registered 'Deed of Trust' (as per schedule C of the rules) should be executed between trustee and issuer which explain the rights and obligations of both parties. The details of trustee registration, duties and responsibilities of trustee are described in Article 9. Besides, duties of trustee in case of default of the issue described in Article 12. What is more, trustee annually reports to the BSEC regarding the instrument, interest payment and other relevant information. BSEC has rights to change the trustee in the event of securities holders claim or in the public interest, if it fits (Article 9 (5)(i)).

(d) Fees: BSEC consent fees at 0.10% of the face value of the securities have to be paid by the issuer within 15 days of issuance of consent letter (Article 7 (1)) and annual maximum trustee fee is 0.25% of the outstanding amount of the securities should be paid by issuer (Article 9 (10)).

(e) Information Memorandum (IM): Article 4 (o) recognized that IM of the issue that prepared by the issuer should contain all relevant information about the issuer, issue and the trustee. The format and contents of such IM are described in schedule B of the rules. The missing point is, there is no obligation to publish the IM to general public or shareholders although they are the stakeholder of the sub-debt issued under Basel framework.

Based on the two legal documents of sub-debt, it can be observed that sub-debt is a debt instrument which contains a tripartite contract agreement among the three legal stakeholders of sub-debt. The legal parties are: (i) issuer of the debt, (ii) trustee of the debt and (iii) debtholders.

Besides, it is evident from the above discussion that sub-debt that is intended to be issued to strengthen the regulatory capital needs both BSEC and BB consent and the trustee plays a vital role in this context.

Critical Views on Regulations of Sub-Debt in Bangladesh

As was we mentioned earlier that as of December 2018 most of the Bangladeshi PCBs issued the sub-debt to maintain minimum capital adequacy ratio. Hence, the important question is what are the institutional cost involved with sub-debt? We observed from the sub-debt regulations that there are two types of costs involved with sub-debt such as (i) transaction cost/issue cost of sub-debt (ii) coupon rate of sub-debt. In this sub-section, we critically examine these two costs from the sub-debt regulations.

(i) Transaction Cost/Issuance Cost of Sub-debt

We mentioned in Sect. 4.2 of this chapter that the 'transaction cost analysis' concept is widely accepted by new the institutional economists. Williamson (1985) categorized transaction cost into two types, *ex ante* and *ex post*. *Ex ante* costs are the costs of drafting, negotiating and safeguarding an agreement to avoid complexities and contingencies involved with a contract (Williamson, 1985, p. 20). These costs ensure the acceptance of the contract among related parties as Williamson (1985) mentioned, '*Ex ante* inter firm safeguards can sometimes be fashioned to signal credible commitments and restore integrity to transaction' (p. 20). On the other hand, *ex post* costs of a contract may arise from four corners such as (i) the maladaptation cost incurred when transaction drift out of alignment, (ii) the haggling cost that incurred to correct ex post misalignments (iii) setup and running costs associated with the governance structures to which disputes are referred and (iv) the bonding cost of effecting secure commitments (p. 21). As sub-debt is a financial contract, are there any transaction costs for sub-debt? If so, what are they? Chowdhury (2019) identified several transaction costs for bond issuance in Bangladesh such as bond registration fees (consent fees of BSEC), stamp duties, annual trustee fees and ancillary charges. However, based on the definition of transaction cost by Williamson (1985) and the mentioned issue cost of sub-debt in the said two legal documents, we

Table 4.3   Transaction cost/issuance cost of sub-debt in Bangladesh

Sl. no	Ex-ante cost	Ex-post cost
1	Consent fees to BSEC which are 0.10% of the total face value (BSEC, 2012, Article 7)	-
2	Initial trustee fee which is 0.25% of the outstanding amount of the debt securities (BSEC, 2012, Article 9)	Annual trustee fee
3	Issue manager/Mandated Lead arranger fee (it depends on agreement)	Any other administrative cost related with post issue matters
4	Legal counsel fee	–
5	Initial rating fees paid to credit rating agencies	Surveillance rating fee till the life of the instrument
6	Printing and advertisement cost or any other expenses	

BB (2009, 2010, 2014) and BSEC (2012)

identified some potential transaction costs of sub-debt which are shown in Table 4.3.

From Table 4.3, it seems that some *ex-ante* costs such as consent fees and trustee fees are fixed by regulators and some costs such as mandated lead arranger (MLA) fees, legal fees and other costs may be dependent on the bank's negotiation strategy. However, *ex-post* costs such as administrative costs seem to be variable costs. What is the real number of transaction costs for the issuance of sub-debt? To answer this let us check the three information memorandums of sub-debt that was issued in 2014 by three different banks. Based on the information memorandums, the *ex-ante* transaction cost of each issue is presented in Table 4.4.

Table 4.4 shows that *ex-ante* costs are, on average, 1.18% for three issues. On the other hand, the *ex-post* transaction costs are trustee fees which are around 0.05% of the face value of the issue and the surveillance rating fees which are BDT 0.3 million per year (it depends on the outstanding amount of the debt). As information memorandums of other banks are not publicly available, the authors cannot compute the transaction costs of individual banks. Anyway, if we consider, the transaction cost (*ex-ante*) is one (1) percent on average of the sub-debt issued by the banks, we can compute the real amount of transaction cost of sub-debt. In Table 4.5, we estimate the total *ex-ante* transaction cost of sub-debt since 2009 that banks had to incur to issue sub-debt as Tier 2 capital.

Table 4.4 Ex-ante transaction cost and coupon rate of three sub-debts issued in 2014 (amount in BDT million)

Sl no	Details	ABBL*	MBL*	SIBL*
1	Total issue amount	2,500	3,000	3,000
2	Rate of return/Coupon rate	11–13%	6-month FDR rate + margin 3%	120% of 180 days MTD rate
3	Consent fees to BSEC (0.10% of the total face value)	2.5	3.0	3.0
4	Trustee fee, rating fees, arrangement fees, legal counsel fees, stamp fees, etc	37.91	30.47	21.21
5	Total transaction cost (ex-ante) (sl no. 3 + 4)	40.41	33.47	24.21
6	Percentage (%) to total issue amount (sl. no 5÷1)	1.62	1.12	0.81

*ABBL-AB Bank Limited, MBL-Mercantile Bank Limited, SIBL-Social Islami Bank Limited
Source Information Memorandum of Subordinated Debt issued by respective banks

Table 4.5 Total ex-ante transaction cost for subordinated debt issued for capital adequacy purposes (amount in USD million)

Year	Amount of sub-debt issue**	Ex-ante cost (@1.00%)
2009*	123	1.2
2010	98	1.0
2011	44	0.4
2012	45	0.5
2013	98	1.0
2014	315	3.2
2015	243	2.4
2016	474	4.7
2017	676	6.8
2018	904	9.0
Total	3,022	30.2

*2009 data included the MPB of IBBL, ** as per average exchange rate shown in Table 4.3 in Annexure

Table 4.5 shows that the total *ex-ante* transaction cost for issuance of sub-debt over last 10 years is approximately USD 30 million. In addition, fixed annual trustee fees, rating fees and other administrative expenses must be paid by issuer banks as *ex-post* transaction costs during the tenure of the bond. It also evident that BSEC had earned USD 3.02 million (i.e., 3,022 X 0.1%) during the period 2009 to 2018 from the banks while providing consent to issue sub-debt which is exclusively used only for bank's capital adequacy purposes. In fact, the real cost of issuance of sub-debt is much higher than our estimated figures as BB in its report mentioned that, 'issuing costs (trustee fee, arranger fee, legal counseling fee, credit rating fee, consent fee, trust deed registration cost, issue management/corporate advisory fee, stamp duty and post issue management fee) and secondary transaction costs (annual depository/listing fee, transaction fee, new issue fee) that amount to nearly 6% of issue size' (BB, 2019, p. 28). As a result, banks had to incur a large amount of expenses as issue cost which ultimately have impact on net income of the bank.

(ii) Coupon Rate of Sub-debt

Besides the high transaction cost related with the issuance of sub-debt, it involves a high coupon rate. As we have seen in Table 4.4, the offer rate of the return/coupon rate is higher than the 6-month fixed deposit rate. Reader may ask, why do banks offer such a high coupon rate against the sub-debt? We presume that there are two reasons that motivate banks to collect high cost bearing debt instruments such as sub-debt from the market. First, when banks have an immense need for sub-debt to maintain their capital ratio, there is competition among banks to offer high interest rates to sell their debts. It is rational that issuers obviously want to sell their debt in the full amount and offer a lucrative interest rate to institutional investors which is higher than the other deposit products in the market. Second, as the debt is unsecured, and therefore not included in the deposit insurance scheme and unlisted in the burses, issuers provide some 'risk premium' to the debtholders. However, the rules have neither offered any fixed ceiling on coupon rate of the sub-debt nor any methodology offered by the central bank while fixation coupon rate which creates an opportunity for the banks to offer a high rate. This is because banks, as mentioned, have an incentive to issue sub-debt. In fact, this is a major institutional loophole that exists in the regulations. In addition, it is observed from the financial statements of all PCBs that they tend to consolidate the 'interest paid against subordinated debt' with 'interest paid on deposits and borrowing'. As a result, we presume that the general shareholders are not aware of the real 'coupon rate' of sub-debt issued by their banks and do not know about the 'transaction cost' involved with sub-debt as there is no disclosure in the annual report regarding these two. There is no provision in the regulations to disclose those expenses separately in the financial statements for the interest of investors.

Wrap-Up Comments on Regulations of Sub-debt in Bangladesh

We observed that the national supervisors have issued two important regulations regarding issuance of sub-debt as regulatory capital and despite of high transaction cost/issue cost and coupon rate, banks frequently issuing sub-debt chiefly to maintain minimum CRAR. We document that there is a huge cost (transaction cost and coupon rate) embedded with sub-debt which the issuing bank must bear. A rational question might arise at this point, why do banks issue such a costly debt instrument as Tier 2 capital without enhancing its' CET 1? Probably the incentive of sub-debt is outweighing its' transaction cost and high coupon rate. However, the alarming concern is the existing institutions of sub-debt fails to put ceiling on these two costs.

4.6 Concluding Remarks

In this chapter we briefly discussed the institutional economists' view on regulation. We also discussed on credit risk quantification approaches in Basel Accord. Then we argued that the standardized approach of Basel Accord advocates the reliance on ECAIs rating for credit risk mainly for homogenization of quantification of credit risk. As regulator advocates for SA, we detailed analyses the ECAIs regulations from institutional perspective. We document that such homogenization of credit risk while relying on ECAIs credit information has a positive impact on non-performing loan growth in Bangladesh. As evidence, we examined the ECAIs regulations from two points and found that within the institutions there is no liability regime for ECAIs rating and the article in the regulations on disclosure is not sufficient to ensure reliance on ECAIs credit rating methodology. Besides, we discussed the institutions of sub-debt in

Bangladesh and found that banks had to incur huge cost against issuance and maintenance of sub-debt. The regulations of sub-debt are silent on these issues which requires to resolve immediately through institutional reforms.

REFERENCES

Akerlof, G. A. (1970). The market for "Lemons": Quality uncertainty and the market mechanism. *The Quarterly Journal of Economics, 84*(3), 488–500.

Alchian, A. A. (1950). Uncertainty, evolution, and economic theory. *Journal of Political Economy, 58*(3), 211–221.

Bangladesh Bank (BB). (2002, November 24). *Master circular on capital adequacy of banks* (BRPD Circular No. 10). Banking Regulation and Policy Department, Bangladesh Bank.

Bangladesh Bank (BB). (2008, September 23). *Guidelines for recognition of eligible External Credit Assessment Institutions (ECAIs)* (BRPD Circular No. 7). Banking Regulation and Policy Department, Bangladesh Bank.

Bangladesh Bank (BB). (2009, October 14). *Guidelines on Subordinated debt for inclusion in Regulatory Capital* (BRPD Circular No. 13). Banking Regulation and Policy Department, Bangladesh Bank.

Bangladesh Bank (BB). (2010, August 3). *Revised guidelines on Risk Based Capital Adequacy (RBCA) for Banks* (BRPD Circular No. 24). Banking Regulation and Policy Department, Bangladesh Bank.

Bangladesh Bank (BB). (2014, December 21). *Guidelines on Risk Based Capital Adequacy (Revised Regulatory Capital Framework for banks in line with Basel III)* (BRPD Circular No. 18). Banking Regulation and Policy Department, Bangladesh Bank.

Bangladesh Bank (BB). (2018). *Financial Stability Report, 2018, Issue 9.* Financial Stability Department, Bangladesh Bank. https://www.bb.org.bd/pub/index.php.

Bangladesh Bank (BB). (2019). *Comprehensive framework on the development of the bond market in Bangladesh.* Bangladesh Bank. https://www.bb.org.bd/pub/publictn.php.

Bangladesh Securities and Exchange Commission (BSEC). (1996). *Credit rating companies rules 1996.* Dhaka, Bangladesh: BSEC. https://www.sec.gov.bd/home/lbook.

Bangladesh Securities and Exchange Commission (BSEC). (2012). *Securities and Exchange Commission (Private Placement of Debt Securities) Rules, 2012.* BSEC. https://www.sec.gov.bd/home/laws.

Basel Committee on Banking Supervision (BCBS). (2006). *International convergence of capital measurement and capital standards a revised framework comprehensive version*. Bank for International Settlements. https://www.bis.org/publ/bcbs128.htm.

Basel Committee on Banking Supervision (BCBS). (2017). *Basel III: Finalising post-crisis reforms*. Bank for International Settlements. https://www.bis.org/bcbs/publ/d424.pdf.

Boot, A. W. A., & Thakor, A. V. (1993). Self-interested bank regulation. *The American Economic Review, 83*(2), 206–212.

Carrigan, C., & Coglianese, C. (2015). Geroge J. Stigler, "The theory of economic regulation". In M. Lodge, E. C. Page, & S. J. Balla (Eds.), *The Oxford handbook of classics in public policy and administration* (pp. 287–299). Oxford University Press.

Chowdhury, S. K. (2019, July 3). Long-term finance and bond market development in Bangladesh. *The Daily Financial Express*, p. 4.

Coase, R. H. (1937). The nature of the firm. *Economica, 4*(16), 386–405.

Coase, R. H. (1960, October). The problem of social cost. *Journal of Law and Economics, 3*, 1–44.

Davis, S., Lukomnik, J., & Pitt-Watson, D. (2016). *What they do with your money*. Yale University Press.

Frexias, X., Leven, L., & Peydro, J. (2015). *Systemic risk, crises, and macroprudential regulation*. The MIT Press.

Hayek, F. A. (1948). *Individualism and economic order*. University of Chicago Press.

Knight, J. (1992). *Institutions and social conflict*. Cambridge University Press.

Laffont, J.-J., & Tirole, J. (1991). The politics of government decision-making: A theory of regulatory capture. *Quarterly Journal of Economics, 106*, 1089–1127.

Langlois, R. N. (1986a). The new institutional economics: An introductory essay. In R. Langlois (Ed.), *Economics as a process: Essays in the new institutional economics* (pp. 1–25). Cambridge University Press.

Langlois, R. N. (1986b). Rationality, institutions, and explanation. In R. Langlois (Ed.), *Economics as a process: Essays in the new institutional economics* (pp. 225–255). Cambridge University Press.

Mourlon-Drulo, E. (2015). 'Trust is good, control is better': The 1974 Herstatt Bank Crisis and its Implications for International Regulatory Reform. *Journal Business History, 57*(2), 311–314. https://doi.org/10.1080/00076791.2014.950956.

Nelson, R. R., & Winter, S. G. (1982). *An evolutionary theory of economic change*. Belknap Press.

North, D. C. (1981). *Structure and change in economic history*. Norton.

North, D. C. (1990). *Institutions, institutional change and economic performance*. Cambridge University Press.

North, D. C. (2005). *Understanding the process of economic change*. Princeton University Press.

Ostrom, E. (1993). Self-governance, the informal public economy, and the tragedy of the commons. In P. L. Berger (Ed.), *Institutions of democracy and development*. ICS Press.

Ostrom, E. (2005). *Understanding institutional diversity*. Princeton University Press.

Ostrom, E., Schroeder, L., & Wynne, S. (Eds.). (1993). *Institutional incentives and sustainable development: Infrastructure policies in perspective*. Westview Press.

Peláez, C. M., & Peláez, C. A. (2009). *Regulation of banks and finance: Theory and policy after the credit crisis*. Palgrave Macmillan.

Posner, R. A. (2013). The concept of regulatory capture: A Short, Inglorious History. In D. Carpenter & D. A. Moss (Eds.), *Preventing regulatory capture: Special interest influence and how to limit it* (pp. 49–66). Cambridge University Press.

Schumpeter, J. A. (1926). *Theorie der wirtschaftlichen Entwicklung* (2nd ed.). Duncker & Humblot.

Schumpeter, J. A. (1934). *The theory of economic development: An inquiry into profits, capital, credit, interest, and the business cycle*. Harvard University Press.

Schumpeter, J. A. (1942). *Capitalism, socialism and democracy*. Allen & Unwin.

Scott, W. R. (2014). *Institutions and organizations: Ideas, interests and identities* (4th ed.). Sage.

Stigler, G. T. (1971). The theory of economic regulation. *The Bell Journal of Economics and Management Science, 2*(1), 3–21.

Stiglitz, J. E., & Weiss, A. (1981). Credit rationing in markets with imperfect information. *American Economic Review, 71*(3), 393–410.

Suzuki, Y. (2011). *Japan's financial slump: Collapse of the monitoring system under institutional and transitional failures*. Palgrave Macmillan.

Williamson, O. E. (1979). Transaction-cost economics: The governance of contractual relations. *Journal of Law and Economics, 22*(2), 233–261.

Williamson, O. E. (1985). *The economic institutions of capitalism: Firms, markets, relational contracting*. The Free Press.

CHAPTER 5

Incentive: The Missing Pillar in the ECAIS Institutions

5.1 Introduction

We have detailed discussed about role of incentive and sanction while formulation of institutions in Chapter 4 from neo-institutional economist perspective and discussed on ECAIs liability regime (a kind of sanction) in the institutions in that chapter. This chapter sheds an analytical light on incentive in the ECAIs institutions that ensure the quality of ECAIs credit information while quantification of credit risk under Basel Accord. To examine the ECAIs incentive for rating accuracy we analyze the institutions in one hand and an empirical investigation in another hand. The discussion will aid to understand the anomaly (i) that we develop in Chapter 1. The chapter is organized as follows: Sect. 5.2 discusses how a CRA's rating is used for regulatory purposes in Bangladesh, and Sect. 5.3 presents detailed a discussion on quality of ECAIs credit information based on in-depth interview conducted in 2018 and 2019 and the relevant articles in ECAIs regulations. Section 5.4 summarizes the findings of research on ECAIs incentive in the existing institutions. Section 5.5 presents the concluding remarks.

5.2   Regulatory Reliance
on CRAs Rating in Bangladesh

The Bangladesh Securities and Exchange Commission (BSEC) first issued 'Credit Companies (CRC) Rules 1996' in June 1996, and it is considered as the first step to ushering in credit rating businesses in Bangladesh (Tsunoda et al., 2013). Later, BB issued the first recognition rules for ECAIs in 2009, in which banks were instructed to follow ECAIs risk rating to compute risk-weighted assets under Basel Accord implementation (BB, 2009). In fact, the BSEC first issued licenses to Credit Rating Companies in 2002 under CRC rules 1996 and Bangladesh Bank recognized the first ECAIs in April 2009. So far, eight CRAs have received licenses from BSEC and all were dully accorded the status of ECAIs by BB (BB, 2017). Tsunoda et al. (2013) fine-tuned the regulatory uses of the credit rating in Bangladesh and pointed out five moments when credit rating agencies 'rating' role received regulatory compulsion/stamp. These are:

1. In 1996, BSEC made it compulsory to use credit rating companies rating when issuing any debt security by any company and public issue of share at premium (including right shares) by any public limited companies.
2. In 2004, BB has instructed all unlisted banks to get them rated before they proceed to IPO.
3. Direct Listing rules 2006 of Dhaka Stock Exchange, which made it compulsory to carry a 'BBB' rating from a recognized CRA when desiring to directly offload shares in the bourse instead of IPO.
4. Capital Adequacy Framework (Basel II) implementation in 2007 which provided regulatory incentives to CRAs.
5. In 2007, 'The Office of the Chief Controller of Insurance' (Now it is 'Insurance Development and Regulatory Authority'—IDRA) simultaneously issued instructions to all general and life insurers to be rated by a CRA every year and every two years, respectively.

Hence, it is apparent that the demand for CRAs in Bangladesh was not fueled by 'market forces'; rather, it was fueled by 'artificial demand' of regulatory requirements. 'Artificial demand' in the sense that Bangladeshi regulators made it compulsory for the firms to use and rely on CRAs rating for various regulatory purposes (Tsunoda et al., 2013) instead of real demand of such ratings raised by investors, which we have observed in the global CRA evolution history in the US and its regulatory reliance on CRAs ratings (see Appendix). Hence, the responsibility for creating incentives for CRAs (to ensure their rating quality) in the institutions are equally borne by the regulators who made CRAs rating compulsory in the financial regulations. We have discussed the existing debate on CRAs' roles in Chapter 3, hence we shall leave that debate here.

5.3 Discussion on Quality of CRAs/ECAIs Credit Information in Bangladesh

We will use secondary data from various publications of national regulators and ECAI's website information in some parts of our discussion. Besides this, the discussion of ECAIs (CRA rule 1996 and ECAIs guidelines 2008) in Chapter 4 will support our discussion to some extent. In short, we keep the legal documents in the one hand and qualitative information in the other hand while exploring the theme of this chapter, what are the incentives offered in the institutions to ECAIs for exposure rating. Our discussion will be based upon three core issues such as:

(a) ECAIs accumulation of credit screening skills
(b) State of competition among ECAI
(c) Pay model of ECAI.

(a) ECAIs Accumulation of Credit Screening Skills

We examine incentives for ECAIs while accumulation of credit screening skill from two points of view. Firstly, how well the internal governance is designed to ensure its credit screening skill and secondly, how well ECAIs dedicate their efforts to accumulating credit risk screening skills.

Internal Governance of ECAIs
While discussing the CRC Rules, 1996 in Chapter 4, we mentioned that there is a board of directors, RC and IRC who are recognized in the rules (see Table 4.1). While interviewing all ECAIs during the field research of the study, one of the authors has confirmed the existence of such three-tier systems in all CRAs of Bangladesh. The statutory organizational structure of ECAIs related with rating can be presented in Fig. 5.1.

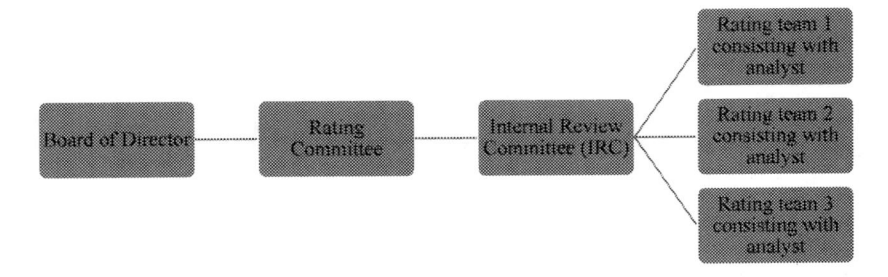

Fig. 5.1 Statutory organizational structure of ECAIs related with rating in Bangladesh

We shall note that under CRC rules 1996, a CRC is a public limited company and hence will follow the Companies Act 1994 while appointing directors. However, as CRC is not a listed public limited company, it is not mandatory for them to follow the corporate governance code that BSEC published in 2006 (latest amendment in 2018) while appointing a board of directors. Hence, all the directors in the board of CRC are shareholders and directors, no independent directors are appointed as board members. While investigation in the total number of members in board of directors and RC of each CRC the study found that one CRA does not disclose its board of directors' names whereas forty percent of CRAs don't disclose their RC members number and the details of RC members expertise on the public website. In short, we can say that ECAI's governance does not follow the corporate governance code of BSEC, and hence they do not publish their full internal governance structure to the public. Besides, it is mentioned in the rules that 'credit rating shall be assigned by rating committee and not by any individual analysts' (BSEC, 1996, Article 9 (1)). The serious missing point in the said rules is that there are no specific requirements, responsibility or remuneration system described explicitly for external members of a rating committee. These issues are not addressed in the BB guidelines as well. Therefore, this undisclosed and un-explained information by both regulatory bodies and CRAs is creating ambiguity or making a 'rating process black box' (Cifuentes, 2008) for understanding how well the governance system of an ECAI works. While interviewing the CRAs, one of the interviewees (among ECAIs) termed the issue as loopholes of the regulations. From this above discussion, we presume that ECAIs maintain a weak governance structure from an institutional perspective which adversely affects the credit information provided to banks.

Efforts on Accumulation of Credit Screening Skills

Although there is no specific regulation described in the rules for the internal rating procedure of ECAIs, each ECAI must develop their own rating procedure under the rules (BB, 2014; BSEC, 1996, Article 9). While investigation, we conducted comprehensive interviews about rating methodologies and the process with the Chief Rating Officers (CRO)/concerned officials of all the ECAIs. Based on the interview information and disclosure on their public websites regarding rating methodologies, the rating process of the entities has six steps (see Fig. 5.2) and can be succinctly explained as follows. There are two types of entity ratings; initial rating (when an entity first rated by an ECAI) and surveillance rating (after the initial rating, a consecutive 2- or 3-years annual rating by the same ECAI as per the agreement). In general, there are multiple steps are involved in the entire rating process. Initially, when the rating clients want to rate their entity for bank loan purposes, then they make an agreement with an ECAI and the rating process starts with the terms and conditions described in the agreement. Then the ECAI assigns two analysts to the entity who collect the necessary information and data. After validating all information, the analysts deliver their initial rating report (without assigning any notch) to the internal review committee and a copy of the same is sent to the client for their comments. After getting no objections from the clients on the information available in the report and being satisfied by internal review committee members, the report is placed before the RC for rating. Finally, the RC assigns a rating to the entity and the surveillance rating is conducted as per agreement. Hence, entity rating is a structural process which requires time and effort to produce a quality report on exposure rating.

When asked about the total time required for completion of steps 1–6, most of the ECAIs responded that it requires at least fifteen (15) days. As there is no compliance by regulators regarding publicly disclose the annual reports of ECAIs, the number of rating reports produced by per analyst per month is not disclosed officially. However, as per the information provided by the ECAI officials during our interview, they have confessed that the working load is too high for the analysts and there is less incentive to improve individual analyst's rating skill as the pricing of rating is controlled. The increasing number of rated corporate exposures and number of international standard professional analysts in the ECAIs have evidence on it. Besides, as it requires several steps (Fig. 5.2) in every

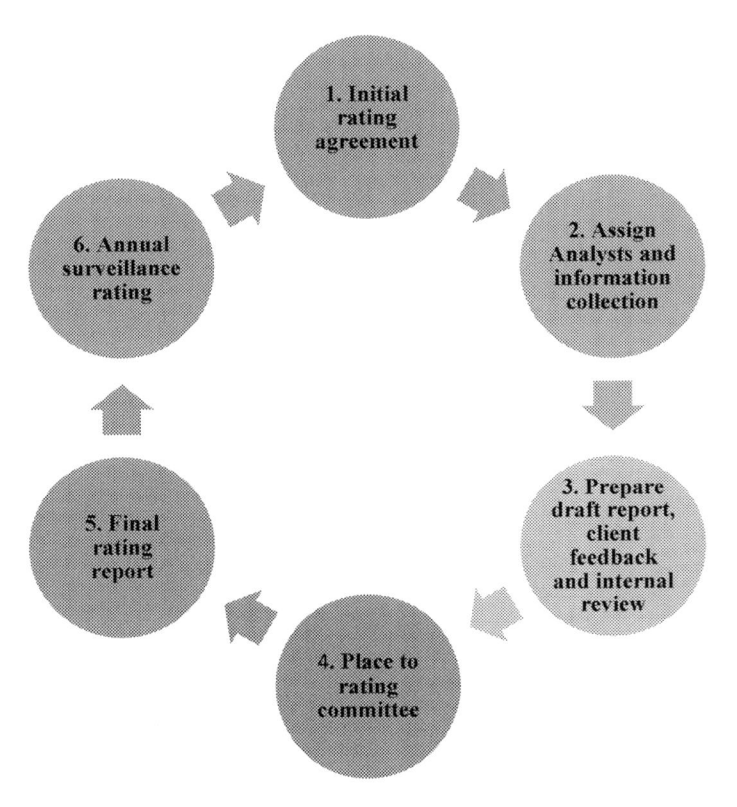

Fig. 5.2 ECAIs exposure rating process in Bangladesh

single deal, it is presumed that the time for proper judgment is quite short for analysts as well as the rating committee to make a judgment on each rating report. The institutional lacuna at this point is, there is no direction regarding the minimum time to produce a report; how many reports can an analyst prepare per month? How does one check the objectivity of the rating by the RC members? We have previously discussed in Chapter 4, (regarding the liability regime of ECAIs) that there are institutional loopholes regarding holding ECAIs responsible for inaccurate ratings. Hence, it is presumed that due to the existence of less incentive on quality ratings, ECAIs put less effort (in terms of time and skilled manpower) into the accumulation of credit screening skills.

(b) State of Competition among ECAIs

There is an academic debate on the level of competition among CRAs. The debate is mainly raised from two perspectives, one is competition through price, and the other is competition deriving from the quantity of CRAs. Some scholars argue that as price will dictate the quality of the rating, the number of rating agencies (duopoly or competitive) does not matter (Chan, 2010; U.S. SEC, 2008). Therefore, the competition should be on price, and the quality of ratings will dictate the price. Some researchers point out that competition within quantity matters as insufficient competition in quantity will lead to dominant CRAs keeping their market share despite their poor rating performance (Darbellay, 2013), as issuers have no other options. But increasing competition could extend the problem rather than minimize the conflict of interest (which arises from CRAs 'issuer-pay' model) because issuers pressure the competing CRAs to relax their standards to obtain business (Coffee, 2011). On the contrary, the US CRA reforms policy suggested to enhance the number of CRAs and remove barrier of entry for new entrants (U.S. SEC, 2012) whereas European regulatory bodies stress quality of the regulation of CRAs, if competition matters (EC, 2016). Interestingly, there is no benchmark published by the regulators to determine how many CRAs are required for a market be it for either developed or developing countries which is the main drawback in contemporary institutions. We presume that institutions have tendered it on each country's national supervisor's jurisdiction and prudence. Table 5.1 shows the number of CRAs in some selected countries which will contribute our discussion further.

Table 5.1   Number of CRAs in some selected countries

Sl no	Name of the country	Number of CRA (as of December 2018)
1	US	10 (NRSRO including 2 foreign affiliated)
2	EU	47 (including 4 non-EU affiliated)
3	Japan	7 (including 5 foreign affiliated)
4	Malaysia	2 (all domestic)
5	India	6 (including 1 foreign affiliated)
6	Pakistan	2 (all domestic)
7	Sri Lanka	2 (including 1 foreign affiliated)
8	**Bangladesh**	**8 (all domestic)**

Source Related countries SEC web portal

We should note that the Bangladesh financial system is bank-based like other South Asian countries, i.e., the household savings are invested in terms of bank deposit instead of investing in securities and the bond market. Corporate firms also depend on bank loans for project financing since the country's bond market is in a very nascent stage (see Table 5.2). Having this reality at the crux of the country's financial system, Table 5.1 shows that Bangladesh has too many CRAs compared to other countries in South Asia and the US in which the financial system is mainly securities-based (Kaufman, 1995) and the top country in the world by market capitalization (WB, 2019) has only ten NRSRO. Why does Bangladesh have so many CRAs? When asking this question to the regulatory officials during our investigation, they would not provide a clear answer. There is no regulatory rationale explained by BSEC or official reports published by the national supervisors for justifying the huge numbers of CRAs in Bangladesh which is the highest number in South Asia and having no guideline to determine the required number of CRAs in the existing institutions. However, regulators may deserve credit for enhancing the number of rated corporate exposures under Basel Accord due to the large number of ECAIs in the market. But at the same time, as the number of non-performing loans has also increased, we assume that it may be the

Table 5.2 Number of companies and amount (in BDT billion) for IPOs (including premium), Sub-debt and Debenture issue

Sl No	FY	IPO		Sub-debt issue		Bond/debenture issue	
		Number	Amount	Number	Amount	Number	Amount
1	2008–2009	7	0.82	3	9.31	1	0.03
2	2009–2010	10	13.99	1	3.55	3	5.88
3	2010–2011	6	11.22	3	7	1	1
4	2011–2012	11	10.47	2	24	–	–
5	2012–2013	13	7.09	2	2.50	2	4
6	2013–2014	17	6.53	4	10.20	2	0.31
7	2014–2015	11	8.08	7	18.50	2	0.06
8	2015–2016	09	3.68	8	24.50	2	0.27
9	2016–2017	6	2.36	2	9	3	4.98
10	2017–2018	11	5.03	19	86.25	–	–
	Total	101	69.27	51	194.81	16	16.53

BSEC (2018)

adverse impact of competition within ECAIs. In other words, competition probably provides ill-incentives to the Bangladeshi ECAIs. Some scholars noted that such competition can lead the CRAs to 'race to the bottom' in the sense that CRAs compete among themselves to lower rating standards instead of focusing on rating quality (Darbellay, 2013). If so, why does regulator provide licenses to eight CRCs in a market where the capital issue is exceptionally low?

In fact, the rationale for encouraging 'competition' in the credit rating industry can be discussed in two ways:

(i) To eliminate the 'dead weight welfare loss' (in economics literature, a common point while advocating for market mechanism) of the issuers and investors. Because if there is a monopoly in the market, ECAIs can charge more which ultimately is paid by borrowers and increases their cost of doing business as a result the loan became costlier, consequently the final product will be costlier, and the consumers will pay the cost. Hence, competition may eliminate the cost of finance for producers and the society will benefit from having more ECAIs in the market.

(ii) The regulatory incentive (use of ECAIs rating for regulatory purposes) provided by the regulators to the ECAIs due to 'competition' may help to build some 'reputational capital' for ECAIs. As the market becomes competitive and an ECAI's line of earning depends on bank exposure ratings, it is expected that ECAIs will invest their resources to enhance their rating quality for achieving market share. In other words, competition can act as a sanction mechanism for low quality ratings of ECAIs in the sense that if any ECAI produced an inflated rating/mis-rating, it loses trust among bankers (who are the consumers of ECAI's rating) and next round will lose market share.

However, the institutions of ECAI present another story. Firstly, BB in its ECAIs recognition guideline (BB, 2014) has instructed all ECAIs to follow a 'uniform pricing policy.' As a result, there is no option to charge high prices for any individual ECAIs which demotivates them to employ skilled and experienced analysts for rating purposes. Because skilled and experienced analysts play a key role in improving the quality of rating, and if ECAIs have no incentive to hire skilled analysts they will not do so. Generally, the rating analysts have no incentive to upgrade their own skill and expertise as ECAIs will not hire them for their advanced skill. This seemingly is a 'convoy' system while controlling the remuneration of ECAIs rating, however, it distorts the capacity (as ECAI has no option to increase revenue by pricing strategy) of ECAIs to hire more professionals in credit analysis, resulting in lowering the overall quality of credit ratings. Surprisingly, in the same guidelines, it has placed all ECAI's ratings in same category in the sense that there is no grading based on ECAI's 'reputation' or 'quality of rating.' As a result, ECAIs have lost another incentive to employ a high paid analyst to produce an accurate rating and hence competition could not help them to build 'reputational capital.' The 'convoy system' by BB in incubating ECAIs in the same pace and direction may have created an ill-incentive, or rather a moral hazard effect for ECAIs to shirk monitoring, resulting in free-riding on the protected profit margin without paying effort to building their reputational capital. Therefore, the high competition in the CRA industry in Bangladesh neither brings any welfare to society nor helps ECAIs to build their reputational capital. To conclude, we presume that thinner profit margins under severer competition may discourage ECAIs to improve the quality of credit information and market forces cannot correct the ECAI's rating quality. Rather excess competition creates a new type of 'moral hazard' for ECAIs while maintaining the quality of rating.

(c) Pay Model of ECAI

We can hypothesize that there is also a potential moral hazard in the ECAI's existing pay model which might affect the ECAI's quality of credit information. We can examine this statement with two sets of logic (i) what are the sources of ECAI's revenue and (ii) how the ECAI's pay model works.

(i) What are the sources of revenue of Credit Rating Companies (CRCs) in Bangladesh?

Based on CRC rules 1996, various BB and IDRA notifications (which were issued from time to time between 2002 and 2018), the main sources of revenue for CRCs in Bangladesh can be broadly categorized into four sets:

- bank exposure rating fees paid to ECAIs by firms directly (corporate and SME)
- annual entity rating fees paid to ECAIs by financial institutions directly (as per existing law advocates banks, non-banks financial institutions (NBFI) and insurance companies to conduct annual rating by (CRC))
- entity rating for IPO and bond rating paid to ECAIs by issuers directly (if any company wishes to issue a bond in the capital market the business entity must be rated by a CRC).
- Consulting/Miscellaneous.

In every case, firms/issuers are liable to pay the rating fees. It indicates that the CRA's pay model is issuer based. While conducting our interviews with ECAIs, one of the major ECAI's senior executive admitted that around 70% of their revenue was derived from bank exposure ratings in 2018 and other interviewees were hesitant to disclose their revenue segmentation. However, the study adopted another approach to locate ECAI's revenue sources. As an ECAI's rating is mandatory for IPO, and debt issuance, Table 5.2 shows the capital market instruments (initial public offer (IPO), sub-debt and debenture issue)) that were issued through BSEC from the period of 2008–2009 to 2017–2018; to aid in understanding the other revenue sources of ECAIs (except bank exposure rating).

It is evident from Table 5.2 that only 101 IPOs, 51 sub-debts and 16 debentures were floated in the capital market during last 10 years. As all sub-debt was issued by the commercial banks, these debt instruments are need not be rated by CRCs because their issuers were already rated by a CRC. Hence, only 117 (101 + 16) companies were rated by the CRCs in last 10 years (only an average of 13 companies per year!) while raising their funds from the capital market. This data endorses that the issuance of capital through BSEC was very marginal in Bangladesh during our investigated period, and hence, the majority of CRC revenue does not depend on the rating of capital market instruments rather the lion's share of revenue is derived from bank exposure ratings. However, in the CRC rules and ECAIs recognition rules, there is no compulsion to disclose the financial statements or annual reports to the public hence authors could not reach the financial statements of CRCs. Future research might explore more information regarding the revenue segmentation of CRCs. Scholars strongly opined that the difference between a serious conflict of interest with CRAs compared to other gate keepers is that CRAs majority revenues come from rating fees (Partnoy, 2006) which compel them to compromise with rating quality. We presume that similar conflict of interests exist in Bangladesh.

In a word, from the above discussion, it is evident that bank exposure rating is the chief revenue source, and we view that this can create a moral hazard for ECAIs. To clarify this issue concretely, next we discuss how the revenue/pay model of ECAIs works in the case of exposure rating.

(ii) How does an ECAI's revenue/pay model for bank exposure rating work?

The revenue model is the most crucial factor as paying customers are the most powerful in a market economy. We referenced earlier that bank exposure ratings by ECAIs are conducted only for Basel Accord implementation and the 'issuer-based' model is debatable among academics and regulators as well. In the exposure rating process, firms are acting as the 'issuer' (like security rating) who collect the funds (loan) from bank using the ECAIs rating notch and banks are 'investors' (like security rating) who invest their money in the firm relying on credit rating assessments by ECAIs. Therefore, like security rating, ECAI's pay model is an 'issuer pay model.' Firms require ECAI ratings as a part of loan documentation paper and thus ECAIs are paid by the firms/individuals who are seeking bank loans. Banks and regulators are the end user of ECAI's ratings and do not pay any fees to ECAIs. Thus, there are four parties involved in exposure rating such as ECAIs, firms, banks, and regulators and only firms pay ECAIs; banks and regulators are end consumers of the ECAIs rating. Figure 5.3 shows and explains this concept.

Figure 5.3 shows the relationship with firms and ECAI; ECAI-Bank-Regulators and Firm-Bank. Firms pay rating fees to ECAIs and ECAIs conduct the rating. Banks and ECAIs are exchanging business information via ECAI's business development team (if they need to validate any information) and banks use the rating notch for computing the regulatory capital that they received via the firm. Finally, ECAIs provide the rating report to regulators and banks prepare and submit the CRAR report to regulators using ECAIs rating grade while computing RWA for credit risk. However, the study found from structured interviews with 25 corporate entities that 80 percent of corporate managers are

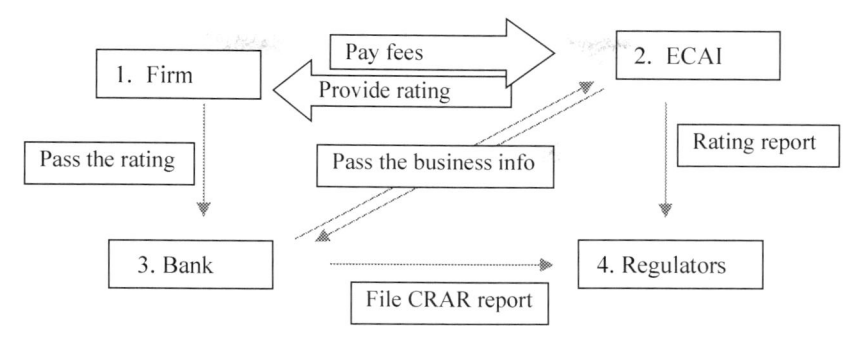

Fig. 5.3 Relationship with firm, ECAI, regulators and bank while exposure rating

agreed that an ECAI's rating was helpful to get a bank loan and the study also confirmed that some banks offer discounted interest rates when lending to high rated clients. We shall note that the fees of exposure rating are the same for all ECAIs as BB instructed (BB, 2014, p. 132), hence, there is no competition with price among ECAIs. Therefore, as ECAI's pay model is firm-paid, there is a conflict of interest (since we document that the lion's share of ECAIs revenue depends on exposure rating). Hence, we presume that this leads to potential a moral hazard for ECAIs. The concern is, as there exists an institutional 'omission' (i.e., no civil liability for irresponsible/mis-rating/inflated rating by ECAIs), the CRA's conflict of interest is to trade-off between pay model and rating quality which leads into a moral hazard (as there is no institutional incentive for ECAI's to allocate resources to rating accuracy). In the following sub-section, we elaborate the potential moral hazard of ECAI that arises from the pay model.

Potential moral hazard of ECAIs from the existing pay model

In case of CRAs, when the market is competitive, issuers/client's behavior is opportunistic, and they prefer a 'rate shopping' strategy (Coffee, 2006). It means that issuers prefer the rater who will rate his instrument with a high notch and the same logic is applied with bank exposure rating. For example, firm 'A' seeks bank finance for business and thus they need to have their business rated by any ECAI, as banks offer low interest rates for high rated clients. So, firm 'A' has an incentive to be rated with the highest notch and it will choose the ECAI which will offer a favorable rating (higher rating). As the market is competitive, ECAIs have to honor firm's expectations otherwise they will lose the business. Therefore, in theory it is possible that a firm/client will shop for their rating from ECAIs which will offer a high rating or the expected rating notch. Here the role of institutions is crucial in the context of Bangladesh. Another comparative advantage to firms is, as ECAI's pay model is 'issuer-based,' firms can bargain with the rating agencies for a high rate. In our previous example, if 'X' rating agency assigns the firm 'A' the 'BBB' rating notch then 'Y' rating agency may assign the same firm the 'A' rating notch to catch the business. Then the rational firm/client will either pick 'Y' rating agency or bargain with 'X' rating agency for assigning rating notch 'A.' In practice, such kinds of 'rate shopping' can create a moral hazard for ECAIs. Consequently, ECAIs are in a 'race to the bottom' in the sense of quality and a 'race to the top' in the sense of rating notches. These 'race to the top' and 'race to bottom' phenomena express the ECAIs moral hazard.

In fact, the dilemma for an ECAI is, the nature of an entity as a 'quasi-regulatory' organization but with a business model as a 'for-profit' organization. The nature and objectives of a 'quasi-regulatory' entity are contradictory with those of a 'for-profit' entity which creates an incentive problem for ECAIs. BB has acknowledged this in the following way, 'though rating agencies have been implicitly playing a quasi-regulatory role, they are for-profit entities, and their incentives may be misaligned with regulatory objectives. Conflict of interests might arise because the rating companies are paid by the entities issuing the securities or extending exposures- an arrangement that has come under fire as a disincentive for the agencies to be vigilant on behalf of investors. Several studies indeed show that the smaller credit rating agencies, whose assessments will also be used in Basel II, tend to assign more favorable credit ratings than those issued by globally reputed credit rating agencies, e.g., rated by Moody's, S&P or Fitch. Moreover, the quality of the rating also depends on the quality and integrity of the persons and institutions that rate others" (BB, 2013, p. 69). Therefore, fundamentally ECAI's firm-pays model has a conflict of interest with its business objectives. In our view, as Bangladeshi ECAIs have no institutional incentives to mitigate the conflict of interest, they fall into the 'moral hazard.'

5.4 Wrap-Up Comments on ECAIs Incentive Issues in the Institutions and Bank Managers Role

To sum up, first, we observed in our previous discussion that the weak internal governance creates a gray zone specifically how external RC members are appointed, and what are the responsibilities of RC members; are not specified, which can affect ECAI's rating quality. Second, there is no incentive-based regulation introduced by the supervisors when regulating ECAIs (i.e., there is no 'rating over ECAIs rating' by regulators which evaluate the rating quality on one hand and ECAIs remuneration control by BB on the other hand). Hence, the study found that ECAIs have no 'incentive' for allocating resources to improve rating quality. In turn ECAIs have accumulated less credit screening skills. Third, 'issuer-pays' business model creates conflict of interests with business. Consequently, there is no 'sanction' tool on the hand of market forces to correct ECAI's inflated/mis-rating, hence 'competition' automatically becomes counterproductive and provides disincentives to ECAIs for quality ratings. In our view, this creates a potential moral hazard for ECAIs.

What is more, naïvely relying on an ECAI's rating is another 'weird behavior' of bank managers in our view. Simply opportunistic behavior may give them short-term incentives however, in the long run no one can skip the bitter outcome of such a strategy. As the regulator has adopted the standardized approach and banks are using ECAI's rating for computing the RWA of credit risk, it is easy for banks to make the excuse that it is regulator, who prepared the Basel Accord implementation guidelines and made it compulsory to depend on an ECAI's rating. However, from the broad interest of the industry, it is indeed banks, who are the ultimate users/consumer of an ECAI's rating and have the lion's stake of the financial industry. Bank managers have close and continuous relationships with firms and prepare the credit risk grading (CRG) as a tool for the borrower selection process. We shall note that central bank (see BB, 2005) has provided a CRG manual for all banks which was updated in 2018. Therefore, it is the banker's professional responsibility to inform the central bank if banks' in-house credit risk grading report and an ECAI's rating have deviated to some extent. Unfortunately, we have found evidence that banks offer discounted interest rates to high rated clients of ECAIs to save their capital charge. Hence, we presume that banks naïvely rely on ECAI's credit information and using the ECAI's rating for quantification of credit risk under Basel framework and take more risk in lending. In our view, bank managers act opportunistically to enhance managerial incentives through using an ECAI's rating notch and give up cross-validation of the ECAI's credit information/rating notch. In fact, bank mangers cannot shift their credit risk management responsibility to the ECAI's shoulders as banks exist as the experts in credit risk screening and monitoring. If ECAIs are doing this job, then bank becomes a redundant economic institution in society. However, it is very important from both industry and bankers' interest to create an incentive in the existing institutions of ECAI for their exposure rating with accuracy.

5.5   Concluding Remarks

Some scholar argued that if ECAIs are private entities they should survive on their 'reputational capital' rather than 'regulatory incentives' (Miglionico, 2019), however, as banking regulators use the ECAI's rating for regulatory purposes ECAIs should be regulated to protect public interest. We have found that poor internal governance structure, less effort on credit screening skills, issuer-pays model and fierce competition contribute to lower the quality of ECAIs credit information and ultimately causes them to fall into a moral hazard situation in Bangladesh case. In contrast, it provides ill-incentive to bank managers. We presume that Bangladeshi CRAs are not surviving based on their rigorous analytical rating or reducing the information asymmetry in the credit market rather regulatory recognition provides them incentive to create more revenue. Hence, to bring financial stability and improve the ECAI's rating quality there is no way but to structurally reform the institutions of ECAI. Besides, we expect that ECAI's ratings should be aligned with loan performance (if their rating is used for regulatory purposes), which hopes to improve their rating quality. In Chapter 8, we provide a comprehensive discussion on this issue and present a possible way out and policy recommendations to the decision makers to bring structural reforms in the existing institutions of ECAIs.

REFERENCES

Bangladesh Bank (BB). (2005). *Risk Grading Manual* (BRPD circular no. 18, December 11, 2005). Banking Regulation and Policy Department, Bangladesh Bank.

Bangladesh Bank (BB). (2009, October 14). *Guidelines on Subordinated debt for inclusion in Regulatory Capital* (BRPD Circular No. 13). Banking Regulation and Policy Department, Bangladesh Bank.

Bangladesh Bank (BB). (2013). *Financial Stability Report, 2013, Issue 4.* Financial Stability Department, Bangladesh Bank. https://www.bb.org.bd/pub/index.php.

Bangladesh Bank (BB). (2014, December 21). *Guidelines on Risk based Capital Adequacy (Revised Regulatory Capital Framework for banks in line with Basel III)* (BRPD Circular No. 18). Banking Regulation and Policy Department, Bangladesh Bank.

Bangladesh Bank (BB). (2017). *Financial Stability Report, 2017, Issue 8.* Financial Stability Department, Bangladesh Bank. https://www.bb.org.bd/pub/index.php.

Bangladesh Securities and Exchange Commission (BSEC). (1996). *Credit rating companies rules 1996.* BSEC. https://www.sec.gov.bd/home/lbook.

Bangladesh Securities and Exchange Commission (BSEC). (2018). *Annual Report 2017–2018.* BSEC. https://www.sec.gov.bd/home/annual_reports.

Chan, S. (2010, April 22). Documents shows internal qualms at rating Agencies. *The New York Times.* https://www.nytimes.com/2010/04/23/business/23ratings.html.

Cifuentes, A. (2008). *Full committee hearing: Turmoil in U.S. credit markets: The role of the credit rating agencies (Testimony of Dr. Arturo Cifuentes, Managing Director, R. W. Pressprich & Co. at the hearings by the Senate Committee on Banking Housing and Urban Affairs).* United States Senate Committee on Banking Housing and Urban Affairs. https://www.banking.senate.gov/hearings/turmoil-in-us-credit-markets-the-role-of-the-credit-rating-agencies.

Coffee, J. C. (2006). *Gatekeepers: The professions and corporate governance.* Oxford University Press.

Coffee, J. C. (2011). Rating reforms: The good, the bad and the ugly. *Harvard Business Law Review, 1,* 231–278.

Darbellay, A. (2013). *Regulating credit rating agencies.* Edward Elgar.

European Commission (EC). (2016). *Study on the state of the credit rating market: Final Report.* European Commission. https://doi.org/10.2874/625016. https://ec.europa.eu/info/system/files/state-of-credit-rating-market-study-01012016_en.pdf.

Kaufman, G. G. (1995). *The U.S. financial systems: Money, markets and institutions* (6th ed.). Prentice Hall.

Miglionico, A. (2019). *The governance of credit rating agencies regulatory regime and liability issues.* Edward Elgar Publishing.

Partnoy, F. (2006). *How and why credit rating agencies are not like other gatekeepers* (University of San Diego Legal Studies Research Paper Series No. 07-46). In Y. Fuchita & R. E. Litan (Eds.), *Financial gatekeepers: Can they protect investors?* Brookings Institution Press & the Nomura Institute of Capital Markets Research.

Tsunoda, J., Ahmed, M., & Islam, M. T. (2013). *Regulatory framework and role of domestic credit rating agencies in Bangladesh* (ADB South Asia Working Paper Series, No. 21). Asian Development Bank. https://www.adb.org/pub lications/regulatory-framework-and-role-domestic-credit-rating-agencies-ban gladesh.

U.S. Securities and Exchange Commission (U.S. SEC). (2008). *Summary report of issues identified in the commission staffs examination of select credit rating agencies.* The Staff of the Office of Compliance Inspections and Examinations Division of Trading and Markets and Office of Economic Analysis, United Stated Securities and Exchange Commission. https://www.sec.gov/news/stu dies/2008/craexamination070808.pdf.

U.S. Securities and Exchange Commission (U.S. SEC). (2012). *Report to congress on assigned credit ratings.* Division of Trading and Markets. United Stated Securities and Exchange Commission. https://www.sec.gov/news/studies/ 2012/assigned-credit-ratings-study.pdf.

World Bank (WB). (2019). *Doing business 2020.* The World Bank.

CHAPTER 6

Subordinated Debt: A Skeptical Component of Regulatory Capital

6.1 Introduction

In the previous chapters (Chapters 4 and 5), we argued that the quantification of credit risk by ECAIs was deviated from the real credit risk, due partly to the low quality of ECAI's credit information, presumably resulting in the huge accumulation of NPLs in Bangladeshi banks. As NPLs are accumulated, the RWA tends to increase. In turn to maintain the minimum CRAR, banks require to increase their regulatory capital as it is the numerator of the capital adequacy ratio. In this sense, the regulatory capital is mattered to maintain minimum CRAR. In this chapter, we shed an analytical light on the funding of the regulatory capital of Bangladeshi banks that enables them to maintain the minimum CRAR. This analysis attempts to solve the anomaly (ii) that we raised in introduction part of the book. Simultaneously, we point out here that their naïve reliance on the subordinated debt, we name this problem as the 'sub-debt trap,' may have undermined the resilience of the Bangladeshi banking industry. To investigate this, we chiefly attempt to examine the overall magnitude of the 'sub-debt trap' through empirical study upon an econometric approach in this chapter. It would help the readers to understand the real performance of Bangladeshi banks if they had not tapped into the 'sub-debt trap.' Then we further analyze the issue from sub-debt funding mechanism perspective. The structure of this chapter is as follows: Sect. 6.2 discusses how sub-debt is institutionally considered as RC in

A K M K. Hasan and Y. Suzuki, *Implementation of Basel Accords in Bangladesh*, https://doi.org/10.1007/978-981-16-3472-7_6

Bangladesh. Section 6.3 presents the details of the econometric model, results and discussion on said results. Section 6.4 demonstrates the overall magnitude of the 'sub-debt trap' in the financial system. Section 6.5 concludes.

6.2   History of the Allowance of Funding 'Subordinated Debt' as a Component of Regulatory Capital in Bangladesh

Bangladesh Bank has identified five core risks in banking areas: these are (i) credit risk (ii) asset liability and balance sheet risk (iii) foreign exchange risk (iv) internal control and compliance risk (v) money laundering risk. Subsequently BB has published the prudential guidelines and regulations to manage such risks (see BB, 2016a, 2016b). For managing the 'credit risk' BB has formulated several prudential regulations for banks such as the policy on capital adequacy of banks, the policy on loan classification and provisioning, the policy on single borrower exposure, the policy for rescheduling of loans and the policy for loan write off (BB, 2014). While upgrading the policy on minimum capital adequacy ratio for banks, BB has abandoned the 'Capital to Liability Approach,' instead replacing it with 'Risk weighted Asset Approach' since 1996 in accordance with the adoption of Basel I (BB, 2002; Rahman et al., 2018). Then, BB revised the regulatory capital framework and prepared the 'Guidelines on Risk Based Capital Adequacy (RBCA)' in line with the adoption of Basel II in 2009 (BB, 2008). BB revised the RBCA in 2014 in line with the adoption of Basel III to make the bank's capital more risk-absorbent and bring financial stability to the entire industry (BB, 2014). As a result of the evolution of the regulatory capital framework, the components of regulatory capital (RC) were revised from time to time. Table 6.1 shows the constituents of RC as per capital adequacy framework under different phases of Basel Accord implementation in Bangladesh.

We shall note from Table 6.1 that the CRAR has been fixed at 9 percent in 2003, 10% in 2007 and 12.5 percent since December 31, 2019. It reflects that although the minimum CRAR was fixed at 8 percent in the Basel framework issued by BCBS, BB has fixed a higher CRAR for Bangladeshi domestic banks. BB did not disclose any rational for setting a higher CRAR for domestic banks while transitioning to the Basel Accords. We presume that for the resilience of banking industry BB has set a higher minimum CRAR than the Basel Accord standard however interestingly BB has fixed the CET 1 at 4.5 percent in all version

Table 6.1 Constituents of regulatory capital (RC) under Basel accord in Bangladesh

Sl. No	Components of capital	1996 (Basel I)	2009 (Basel II)	2014 (Basel III)
1	Core capital (Tier 1 capital)			
	Paid-up capital	✓	✓	✓
	Non-repayable share premium account	✓	✓	✓
	Statutory reserve	✓	✓	✓
	General reserve	✓	✓	✓
	Retained earnings	✓	✓	✓
	Minority interest in subsidiaries	✓	✓	✗
	Dividend equalization account	✓	✓	✓
	Non-cumulative irredeemable preference shares	✓	✓	✗
	Additional Tier 1 capital (AT 1)	✗	✗	✓
	Instruments issued by the banks that meet the qualifying criteria for AT1 (such as perpetual subordinated debt)	✗	✗	✓
	Minority interest, i.e., AT 1 issued by consolidated subsidiaries to third parties	✗	✗	✓
2	Supplementary capital (Tier 2 capital)	✓	✓	✓
	General provision (1% of unclassified loans)	✓	✓	✓
	Subordinated debt (maturity ≥5 years)	✗	✓	✓
	Perpetual subordinated debt	✓	✗	✗
	Minority interest, i.e., Tier 2 issued by consolidated subsidiaries to third parties	✗	✗	✓
	Revaluation reserves (maintained for fixed assets, securities and equity instrument)	✓	✓	✗
	All other preference shares	✓	✓	✗
	Exchange Equalization account	✓	✓	✗
3	Tier 3 capital (additional supplementary capital)	✗	✓	✗
	Subordinated debt (original maturity less than or equal to five years but greater than or equal to two years) would be solely for the purpose of meeting a proportion of the capital requirements for market risk	✗	✓	✗
4	Total regulatory capital	(Sl 1 + 2)	(Sl 1 + 2 + 3)	(Sl 1 + 2)

(continued)

Table 6.1   (continued)

Sl. No	Components of capital	1996 (Basel I)	2009 (Basel II)	2014 (Basel III)
5	Minimum Tier 1 capital (to total RWA) (Common Equity Tier 1—CET 1 ratio)	≥4.5%	≥4.5%	≥4.5%
6	Capital to risk weighted asset (CRAR) (including 2.5% capital conservation buffer under Basel III)	≥9% (since June 30, 2003)	≥ 10% (since December 31, 2007)	≥12.5% (since December 31, 2019)

Source (BB, 2002, 2010, 2014)

of Basel guidelines. In fact, we are concerned about the 'subordinated debt' which has been allowed as a new component of RC in the Basel Accord implementation process. Subordinated debt was first introduced by naming 'perpetual subordinated debt' in 2002 as Tier 2 capital and it was replaced by 'subordinated debt' in 2008 as per BRPD circular no. 13, October 14, 2009. Some revaluation reserves[1] were delisted as Tier 2 capital, while Basel Accord III was implemented. However, BB has designed a transitional arrangement for the deduction of such reserves as 'phase-in deductions' (BB, 2014, p. 14). We shall note that paid-up capital/equity capital, share premium, statutory reserve, general reserve and retained earnings are considered as Tier 1 capital components since the inception of the Basel Accord in Bangladesh. In Common Equity Tier 1 (CET 1) capital, the components of equity and retained earnings are of most concerned by bank owners and executives (while realizing their stakes from bank) as increase in equity will dilute the ROE. We will discuss this dimension in the later part of this chapter. In addition, BB has acknowledged three types of components as Tier 2 capital under the adoption of Basel Accord III; these are (i) general provisions (ii) subordinated debt and (iii) minority interest (BB, 2014). Therefore, from this

---

[1] Such as 'asset revaluation reserve', 'investment in securities revaluation reserve' (these reserves represent the difference between the book value and re-valued amount of bank's fixed assets and investment in securities respectively). The increased amount is credited directly to the equity under the heading of 'asset revaluation reserve' as per International Accounting Standard –16 and 'revaluation reserve of securities' as per BB instruction.

discussion, it is clear that BB has made the CRAR more stringent without enhancing the CET 1 (i.e., keeping it at 4.5%), which creates an opportunity for banks to keep the minimum CRAR by enhancing Tier 2 capital. In fact, this is a kind of weakness in the RBCA guidelines that provides a scope for the banks to maintain a thin CET 1 capital ratio within the legal cover. However, there is no rationale explained in the regulations for fixation of such a thin CET 1 ratio. As a result, banks have issued bulk amounts of sub-debt as Tier 2 capital to maintain minimum CRAR. In our view, such option within the regulation has provided an (ill) incentive to the banks. We briefly discuss this in the following section with empirical illustration.

6.3   Impact of Sub-debt on Bangladeshi Banks Performance

This section offers an econometric analysis regarding the impact of subordinated debt as RC in CRAR as well as on bank performance in the special context of Bangladesh. To begin, let us look at the overall banking sector performance in introduction chapter (also see Table 1.2 in Annexure). As was mentioned that when banks accumulated huge NPL (see Fig. 6.1), to compensate for the impact of NPL on the minimum CRAR, banks need to enhance the regulatory capital (RC) base, i.e., either increase Tier 1 capital or increase Tier 2 capital. We also refer earlier that paid-up capital and retained earnings are the main components of Tier 1 capital (see Table 6.1). However, since Bangladeshi banks tend to steadily pay out cash dividends (7.07 percent in 2009–2018 on average, see Fig. 6.2), the component of retained earnings was not enough as the base for the banks to enhance Tier 1 capital. Accordingly, to tap into sub-debt as Tier 2 was left as the only option to maintain the minimum CRAR. In fact, the total amount of issuance of sub-debt jumped to the size of no less than BDT 242.75 billion since 2009.

Figure 6.2 shows that the average 'stock and cash' dividend rate was 19.93 percent between 2009 and 2018 whereas the average 'cash' dividend rate was 7.07 percent during the same period. It attests to the fact that, while the banks were accumulating huge NPLs, they were paying attractive dividends to their shareholders. Presumably, tapping into sub-debt, particularly since 2009, made them do this covert action. Hence a follow-up question is what the relationship among CRAR, sub-debt and bank performance. To investigate the following section, we empirically analyze the effect of sub-debt on bank performance yardsticks and attempt to investigate why and how banks tapped into the 'sub-debt trap.'

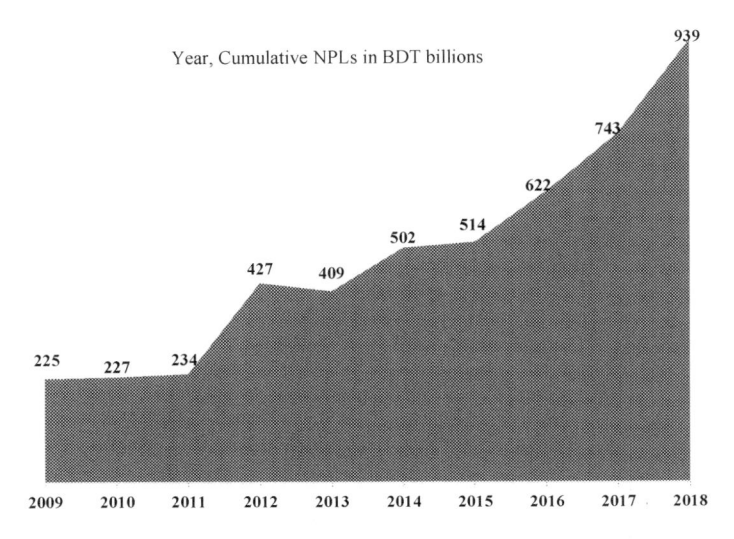

Fig. 6.1 Banking sector NPL (in BDT billion) (*Source* BB Financial Stability Reports)

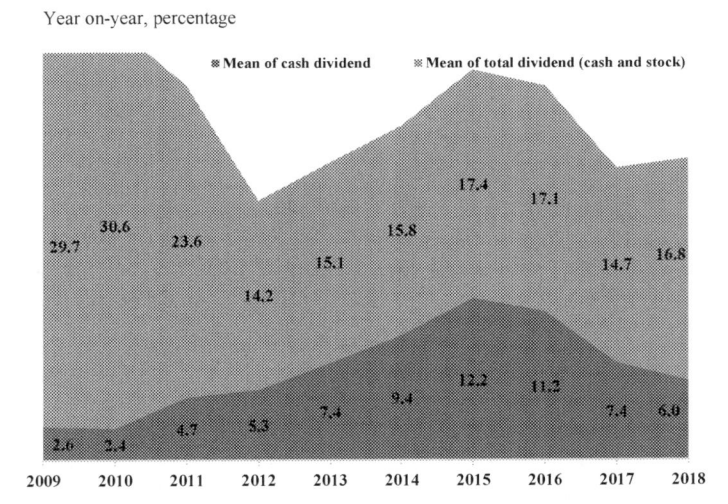

Fig. 6.2 Average dividend rate of PCBs between 2009 and 2018 (*Source* Computed by the author based on 29 PCBs Annual Report on various years)

Empirical Analysis of the Effect of Sub-debt on CRAR and Bank Performance

Let us elaborate on the effect of sub-debt on CRAR by using an econometric method. In this model we use the panel data for 42 banks between 2009 and 2018 and the core regression model is:

$$Y_{it} = \alpha + x_{it}\ \beta + \mu_{it}$$

$$\text{where, } i = 1, \ldots \ldots 329,\ i = 1, \ldots \ldots 10$$

where i denotes the cross-sectional dimension and t indicates the time dimension, Y_{it} is the bank i's capital adequacy measures at time t, x_{it} is a $1 \times K$ vector of observations on K, β is a $K \times 1$ vector of parameters explanatory variables for the ith bank in the tth period, μ_{it} is a disturbance term and is defined as

$$\mu_{it} = \mu_i\ + V_t$$

where μ_i denotes the unobservable individual effect and V_t denotes the remainder disturbance.

The empirical model specification is as follows:

$CRAR_{it} =$

$$\beta_0 + \beta_1 AD\ ratio_{it} + \beta_2\ ROE_{it} + \beta_3\ NPL_{it} + \beta_4\ COF_{it}$$
$$+\ \beta_5 10\% \text{ above capital loan}_{it} + \beta_6\ SME\ fin_{it}$$
$$+\ \beta_7 \text{ Dividend (cash \& stock)}_{it} + \beta_8 \text{ Cash Dividend}_{it}$$
$$+\ \beta_9 \text{ Capital market growth GDP}_{it} + \beta_{10} BM_{it}$$
$$+\ \beta_{11} \text{ PE ratio of the banking sector}_{it} + \varepsilon_{it} \qquad (6.1)$$

where,

AD ratio $_{it}$ = Advance-deposit ratio of bank i at time t,
ROE_{it} = Return on equity of bank i at time t,
NPL_{it} = Percentage of non-performing loan to total loan and advances of bank i at time t,
COF_{it} = Ratio of total cost of deposit (including administrative expenses) to total weighted average deposit of bank i at time t,

10 % above capital loan$_{it}$ = The large loan (10% above capital loan) of bank i at time t,

SME Fin$_{it}$ = Percentage of SME Finance comparing to total loans and advances of bank i at time t,

Dividend (cash and stock)$_{it}$ = Dividend paid to the shareholders as a form of cash and stock of bank i at time t,

Dividend (cash)$_{it}$ = Cash dividend paid to the shareholders of bank i at time t,

Capital market capitalization growth$_{it}$ = Market capitalization growth of DSE for bank i at time t,

BM$_{it}$ = Broad money growth rate of the country for bank $\underline{i}$ at time t,

PE ratio$_{it}$ = Price-earning ratio of banking sector at DSE for bank i at time t,

$\beta_1 - \beta_{10}$ = coefficients of the related variables,

ε_{it} = error term of firm i at time t.

While analyzing the panel data, we have the following three broad objectives.

(a) Estimate the transitional effect of the implementation of the Basel Accords: To evaluate the transitional effect of Basel Accord implementation, we consider three time-horizons such as between 2009 and 2018, 2009 and 2013 and 2014 and 2018. The panel data included in the time series between 2009 and 2018 which indicates the full-range effect on CRAR, the 2009 to 2013 time series data indicates the effect in the implementation of Basel II and finally the 2014 to 2018 time series data indicates the effect in the transition from Basel II to Basel III by our proposed model.

(b) Estimate the effect in each bank category: We regress our model in each bank category; all the banks, only private banks (PCBs), only Islamic Banks, only state-owned commercial banks (SCBs) and only new banks (which started their operations in FY 2013 and 2014).

(c) Sensitivity analysis of sub-debt: To examine the impact of sub-debt in the CRAR, our analysis considers the following two scenarios and run all our specified models used in (a) and (b) within two scenarios.

Scenario #1, Sub-debt is considered as a component in Tier 2 capital. Therefore, we compute the CRAR with sub-debt by the following formula.

CRAR $_{it}$ = (Regulatory capital (of i bank at time t) with sub-debt*) divided by risk.
weighted assets* of i bank at time t,

Scenario #2, A hypothetical CRAR of a specific bank is estimated when the sub-debt is not counted as Tier 2 capital. To compute the CRAR without sub-debt, we use the following formula.

CRAR $_{it}$. = (Regulatory capital (i bank at time t) without sub-debt) divided by risk.
weighted assets of i bank at time t,
*Risk-weighted assets and sub-debt are disclosed in the annual report of each bank under the Basel accord disclosure.

To show the two scenarios in a micro-sense, let us take 'Dhaka Bank Limited' as a sample and compute the CRAR with debt and without debt, respectively, as of December 31, 2018 (see Table 6.2).

Table 6.2 Computation of CRAR with debt and without debt

Sl no	Particular	With debt	Without debt
A	Total Tier-1 Capital (A)	1,540.29	1,540.29
B	Tier-2 Capital (going concern capital)		
	General provision	581.73	581.73
	Asset revaluation reserve account	6.48	6.48
	Revaluation Reserve for HFT & HFT securities	0.62	0.62
	Non-convertible subordinated debt	780.33	–
	Total Tier-2 Capital (B)	1,369.17	588.83
C	Total eligible regulatory capital (A + B)	2,909.46	2,129.12
D	Total risk weighted assets	21,024.04	21,024.04
E	Capital to risk-weighted asset ratio (CRAR) (C/D)	13.84%	10.13%

Source Dhaka Bank Annual Report (2018, pp. 285–286). https://dhakabankltd.com/financial-statem ents-reports/

The study recomputes the CRAR with debt and without debt for all sample banks with same approach, which we describe as 'summary statistics of CRAR' (see Table 6.4). Finally based on the above-mentioned three objectives (a), (b) and (c), we prepare a set of panels of data to the test the model (in Eq. (6.1)) and each panel data is tested considering the scenario #1 and scenario #2 over the investigated period 2009–2018, 2009–2013 and 2014–2018.

We use the Model 1.1 for analyzing the panel data 1 to 8 while Model 1.2 is used for panel data 9 to 13

$$
\begin{aligned}
CRAR_{it} = {} & \beta_0 + \beta_1\, AD\,ratio_{it} + \beta_2\, \text{ROE}_{it} + \beta_3\, \text{NPL}_{it} \\
& + \beta_4\, \text{COF}_{it} + \beta_5\, 10\%\,\text{above capital loan}_{it} + \beta_6\, \text{SME fin}_{it} \\
& + \beta_7\, \text{Dividend (cash \& stock)}_{it} + \beta_8\, \text{Cash Dividend}_{it} \\
& + \beta_9\, \text{Capital market growth GDP}_{it} + \beta_{10}\, \text{BM}_{it} + \varepsilon_{it}
\end{aligned} \tag{1.1}
$$

$$
\begin{aligned}
CRAR_{it} = {} & \beta_0 + \beta_1\, AD\,ratio_{it} + \beta_2\, \text{ROE}_{it} + \beta_3\, \text{NPL}_{it} \\
& + \beta_4\, \text{COF}_{it} + \beta_5\, 10\%\,\text{above capital loan}_{it} \\
& + \beta_6\, \text{SME fin}_{it} + \beta_7\, \text{Dividend (cash \& stock)}_{it} \\
& + \beta_8\, \text{Cash Dividend}_{it} + \beta_9\, \text{Capital market growth GDP}_{it} \\
& + \beta_{10}\, \text{PE ratio of the banking sector}_{it} + \varepsilon_{it}
\end{aligned} \tag{1.2}
$$

The panel data is stationary, and we use one step GMM estimator to explain the explanatory variables. We estimate it using the Random Effect Model (REM) based on Hausman test (Hausman, 1978). The probability of 'f' tests (prob. >F) of all regression models is less than 0.005 (<0.05) which validates the model's acceptability. There are three types of variables used in our model such as bank performance indicators, industry specific variables and macroeconomic variables. Table 6.3 provides list of variables used in the diagnostic tests. This study considers 42 banks out of 57 scheduled banks. Foreign banks are excluded from our sample size as these banks are operating in the country as subsidiary of their parent banks. In fact, our sample size represents 87.5 percent of all domestic scheduled banks of the industry.

Table 6.3 List of variables

Variables	Symbols
A. *Dependent variable*	
Capital to Risk-weighted Asset Ratio (CRAR)	*CRAR with debt*
	CRAR without debt
B. *Main Explanatory Independent variables*	
Return on Assets	*ROA*
Return on Equity	*ROE*
Dividend rate	*Dividend*
Cash dividend rate	*Cash dividend*
Non-performing loans to total loans and advances	*NPL*
Cost of fund	*COF*
Advance-deposit ratio	*AD Ratio*
C. *Industry specific variables*	
10% above the capital loan (large Loan)	*10% above capital*
SME finance to total loans and advances	*SME finance*
Price-earning (PE) ratio of banking sector	*PE ratio of banking sector*
Capital market capitalization growth	*Capital market cap growth*
Banking sector net interest margin**	
D. *Macroeconomic variables*	
Broad Money growth rate	*BM*
Pvt. Sect Credit growth**	
CPI**	
Risk premium**	
GDP**	
Domestic credit to private sector by banks % of GDP**	

** = included to check multicollinearity and correlation coefficient and finally dropped from the regression

Key Findings on Empirical Results

We compute the CRAR for all sample banks for the years 2009–2018, 2009–2013 and 2014–2018 considering sub-debt and without sub-debt (see Table 6.4). This has shown that the CRAR has relatively increased by tapping into sub-debt (in row (2)). When we exclude sub-debt

Table 6.4   Summary statistics of CRAR (all sample banks in the panels)

	2009–2018		2009–2013		2014–2018	
	CRAR with debt	CRAR without debt	CRAR with debt	CRAR without debt	CRAR with debt	CRAR without debt
Observations	330	330	165	165	165	165
Mean	0.114417	0.104515	0.110765	0.107197	0.118068	0.101833
Standard deviations	0.027084	0.02625	0.028481	0.028695	0.025171	0.023333
Max	0.1891	0.1891	0.1891	0.1891	0.1704	0.1367
Min	−0.0867	−0.0867	−0.0867	−0.0867	−0.066	−0.066

from our sample banks' CRAR, the growth rate of CRAR between 2009 and 2013 and 2014–2018 is −5.00 percent (i.e., (0.101833–0.107197)/0.107197)), whereas it was +6.59 percent (i.e., (0.118068–0.110765)/0.110765)) when we compute the CRAR with sub-debt in the same period. Therefore, it attests to the fact that by issuing sub-debt, banks increase their CRAR. In other words, in a stringent capital regulation regime, banks issued more sub-debt to maintain the minimum CRAR.

Results of diagnostic tests:
All results of our diagnostic tests are shown in Tables 6.5, 6.6, 6.7, 6.8, and 6.9. There are multiple independent variables which are used in the regression model; however, we specially focus on the alignments of three independent variables (ROA, ROE and Cash dividend) with dependent variable to make our discussion relevant with the hypothesis we developed. In fact, Tables 6.5, 6.6, 6.7, 6.8, and 6.9 show that these three variables also have significant relationship with CRAR. We analyze the regression result of these three variables with independent variable in the following sub-sections.

Relationship between ROA and CRAR: In our estimation, the ROA of PCBs has a positive relationship with CRAR during the period 2009–2018, even in the case that they did not tap into sub-debt (Table 6.6). During the period 2009–2013, the relationship between CRAR and ROA was negative (Table 6.6 and 6.7) for PCBs and Islamic banks and a mean of the same panel ROA per se in 2014–18, it dropped by 45.55 percent from that of 2009–2013 (Table 6.7). However, the relationship turned out to be positive during the period 2014–2018 for all PCBs

Table 6.5 Co-efficient and *t*-statistics (in parentheses) of panels (all sample banks)

Explanatory Variables	2009–2018		2009–2013		2014–2018	
	CRAR with debt	CRAR without debt	CRAR with debt	CRAR without debt	CRAR with debt	CRAR without debt
Constant (C) (CRAR)	0.150579 (8.16684)	0.086872 (3.029601)	0.110331 (2.378229)	0.134699 (3.399124)	0.110353 (6.835083)	0.113767 (7.194029)
AD ratio	0.010045 (0.692908)	0.008968 (0.368466)	−0.01694 (−0.509374)	−0.01591 (−0.484295)	0.022418 (1.635578)	−0.01067 (−0.768593)
ROA	0.255639 (1.508444)	0.10196 (0.80231)	0.369213 (1.593918)	0.472042* (1.979983)	−0.026745 (−0.067498)	0.631095 (1.655113)
ROE	0.04875** (7.230478)	0.070213** (6.091801)	0.044594** (5.397775)	0.041536** (4.910208)	0.069427** (3.95234)	0.033384* (2.040959)
NPL	−0.075021** (−3.791704)	−0.1211** (−3.437108)	0.05308 (0.416353)	−0.02317 (−0.746757)	−0.106857** (−4.649943)	−0.06297** (−2.757317)
COF	−0.045745 (−0.677799)	0.214352* (2.49677)	−0.03546* (−2.240614)	0.027913 (0.211132)	−0.123878 (−1.654092)	0.04266 (0.520674)
10% above capital	−0.0189** (−2.158036)	−0.01557 (−1.272334)	0.046264 (0.99729)	−0.0265 (−1.636574)	−0.001565 (−0.164804)	−0.01636 (−1.75044)
SME Finance	0.003969 (0.412287)	0.021674 (1.468438)	0.003992 (0.224437)	0.001576 (0.08722)	0.01593 (1.38024)	0.006057 (0.456672)
Dividend	0.000207 (0.019442)	−0.01525 (−1.510083)	−0.00096 (−0.048399)	−0.00128 (−0.063444)		
Cash dividend	0.034458* (2.335383)	0.006182 (0.34918)	0.010204 (0.372906)	−0.00863 (−0.303139)	0.013868 (0.974607)	0.018819 (1.289591)
Capital market cap growth	−0.00474 (−1.025166)	−0.00471 (−0.841412)	−0.00436 (−0.562811)	−0.00535 (−0.681978)	−0.022045* (−2.486648)	0.012018 (1.375198)

(continued)

Table 6.5 (continued)

Explanatory Variables	2009–2018		2009–2013		2014–2018	
	CRAR with debt	CRAR without debt	CRAR with debt	CRAR without debt	CRAR with debt	CRAR without debt
BM	−0.243687** (−3.346112)	−0.04428 (−0.478914)	−0.17895 (0.952529)	−0.10429 (−0.543668)		
PE ratio of banking sector					−0.001011 (−0.044112)	−0.09427 (−1.128843)
Observations	329	329	164	164	165	165
R-squared	0.407833	0.403914	0.319397	0.298335	0.53086	0.491949
S.E. of regression	0.020281	0.01805	0.022098	0.022375	0.012645	0.009931

**,*marks denotes the statistical significance at the 1% and 5% level, respectively

Table 6.6 Co-efficient and *t*-statistics (in parentheses) of panels (PCBs)

Explanatory Variables	2009–2018		2009–2013		2014–2018	
	CRAR with debt	CRAR without debt	CRAR with debt	CRAR without debt	CRAR with debt	CRAR without debt
C	0.126109 (6.348115)	0.092919 (4.443662)	0.104299 (3.660365)	0.088498 (2.860539)	0.070705 (3.658456)	0.097255 (5.130274)
AD ratio	0.027912 (1.703305)	−0.0063 (−0.357182)	−0.004409 (−0.187347)	−0.003532 (−0.135048)	0.032646 (1.801032)	0.003629 (0.199536)
ROA	0.138685 (0.881807)	0.311595 (1.941556)	−0.007629 (−0.044608)	0.111918 (0.597617)	0.328996 (0.807779)	1.045317** (2.643204)
ROE	0.0426** (5.415484)	0.039289** (5.117451)	0.012639 (1.523983)	0.012788 (1.453626)	0.055612** (3.088328)	0.019941 (1.190231)
NPL	−0.0579** −(2.896176)	−0.050985** (−2.520753)	0.030667 (1.427227)	0.031386 (1.368861)	−0.15616** (−5.751426)	−0.077957** (−2.692739)
COF	0.000245 (0.003936)	0.100499** (1.468982)	0.15654 (1.71374)	0.133906 (1.252685)	0.000743 (0.009166)	0.032835 (0.4019)
10% above capital	−0.0166** (−2.026906)	−0.02168* (−2.416173)	−0.015709 (−1.402787)	−0.010645 (−0.831706)	−0.00966 (−0.981492)	−0.014027 (−1.368259)
SME Finance	0.004758 (0.553626)	0.004251 (0.397461)	−0.005076 (−0.435075)	0.000914 (0.064902)	0.009377 (0.849478)	0.003803 (0.27192)
Dividend	0.001565 (0.162179)	−0.010416 (−1.072231)	−0.006628 (−0.491948)	−0.005398 (−0.374388)		
Cash dividend	0.037111** (2.840399)	0.024328 (1.80266)	0.012365 (0.683942)	−0.000895 (−0.044517)	0.040307** (2.717496)	0.019242 (1.329738)
Capital market cap growth	−0.00529 (−1.220766)	−0.008638* (−2.042253)	−0.004908 (−0.945408)	−0.005585 (−1.020065)	−0.038473** (−3.722958)	0.00897 (1.007967)
BM	−0.20463** (−2.876264)	0.077149 (1.107915)	0.026589 (0.208928)	0.077082 (0.575186)		

(continued)

Table 6.6 (continued)

Explanatory Variables	2009–2018		2009–2013		2014–2018	
	CRAR with debt	CRAR without debt	CRAR with debt	CRAR without debt	CRAR with debt	CRAR without debt
PE ratio of banking sector					0.292522** (2.95324)	−0.059914 (−0.688356)
Observations	289	289	144	144	145	145
R-squared	0.281015	0.253367	0.124222	0.069048	0.619398	0.519631
S.E. of regression	0.017768	0.01711	0.013875	0.014475	0.0124	0.009886

**,*marks denotes the statistical significance at the 1% and 5% level, respectively

Table 6.7 Co-efficient and *t*-statistics (in parentheses) of panels (Islamic banks)

Explanatory Variables	2009–2018		2009–2013		2014–2018	
	CRAR with debt	CRAR without debt	CRAR with debt	CRAR without debt	CRAR with debt	CRAR without debt
C	0.181473 (2.822804)	0.124694 (1.694328)	0.074075 (0.55956)	0.056014 (0.41452)	0.023352 (0.388624)	0.093775 (3.031039)
AD ratio	−0.08361 (−1.206649)	−0.134664 (−1.972873)	0.122572 (0.760546)	0.162231 (1.038454)	−0.020861 (−0.296055)	−0.069475 (−1.794413)
ROA	−0.122529 (−0.285116)	0.710815 (1.417217)	−0.401819 (−1.001137)	−0.083844 (−0.167279)	−1.12872 (−1.307949)	−0.063262 (−0.138812)
ROE	−0.005429 (−0.071699)	0.000371 (0.004059)	−0.088292 (−1.600021)	−0.090442 (−1.605472)	0.195735 (1.799015)	0.102789 (1.634586)
NPL	0.291908** (2.884257)	0.314388 (1.675353)	0.280341 (0.953502)	0.37489 (1.205329)	0.589783** (5.957058)	0.397888** (2.894119)
COF	0.134893 (1.228678)	0.417992** (2.875018)	−0.246761 (−0.855979)	−0.302447 (−0.949334)	0.503908* (2.468172)	0.388157** (3.259444)
10% above capital	0.00724 (0.418035)	0.014311 (0.767222)	0.046538 (1.724865)	0.056346 (1.906796)	−0.016298 (−0.874154)	0.036298 (1.974831)
SME Finance	0.035465** (2.235421)	0.060316 (3.525966)	−0.010577 (−0.303532)	−0.023865 (−0.704976)	0.055** (4.433723)	0.062774 (4.49284)
Dividend	0.075735** (2.277094)	0.02603 (0.70524)	0.064214 (1.339583)	0.057197 (1.19457)		
Cash dividend	−0.014888 (−0.41231)	−0.004843 (−0.150689)	0.053574 (0.682184)	−0.006115 (−0.059835)	−0.010482 (−0.36602)	0.031734 (1.656055)
Capital market cap growth	0.003508 (0.582936)	−0.002494 (−0.415392)	−0.001927 (−0.155867)	−0.001702 (−0.131595)	−0.010482 (0.851684)	−0.331549 (−2.359257)
BM	−0.208657 (−1.929078)	0.126786 (0.917104)	−0.288088 (−0.840283)	−0.388089 (−1.157318)		
PE ratio of banking sector					0.266767 (0.851684)	−0.331549 (−2.359257)

(continued)

Table 6.7 (continued)

Explanatory Variables	2009–2018		2009–2013		2014–2018	
	CRAR with debt	CRAR without debt	CRAR with debt	CRAR without debt	CRAR with debt	CRAR without debt
Observations	60	60	30	30	30	30
R-squared	0.240018	0.327291	0.266392	0.25895	0.590905	0.836741
S.E. of regression	0.014485	0.015093	0.016833	0.018226	0.01079	0.007881

**,*marks denotes the statistical significance at the 1% and 5% level, respectively

Table 6.8 Co-efficient and *t*-statistics (in parentheses) of panels (SCBs)

Explanatory Variables	2009–2018		2009–2013		2014–2018	
	CRAR with debt	CRAR without debt	CRAR with debt	CRAR without debt	CRAR with debt	CRAR without debt
C	0.212545 (2.352017)	0.177249 (1.991502)	0.553293 (1.192189)	0.553293 (1.192189)	0.012684 (0.121872)	0.162853 (1.237414)
AD ratio	−0.085375 (−1 261874)	−0.092221 (−1.383963)	0.117266 (0.216164)	0.117266 (0.216164)	−0.057002 (−1.296078)	−0.043611 (−0.784143)
ROA	2.1 :0797 (1.249869)	1.889257 (1.125176)	7.516482 (1.492111)	7.516482 (1.492111)	−5.02511 (−0.569566)	−0.950327 (−0.085178)
ROE	0.000891 (0.020634)	0.005757 (0.135293)	−0.114651 (−0.991251)	−0.114651 (−0.991251)	0.405599 (0.749971)	0.122122 (0.178566)
NPL	−0.132846 (−0.970594)	−0.160047 (−1.187248)	0.172484 (0.334668)	0.172484 (0.334668)	0.032687 (0.425243)	0.0392 (0.403285)
COF	−0.497258 (−0.851975)	−0.265899 (−0.462562)	−2.365681 (−0.960772)	−2.365681 (−0.960772)	0.971254 (1.27095)	−0.129091 (−0.133583)
10% above capital	−0.016872 (−0.273829)	−0.026241 (−0.43243)	−0.003321 (−0.960772)	−0.003321 (−0.960772)	0.010111 (0.240324)	−0.017232 (−0.32389)
SME Finance	0.176765 (1.042101)	0.173471 (1.038364)	−2.679175 (−0.752611)	−2.679175 (−0.752611)	0.048905 (0.674752)	0.036857 (0.402137)
Dividend	0.199804 (1.326793)	0.245233 (1.653428)	0.393964 (0.876064)	0.393964 (0.876064)		
Cash dividend	−0.785872 (−1.196087)	−0.769217 (−1.188687)	−2.706899 (−1.758183)	−2.706899 (−1.758183)	0.002791 (0.019305)	0.061943 (0.338759)
Capital market cap growth	−0.004715 (−0.186031)	−0.00763 (−0.305651)	0.052703 (0.455808)	0.052703 (0.455808)	−0.07699 (−1.46107)	0.038629 (0.579708)
BM	−0.089292 (−0.224415)	0.075239 (0.191994)	−1.110223 (−0.271108)	−1.110223 (−0.271108)		

(continued)

Table 6.8 (continued)

Explanatory Variables	2009–2018		2009–2013		2014–2018	
	CRAR with debt	CRAR without debt	CRAR with debt	CRAR without debt	CRAR with debt	CRAR without debt
PE ratio of banking sector					0.386294 (0.729941)	−0.547582 (−0.818232)
Observations	40	40	20	20	20	20
R-squared	0.611269	0.620493	0.776286	0.776286	0.482975	0.412835
S.E. of regression	0.03474	0.034216	0.05583	0.05583	0.013409	0.016957

Table 6.9 Co-efficient and *t*-statistics (in parentheses) of panels of new banks

Explanatory Variables	CRAR with debt	CRAR without debt
C	−0.479981	−0.479981
	(−1.597916)	(−1.597916)
AD ratio	0.10511	0.10511
	(0.459569)	(0.459569)
ROA	−0.073251	−0.073251
	(−0.184469)	(−0.184469)
ROE	−0.326643	−0.326643
	(−0.860169)	(−0.860169)
NPL	−3.681275	−3.681275
	(−1.67981)	(−1.67981)
COF	2.91081	2.91081
	(1.931975)	(1.931975)
10% above capital	0.240889	0.240889
	(1.844118)	(1.844118)
SME Finance	0.491599**	0.491599**
	(2.477498)	(2.477498)
Cash dividend	0.697292	0.697292
	(1.699134)	(1.699134)
Capital market cap growth	−0.163328	−0.163328
	(−0.694262)	(−0.694262)
PE ratio of banking sector	2.521463	2.521463
	(0.960816)	(0.960816)
Observations	23	23
R-squared	0.557839	0.557839
S.E. of regression	0.081846	0.081846

(Table 6.6). Particularly in the case of CRAR without sub-debt, our estimation suggests that the ROA was increased by 217.73 percent from the period 2009–2013 to the period 2014–2018. It is apparent that the profitability of Bangladeshi banks in general was not very much improved during the period of 2014–2018, because their ROA per se was hampered. The positive relationship between ROA and CRAR was, presumably, attributable to the huge loan write-off (BDT 234.11 billion) during the period 2014–2018. This interpretation is supported by our estimation of new banks which had not yet started to write-off bad loans. In fact, the relationship with CRAR and ROA for new banks was negative (see Table 6.9).

Relationship between ROE and CRAR: Table 6.10 suggests that the mean of ROE for all banks declined in 2014–2018 by 35.55 percent when compared with that of 2009–2013. In spite of this, during the period of

Table 6.10   Percentage of changes in mean of explanatory variables

Banks type	Period	AD ratio	ROA	ROE	NPL	COF	10% above cap	SME Finance	Cash dividend	Cap market growth	BM
All	2009–2013	0.82	0.02	0.15	0.06	0.09	0.29	0.18	0.05	0.39	0.18
	2014–2018	0.81	0.01	0.10	0.08	0.08	0.36	0.21	0.09	0.11	0.09
	Change*	−1.01	−44.59	−35.55	27.41	−16.09	22.06	15.73	93.28	−70.88	−50.72
PCB	2009–2013	0.83	0.02	0.18	0.04	0.09	0.28	0.19	0.05	0.39	0.18
	2014–2018	0.84	0.01	0.10	0.06	0.08	0.36	0.22	0.09	0.11	0.09
	Change*	0.35	−45.56	−42.27	41.41	−17.30	26.95	13.01	86.59	−70.88	−50.72
IB	2009–2013	0.89	0.02	0.16	0.03	0.10	0.22	0.25	0.02	0.39	0.18
	2014–2018	0.88	0.01	0.11	0.05	0.08	0.32	0.32	0.10	0.11	0.09
	Change*	−1.00	−48.63	−27.68	73.60	−13.14	46.65	28.73	310.14	−70.88	−50.72
SCB	2009–2013	0.68	0.00	−0.08	0.20	0.08	0.37	0.08	0.02	0.39	0.18
	2014–2018	0.59	0.00	0.04	0.21	0.08	0.35	0.13	0.03	0.11	0.09
	Change*	−13.12	22.07	−143.33	4.59	−5.82	−5.46	63.76	25.00	−70.88	−50.72

*Change = Percentage of change in 2014–2018 over 2009–2013

2014–2018, we should note that the change in declining ROE was not as severe for all types of banks as that in declining ROA (decreased by 44.59 percent). Theoretically, the relative increase in ROE to ROA may suggest the result of *quasi*-leveraging by the banks (Suzuki, 2011). On the other hand, in case of PCBs, we find a very strong positive and significant relationship between CRAR and ROE during the period 2009–2018 and 2014–2018 when sub-debt is considered as the regulatory capital (see Table 6.6 in with debt column). The relationship was more significant than that of our estimation of CRAR without debt. It suggests that sub-debt contributed to enhancing the ROE of PCBs in our investigated period. The relation with CRAR and ROE of PCBs has raised by 340 percent in 2014–2018 compared to that of 2009–2013. The same trend was observed in the cases of Islamic banks and SCBs. In the case of new banks which did not issue any sub-debt, the CRAR had a negative correlation with ROE. Again, we should note that the profitability per se in Bangladeshi banks was not improved, while the relative increase in ROE to ROA was, in general, observed. We assume that since they were allowed to tap into sub-debt for writing off NPLs, they could take the 'leveraging' strategy for seeking a short-sighted profit, resulting in the ostensibly positive relationship between CRAR and ROE.

Relationship between Cash dividend and CRAR: Table 6.10 shows that the mean of cash dividend rate has increased by 86.59 percent in 2014–2018 compared to that of 2009–2013. In the case of Islamic banks, it shows a 310.14 percent increase during the same period. In fact, there exists significant strong positive correlation between cash dividend and CRAR (Table 6.5 and 6.6). The significant positive relation with CRAR and cash dividend has attested that banks owners were instrumentalizing the sub-debt to maximize their interest (cash dividend). We also assume that the PCBs had a pressure of increasing the cash dividend to the shareholders even under the situation the NPL was rapidly accumulated. They were forced to tap on the sub-debt as the resources not only for writing off the NPL, but also paying the cash dividend. The bank owners perhaps gave the bank managers a pressure of maintaining and increasing the cash dividend. Both bank owners and managers are to be blamed for leaving the banks to fall into the 'sub-debt trap.' In addition, the regulator is to be blamed, too. This is because that an ill-designed adoption of Basel-type capital adequacy requirement allowed the bank owners and managers to take an easygoing strategy by tapping on the sub-debt, consequently losing their incentives for increasing the retained earnings as Tier 1 capital.

Summary on Econometric Analysis

Within this empirical study we examine the effects of banking performance-related indicators on CRAR while considering two scenarios (i) CRAR with subordinated debt (ii) CRAR without subordinated debt. A theory highlights that the marginal change in banks capital structure (while utilizing the subordinated debtholders) could bring market discipline as well as complement to regulatory oversight (Evanoff, 1994, p. 514; Evanoff & Wall, 2000, 2001, 2002; Evanoff et al., 2011; Goodhart, 2011, pp. 197–205). However, we argue that sub-debt can be used as a 'quasi leveraging' instrument and hence can increase ROE (Suzuki, 2011), which hinders getting potential benefits from capital adequacy ratio in Bangladesh. We investigate the effects of banking performance from three perspectives. First, we test the effects of banking performance with Basel Accord implementation periods (2009–2018, 2009–2013 and 2014–2018). Second, we examine the same effects on banks typology-wise (all banks, PCBs, only Islamic banks, only SCBs and only new banks). Third, we introduce one industry specific variable (PE ratio of banking sector) as a new variable while conducting an estimation of the regression for our panel data on 2014–2018 to check the effects of cash dividend and PE ratio on CRAR. The entirety of the discussion on the empirical results can be summarized as follows. The results provide strong evidence regarding the effects of ROE on CRAR. We observed that when sub-debt is included in the CRAR as a Tier 2 capital, PCBs' ROE is positively correlated with CRAR. We have also documented that the cash dividend and price-earnings ratio of the banking sector in DSE have a significant and positive alignment with CRAR during the same period. In the case of SCBs and new banks' dataset, we did not any find such alignment. These results provide evidence that banks' ROEs have been increased by the quasi-leveraging effects of sub-debt. Besides, banks offered a steady rate of cash dividends to the equity-holders, and in turn the PE ratio of the banking sector responded positively in the stock exchange. ROA has a positive relationship with CRAR during the period of 2009–2018. We also observed a strong negative alignment with NPLs and CRAR for all banks during the same period. We shall note that BB has allowed its regulated banks to write off bad loans and the written off loans during this period were BDT 410.71 billion. We presume that the write-off policy has contributed to offsetting NPLs and positively contributed to an increased ROA. Finally, we also observe that capital market capitalization growth has a significant negative impact on CRAR during the period of 2014–2018. It reflects that due to the investment in sub-debt, the institutional investors (financial institutions) of the capital market might be tapped into sub-debt and lose their incentive to invest in the capital market. To sum up we find evidence from our empirical results that Bangladeshi banks are stuck in the 'sub-debt trap' as there is a positive relationship with bank performance and sub-debt.

6.4   Magnitude of 'Sub-debt Trap' in Bangladesh

At this point, readers may ask what the magnitude is so called 'sub-debt trap.' In this section we attempt to discuss this rationale query based on the following two questions (i) who sustained the 'sub-deb trap' in Bangladesh and how severe it is on banks' resilience? (ii) How long (and under what conditions) will the 'sub-debt trap' last? We also discuss on how sub-debt creates systemic risk/negative effects on banking sector resilience.

(i) Who sustained the 'Sub-debt trap' in Bangladesh and how severe it is on banks' resilience?

We have mentioned earlier that the tenure of the debt is minimum five years and amortized in the last five (05) years of the sub-debt life (BB, 2014). We observed that most sub-debt's tenures are seven (07) years and amortization start from the third year of issuance of the debt. As a result, banks are issuing new sub-debt before fully redeeming existing debt, otherwise their CRAR will go below the minimum level. We shall note that sub-debts are not traded in the stock market (excepting one specific sub-debt), rather it subscribes through private placement. Hence it is relevant to investigate who are the investors in sub-debt? To investigate this, let us analyze the sub-debt investors' data from a specific bank named 'One Bank Limited' from our sample bank database. We picked 'One Bank Limited' to analyze the case, as very few banks' annual reports had disclosed detailed information about the investors of sub-debt and the bank has provided a detailed investors list. 'One Bank Limited' has issued three sub-debts to maintain CRAR since 2013. Details are in Table 6.11.

Table 6.11 shows that the total outstanding balance of sub-debt for One Bank Limited was BDT 7,280 (i.e., 880 + 4,000 + 2,400) million

Table 6.11 Sub-debt investors list of 'One Bank Limited' (Outstanding balance in BDT millions as on December 31, 2018)

Name of the investors	Sub-debt I* (issued in 2013)	Sub-debt II (issued in 2016)	Sub-debt III (issued in 2018)
Janata Bank Limited	200	500	–
Agrani bank Limited	200	–	–
Rupali Bank Limited	200	200	
Bangladesh Development Bank Limited	80	–	–
Pubali Bank Limited	40	1,000	–
Bangladesh Commerce Bank Limited	40	–	–
Uttara Bank Limited	40	–	–
Sonali Bank Limited	–	1,000	800
Southeast Bank Limited	–	500	–
Trust Bank Limited	–	400	–
Dhaka Bank Limited	–	300	300
Mutual Trust Bank Limited	–	100	–
Jamuna Bank Limited	–	–	1,300
Saudi-BD Industrial and Agri Co (SABINCO)	80	–	–
Total outstanding balance as on December 31, 2018	880	4,000	2,400

One Bank Limited (2018, pp. 185–187)
*total sub-debt issued for BDT 2,200 million and balance shows after 60% redemption

of which ninety-nine (99) percent is funded by peer banks in the industry. Interestingly some of these peer banks also issued sub-debt to maintain CRAR. Table 6.12 provides evidence in detail that One Bank Limited has also invested in another banks' sub-debt.

Indeed, it is evident from Tables 6.11 and 6.12 that One Bank Limited has issued sub-debt to maintain its' capital deficit on the one hand and take another bank's capital deficit risk on the other hand. Having these scenarios, a fundamental question is, to what extent One Bank Limited will be able to take other bank's unexpected loss risk as the bank itself has

Table 6.12 Outstanding balance of investment of 'One Bank Limited' in sub-debt issued by other banks as on December 31, 2018 and 2017 (amount BDT millions)

Sl no	Name of the sub-debt	2018	2017
1	City Bank 2nd Subordinated Debt	1,000	1,000
2	City Bank 3rd Subordinated Debt	1,300	–
3	National Bank Limited 2nd Subordinated Debt	250	250
4	United Commercial Bank Limited 3rd Subordinated Debt	750	750
5	Mercantile Bank Limited Subordinated Debt	300	400
6	Bank Asia Limited Subordinated Debt	480	600
7	Prime Bank Limited Subordinated Debt	480	600
8	Eastern Bank Limited Subordinated Debt	480	600
	Total investment in Subordinated Debt	5,040	4,200

One Bank Limited (2018, p. 175)

issued sub-debt to tackle its' own capital shortfall. We have found that the total outstanding sub-debt as of December 31, 2018 was BDT 234.71 billion (according to all sample banks' balance sheet) whereas the balance of outstanding investment in sub-debt was BDT 225.60 billion in the same period. In other words, 96.12% of outstanding sub-debts are held by banking sector players themselves. This means that financial institutions, especially banks, are the main investors in the sub-debts issued by their peers. To elaborate on this, let us consider that A, B, C, D, E, F and G banks are the issuers and investors in sub-debt in the Bangladeshi Banking sector that is issued for capital adequacy purposes. Then the real picture is 'A' bank's sub-debt investors are 'B' bank and 'C' bank. 'B' bank's sub-debt investors are 'C,' 'F' and 'G' bank and so on.

From the above discussion it is evident that sub-debt issuing banks are holding another bank's sub-debt in turn it creates weak resilience in the entire banking industry. The logic is that banks are issuing sub-debt to strengthen their own capital deficit which was raised from accumulation of NPL/higher RWA. In other words, although the objective of maintaining minimum capital is to absorb unexpected loss and prevent a bank run (see Chapter 1), Bangladeshi Bank's own capital is not enough to absorb such loss. However, the dilemma is, such weakly capitalized banks invest in another banks sub-debt (which aims to absorb the risk of unexpected loss). We should note that sub-debts are not insured by the deposit insurance scheme of the country (BB, 2014), hence there is no residual value of sub-debt in the case of failure of the issuing bank. It is worth mentioning here that BB (2005, 2012, 2016a, 2016b) has instructed all scheduled banks to form an 'Asset and Liability Committee (ALCO)' with senior management to oversee the growth and stability of the assets and liabilities, as well as future expected capital requirement due to the asset growth forecasted and monitor the liquidity risk. It provides an evidence regarding lack of prudence of bank's ALCO when it decides to fund another bank's sub-debt which was solely issued for maintaining minimum CRAR. Because this imprudent funding decision creates a systemic risk in the entire banking industry and undermines the resilience of the banking industry and quality of capital. Why a bank's ALM takes such an imprudent decision to invest in sub-debt is a crucial question at this stage. Although it is difficult to judge why banks are netting themselves in sub-debt, we presume that a lucrative bond yield attracts institutional investors to invest in sub-debt. Another possible reason is the nexus between bank managers and bank owners is responsible for this. Whatever the reason is, the magnitude of the 'sub-debt trap' is very severe which arises from the lack of prudence of the ALMs of banks. The ultimate impact is banks were tapped into the 'sub-debt trap' and expanding their loan portfolio or investing in risky projects, in turn banks were accumulating more non-performing assets. Hence such risky and unprofessional decision of the bank's ALM put the depositors' interest at risk and the taxpayers' interest are finally unprotected because of a bailout plan. What is more, according to 'Risk Management Guidelines for Banks' (BB, 2018), the Board of Directors and senior management of the bank are responsible for assessing the risk appetite of the bank, developing a comprehensive 'Capital Plan' for the bank and maintaining an appropriate capital level that ensures balance between maximizing shareholder return and protecting the interest of depositors and other creditors. However, our econometric analysis in this chapter shows that sub-debt is only maximizing the shareholders' return and putting the depositors' interest at risk. From this point of view, the RMD/senior management of the banks cannot skip their responsibility for the 'sub-debt trap.' It seems that the 'sub-debt trap' is created by themselves to ensure their managerial incentives and for maximizing shareholder return. In addition, the alarming side of this trap is, if a chain of bankruptcies occur in the Bangladeshi banking sector, depositors have to forgo their entire savings in failed banks except BDT 200,000 (equivalent to USD 2400) (as maximum BDT 200,000 deposit are insured by Deposit Insurance System [BB, 2020; FID, 2020]). This means that existing regulations will not protect the depositors' interest over USD 2,400. Therefore, taxpayers' money will have to be injected to bail out the banking sector to protect depositors' interest (we shall recall that the govt. had injected BDT 7.15 billion to bailout the Farmers Bank Limited in 2018). To sum up we can say that the lack of prudence of ALCOs and risk management committees of the banks letting them to fall into the 'sub-debt trap' which creates a potential systemic risk in the banking sector and puts the depositors' interest at risk.

(ii) How long (under what conditions) will the 'sub-debt trap' last?

At this point, a fundamental question is, how long (under what circumstances) will the 'sub-debt trap' last? To answer this, initially we need to understand the following question—what is the opportunity cost of the 'sub-debt trap'? There are four SCBs (Sonali Bank, Janata Bank, Agrani Bank and Rupali Bank) in our sample dataset and their (four SCBs) investment (outstanding balance) in sub-debt in 2018 stood at BDT 142.42 billion which is 60.68 percent of total the outstanding balance (BDT 234.72 billion) of issued sub-debt by the banks. It reflects that a significant percentage of sub-debts were funded by four SCBs. This may raise a moral hazard for private banks as they can rely on SCBs funding/governmental funding and become reckless in lending. Besides, we presume that other important sectors of the economy such as small and medium enterprises or key state-owned enterprises will get less funding from SCBs since their (SCBs) funds have already been invested in private commercial bank's sub-debt. In addition, what is the capacity of the SCBs to absorb sub-debt or what is the capacity of the industry/economy to absorb the sub-debt issued by banks is a crux query in Bangladesh context. Obviously, it depends on budgetary allocation to SCBs by the Ministry of Finance to absorb the sub-debt. However, we can predict that when SCBs will face scarcity of funds or MOF requires more budgetary allocation to other sector (for instance due to COVID-19 govt. need to allocate more fund to health sector and implementation of stimulus packages), they will stop to investing in sub-debt. In such a case, sub-debt issuing banks will tend to sell their debt instrument to other institutional investors (non-bank financial institutions, insurance companies, co-operative societies, pension funds) or through the stock market. In this respect, another rational question is, if there are more profitable investment opportunities available to the institutional investors, will they invest in sub-debt? If so, to attract the institutional investors, banks have to offer a higher coupon rate, but this initiative will increase the operating cost of the bank and ultimately lower its profitability. Besides, Bangladeshi stock market is too shallow to absorb the bulk amount of sub-debt from banks. Therefore, it is a very deep concern for Bangladeshi private commercial banks to think about the future of sub-debt as Tier 2 capital or what to do after the redemption of existing sub-debt in the year 2024 or 2025.

Indeed, there are very few realistic and pragmatic approaches available in hand to Bangladeshi commercial banks to get out of the 'sub-debt trap.' Banks must increase the CET 1 capital components as an alternative to sub-debt to maintain CRAR. To do so, banks either have to issue new equity (as Right shares or stock dividend) or enhance the retained earnings or both. If bank owners prefer to issue new shares or issue stock dividends, the CET 1 will be increased, in contrast this will dilute the EPS and ROE. Therefore, it is a concern for existing shareholders of the bank. On the other hand, to enhance the retained earnings banks have two options (i) reducing NPLs or make the non-performing assets into performing assets, which requires less loan loss provision, in turn has a positive impact on retained earnings (ii) stop taking cash dividends from banks which will strengthen the retained earnings balance. However, the former option depends on managerial incentives. If managers are provided appropriate incentives for improving credit risk screening and loan recovery, hopefully they will refrain from risky investments and extending loan growth. The side effect of such a shrink in the loan growth might lead to a credit crunch and increase the lending rate which might adversely affect economic growth. The latter option depends on the 'shareholders commitment' to the bank to make it resilient and risk absorbent. Refraining from taking cash dividends from the banks obviously shows the bank owners long-term commitment to banks.

To conclude, SCB's investment in sub-debt is an inefficient step to sustain the sub-debt market. It is not the SCB's business to invest in sub-debt, as they have to invest in more productive sectors which directly contribute to the country's economic growth. This imprudence of funding in bank's regulatory capital encourages banks to take more risk and put less effort into improving their ROA. Besides, the capacity of the SCBs or country's banking industry/entire economy to absorb sub-debt is a crucial matter. Hence, it is expected from the regulator as a public entity, to pressure banks to improve their ROA which ultimately protects the general taxpayers' interest. Country's banking regulator should strictly supervise and monitor the commercial banks to improve their ROA rather than allowing its regulated banks to issue sub-debt. Such mechanism to maintain banks minimum CRAR and enhance ROE in the name of the 'investors return' (someone might argue to enhance the banks' ROE and favor sub-debt instead of equity share or Tier 1 capital, as commercial banks are listed in the local bourses) will fundamentally weaken the resilience of the country's financial system. However, future research on sub-debt in the context of Bangladesh should go together with the debate of 'sub-debt trap.'

6.5   Concluding Remarks

To sum up, from the above theoretical and empirical discussion on 'sub-debt trap' in this chapter, we observed a 'transitional failure' (transition from Basel I to Basel II and Basel II to Basel III) of Bangladesh while implementing the Basel Accords, in the sense that neither sub-debt has facilitated market discipline nor have banks put sufficient efforts into improving their asset quality. Further, it is an 'institutional failure' that sub-debt failed to bring financial stability and market discipline in the banking industry of Bangladesh and appeared as a skeptical component of regulatory capital. We are afraid that the strategy of issuance of sub-debt creates a systemic risk in the entire banking industry as commercial banks are tapped into the 'sub-debt trap'. However, it is also a weakness of the Basel Accord III in which the BIS has failed to forecast the potential ill impact of subordinated debt on the entire industry (when sub-debt is considered as Tier 2 capital). In Bangladesh's case, we have found evidence from empirical investigation that sub-debt maximizes the equity holder's benefit instead of imposing discipline on banks. In a nutshell, due to a such institutional failure, the outcome of the implementation of the Basel Accords in Bangladesh is, Bangladeshi banks fall into the 'sub-debt trap' and the philosophy of Basel Accords seems futile in Bangladesh. It is deserved by the depositors, taxpayers and entire society to receive from the public economic entities of the country, a rational, far-sighted and effective prudential regulations which helps to maintain assurance in the banking system, brings confidence among depositors, ensures financial stability and prevents systemic risk. The effectiveness of a prudential regulation is essential not only to prevent bank runs or enhancing banking resilience but also to guarantee the depositors' money and reduce the burden on taxpayers which in turn will maximize societal welfare.

REFERENCES

Bangladesh Bank (BB). (2002, 24 November). *Master circular on capital adequacy of banks* (BRPD Circular No. 10). Banking Regulation and Policy Department, Bangladesh Bank.

Bangladesh Bank (BB). (2005, December 11). *Risk Grading Manual* (BRPD Circular No. 18). Banking Regulation and Policy Department, Bangladesh Bank.

Bangladesh Bank (BB). (2008, December 31). *Guidelines on 'Risk Based Capital Adequacy for Banks' (Revised regulatory capital framework in line with Basel II)* (BRPD Circular No. 9). Banking Regulation and Policy Department, Bangladesh Bank.

Bangladesh Bank (BB). (2010, August 3). *Revised Guidelines on Risk Based Capital Adequacy (RBCA) for Banks* (BRPD Circular No. 24). Banking Regulation and Policy Department, Bangladesh Bank.

Bangladesh Bank (BB). (2012, February 15). *Risk Management Guidelines for Banks* (DOS Circular No. 2). Department of Off-site Supervision, Bangladesh Bank.

Bangladesh Bank (BB). (2014, December 21). *Guidelines on Risk Based Capital Adequacy (Revised Regulatory Capital Framework for banks in line with Basel III)* (BRPD Circular No. 18). Banking Regulation and Policy Department, Bangladesh Bank.

Bangladesh Bank (BB). (2016a).*Guidelines on Credit Risk Management (CRM) for Banks*. Bangladesh Bank. https://www.bb.org.bd/aboutus/regulationguideline/guidelist.php.

Bangladesh Bank (BB). (2016b). *Managing core risks in banking: Asset Liability Management (ALM) guidelines*. Bangladesh Bank. https://www.bb.org.bd/aboutus/regulationguideline/guidelist.php.

Bangladesh Bank (BB). (2018). *Financial Stability Report, 2018, Issue 9*. Financial Stability Department, Bangladesh Bank. https://www.bb.org.bd/pub/index.php.

Bangladesh Bank (BB). (2020). *Annual Report 2018–2019*. Bangladesh Bank.

Dhaka Bank Limited (DBL). (2018). *Annual Report 2018*. https://dhakabankltd.com/financial-statements-reports/.

Evanoff, D. D. (1994). Capital requirements and bank regulatory reforms. In C. A. Stone & A. Zissu (Eds.), *Global risk based capital regulation Volume 1: capital adequacy*. Irwin Professional Publishing.

Evanoff, D. D., & Wall, L. D. (2000). *Subordinated debt as bank capital: A proposal for regulatory reform (WP 2000–07)*. Federal Reserve Bank of Chicago.

Evanoff, D. D., & Wall, L. D. (2001). Sub-debt yields spreads as bank risk measures. Subordinated debt as bank capital: A Proposal for Regulatory Reform. *Journal of Financial Services Research, 20*(2/3), 121–145.

Evanoff, D. D., Jagtiani, J. A., & Nakata, T. (2011). Enhancing market discipline in banking: The role of subordinated debt in financial regulatory reform. *Journal of Economics and Business, 63*, 1–22.

Evanoff, D. D., & Wall, L. D. (2002). Measures of the riskiness of banking organizations: Subordinated debt yields, risk-based capital, and examination ratings. *Journal of Banking & Finance, 26*, 989–1009.

Financial Institutions Division (FID). (2020). *Draft Amanat Surokka Ain 2020 (Deposit Protection Act 2020): Department of Banks and Financial Institutions*. Retrieved February 4, 2021, from Financial Institutions Division, Ministry of Finance, Government of the People's Republic of Bangladesh: https://fid.gov.bd/sites/default/files/files/fid.portal.gov.bd/draft_law/b55 929ed_9767_4cd9_8f5b_b5b8cad36862/%E0%A6%B8%E0%A7%81%E0% A6%B0%E0%A6%95%E0%A7%8D%E0%A6%B7%E0%A6%BE%20%E0%A6% 86%E0%A6%87%E0%A6%A8.pdf.

Goodhart, C. (2011). *The Basel Committee on banking Supervision: A history of the early years 1974–1997. Central Bank and the Financial System*. Cambridge University Press.

Hausman, J. (1978). Specification tests in econometrics. *Econometrica, 46*(6), 1251–1271.

One bank Limited. (2018). *Annual Report 2018*. https://www.onebank.com. bd/home/financial/annual-reports/.

Rahman, M. M., Zheng, C., Ashraf, B. N., & Rahman, M. M. (2018). Capital requirements, the cost of financial intermediation and bank risk-taking: Empirical evidence from Bangladesh. *Research in International Business and Finance, 44*, 488–503.

Suzuki, Y. (2011). *Japan's Financial Slump: Collapse of the monitoring system under institutional and transitional failures*. Palgrave Macmillan.

CHAPTER 7

Cases of Bank Distress

7.1 Introduction

The grave financial indiscipline and irregularities during the period 2009–2018 put several Bangladeshi commercial banks into a distress condition, which became a major concern for academics as well as policymakers. This chapter provides the readers with the case analysis of banks distress to analyze how once profitable PCBs and SCBs were turned into troubled banks only within a couple of years. Here we raise the cases of the Farmers Bank Limited (FBL), AB Bank Limited (ABBL) and Janata Bank Limited (JBL). The structure of the chapter is as follows. Section 7.2 describes the cases of above-mentioned three banks distress in Bangladesh. Section 7.3 looks at the BB Order 1972 to point out the unsolved issues in the supervision by the BB as concluding remarks to this chapter.

7.2 Cases of Banks Distress in Bangladesh

Farmers Bank Limited Case

We can raise the failure of The Farmers Bank Limited (FBL) as the result of the ill-designed adoption of Basel regulations in Bangladesh. This case study examines the magnitude of NPL that led to a classic bank run which was the first of this kind in Bangladesh. The bank got the banking license from BB in 2013 to operate as a commercial

157

A K M K. Hasan and Y. Suzuki, *Implementation of Basel Accords in Bangladesh*, https://doi.org/10.1007/978-981-16-3472-7_7

bank with paid-up capital of BDT 4.0 billion (BB, 2013; FBL, 2013) and became a hotbed for financial indiscipline in less than four years of operation. Sponsors shareholding structure of FBL is shown in Fig. 7.1 which shows that individual sponsors, institutional sponsors and non-institutional sponsors shareholding compositions were 73.1 percent, 24.9 percent and 2.0 percent, respectively, as of December 2013.

According to the latest publicly disclosed annual report 2016, the bank's some key performance indicators are shown in the following Table 7.1.

Table 7.2 reports the CRAR position of the bank from 2013 to 2017 which revealed that due to NPL, the RWA for credit risk and operational risk has increased rapidly and CRAR has dropped from 29.56% in 2014 to

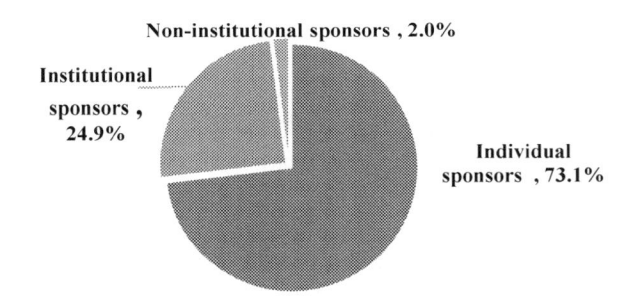

Fig. 7.1   Sponsors shareholding structure of FBL as of December 31, 2013

Table 7.1   FBL's key performance indicators (amount in BDT billion)

Particulars	2013	2014	2015	2016
Shareholders' equity	4.05	4.08	4.38	4.44
Total deposits (including bills payable)	1.87	11.48	34.83	50.64
Loans and advances	0.11	10.07	25.74	44.13
Total assets	6.06	16.76	41.08	58.99
Net profit before tax	0.053	0.061	0.35	0.38
Number of branches	10	26	38	52
ROA	0.75%	0.23%	0.51%	0.39%
ROE	0.94%	0.76%	4.84%	5.19%
NPL*	–	0.22%	1.61%	4.01%

*NPL was 57.82% at end of September 2018 (Alo, 2018)
Source FBL (2016)

Table 7.2 Capital requirement and capital adequacy ratio (2013–2017) (amount in BDT billion)

	2013	2014	2015	2016	2017
RWA for credit risk	2.269	12.866	35.447	41.334	38.651
RWA for market risk	0	0.52	0.996	0.972	0.789
RWA for operational risk	0.345	0.642	1.184	2.188	2.962
Total RWA	2.614	14.028	37.627	44.494	42.402
% of RWA for credit risk to total RWA	86.80%	91.71%	94.21%	92.90%	91.15%
Total regulatory capital	4.055	4.146	4.507	4.732	3.396
CRAR	155.14%	29.56%	11.98%	10.64%	8.01%

Source Basel disclosure of The Farmers Bank Ltd. 2013–2017

11.98% in 2015. Then further slumped in the following years. In 2017, its RWA for credit risk to total RWA was 91% (see Table 7.2) which attest that its major risk was credit risk.

The case can be summarized as follows. The turmoil began in November 2017 when the media reported that FBL has failed to repay the interbank short-term loans for BDT 7 billion, and also failed to repay on the maturity of fixed-term deposits for BDT 2.21 billion to Bangladesh Climate Change Trust Fund (BCCTF) as well as BDT 1.80 billion fixed deposit to Chittagong Port Authority (Islam, 2018, 2019; Rahman & Uddin, 2017; Star, 2019). This news eroded the bank's credibility among the money market and urged the depositors to withdraw their savings, leading to bank panic and subsequently creates serious financial turmoil in the entire banking sector during November–December 2017. During this period, the bank has failed to meet the settlement claims and to collect money from interbank market offering interest rates over 12%, against the 4–8% rates offered by other banks (Islam et al., 2017). To stop the bank panic, BB had instructed in last week of November in 2017 to step down the Chairman of the Board of Directors and chairman of the audit committee of the bank. However, both the institutional depositors and retail depositors did not stop to run to the bank and desperately trying to take their savings out of the bank (CPD, 2018). For example, as of December 13, 2017, FBL had deposits of BDT 47 billion, down from BDT 56.60 billion on October 30, which endorsed that within last 45 days the withdrawn deposit amount was BDT 0.96 billion and within first few days of December, depositors withdrawn amount reached to BDT 12 billion while there are no new deposits (CPD, 2018, p. 179).

The FBL cash crunch creates mistrust and suspect among all banks and call money rate reached the peak. In a word, there observed serious financial chaos in the entire banking sector during November–December 2017 which triggered by FBL. Finally, the Ministry of Finance (MoF) stepped in and announced the bailout plan for BDT 11 billion to FBL (CPD, 2019). Four state-owned commercial banks (Sonali Bank Ltd., Janata Bank Ltd., Agrani Bank Ltd. and Rupali Bank Ltd.) and one state-owned investment company, Investment Corporation of Bangladesh (ICB), were bought equity shares of FBL worth BDT 7.15 billion under the bailout package (CPD, 2019; Uddin, 2018). Later, the reshuffled Board of Directors of the bank took charge and renamed the FBL as 'Padma Bank Limited' in 2019 (BB, 2019). A chronology of the events of FBL is shown in Table 7.3.

There is evidence that FBL cash crisis has started due to NPL problem and the bank faces cash crunch as its borrowers fail to repay the loans which ultimately leads to bank run. We shall note that FBL's major risk was credit risk which dominant in the total RWA of the bank (see Table 7.2). The failure of FBL has exposed the flaws of the banking regulations and undermine the resilience of the entire financial system. Firstly, FBL was Basel compliant bank however, we have observed that the capital regulation fails to control the bank risk appetite in turn CRAR sharply fell within the year 2014 to 2015 (see Table 7.2). Besides, it documents that capital cannot alone cover the unexpected loss, rather the bank managers and owners tend to take more risk without considering the consequences when the capital buffer is exceeding the minimum

Table 7.3 Chronicles of FBL events

2013	*Founded with BDT 4 billion paid-up capital*
Since November 2017	The bank has failed to repay the institutional and individual depositors' claim which create bank panic
November–December 2017	Bank's Chairman, audit committee chairman and managing director had stepped down
February 2018	Five state-owned financial institutions inject BDT 7.15 billion as equity capital which is 1.78 times higher than FBL's initial capital
September 2018	NPL stood at 57.82% (BDT 30.71 billion) out of the total outstanding loans BDT 53.11 billion
January 2019	FBL was renamed as 'Padma Bank Limited'

threshold level. Second, the bank follows the ECAIs rating to compute CRAR while we observed that ECAIs rating fails to capture the real credit risk associated with FBL's exposures. Third, the objectives of bailout plan can be questioned as at the time of bailout, and the sponsors shares were not forfeited/transferred rather public money has been injected as fresh equity to calm down the panic. Certainly, it gave a wrong message to the financial market that aftermath of taking more risk and putting less effort to monitoring, screening and supervision of the banking assets, the bank owners would lose nothing.

AB Bank Limited Case

AB Bank Limited (ABBL), a first-generation bank established in 1983 by local entrepreneurs. As of December 31, 2018, the bank's asset size and deposit stood at BDT 322.53 billion and BDT 235.44 billion, respectively. The bank asset quality sharply declines in 2018 and NPL reached at 33.07% (see Table 7.4), in turn its shortfall in capital reached to BDT 6.09 billion. We summarize the ABBL key performance indicators in Table 7.4.

The episode of ABBL can be summarized as follows. The bank involved in risky investment since 2011 and accumulated NPL proportionately, in turn the profitability of the bank eroded drastically. As observed the erosion of capital has been started since 2013 (see Fig. 7.2), and to maintain CRAR, the bank issued first trench of sub-debt in 2014 for BDT 2.5 billion. However, as the asset quality has been further soured, the erosion of capital continued, and the bank solely relied on sub-debt to maintain CRAR. In turn the outstanding balance of sub-debt stood at 8.7 billion as of December 2018 (see Table 7.4). It is observed from Table 7.5 that the bank's average 89.34% of RWA derives from credit risk between 2013 and 2018 which document that ABBL risk-weighted assets have expanded by leveraging with sub-debt. That is the bank expanded the credit portfolio and accumulated fresh NPL over the years. The situation getting worse when the central bank made a special investigation on ABBL's banking assets and identified that there is loan loss provision shortfall of BDT 61.71 billion against total loan loss in 2018 (ABBL, 2018, p. 170). However, a deferral facility was given to ABBL by allowing to keep the shortfall of the loan loss provision in next 10 years equally from 2019 to 2028. Readers may presume that because of such deferral facility of loan loss provision, owners of the bank finally

Table 7.4 Performance of ABBL (in billions BDT otherwise stated)

	Profit after tax	Common share dividend	Retained earnings	Outstanding balance of sub-debt*	Write-off loans during the period	Div. payout ratio (%)**	Cash div. rate (%)	NPL ratio (%)	CET capital ratio (%)	Total CRAR (%)	ROA (%)	ROE (%)	P/E ratio (in times)	Debt/Equity ratio (in times)	Capital surplus/(deficit)***
	1	2	3	4	5	6	7	8	9	10	11	12	13	14	15
2009	3.36	0.51	3.54	-	0.63	15.22	20	2.75	9.39	11.09	3.52	39.44	26.53	9.53	1.07
2010	3.70	0.32	4.77	-	0.00	8.60	10	2.11	8.39	9.91	3.08	30.77	32.42	8.59	1.35
2011	1.33	0.18	5.29	-	0.00	13.86	5	2.82	9.56	11.37	0.93	9.25	38.99	9.30	1.92
2012	1.44	0.00	5.16	-	0.99	-	-	3.32	9.99	11.73	0.88	9.31	17.76	9.84	2.53
2013	1.01	0.25	4.99	-	0.00	24.53	5	3.37	8.95	10.80	0.53	6.13	19.65	11.28	1.39
2014	1.26	0.00	6.77	2.5	1.72	-	-	3.86	7.50	10.32	0.54	6.95	17.99	13.03	0.71
2015	1.27	0.00	6.83	6.5	1.83	-	-	3.16	7.18	11.09	0.48	6.03	12.47	11.50	2.78
2016	1.31	0.00	6.81	6.5	3.04	-	-	5.19	6.58	10.79	0.44	5.68	12.96	12.62	0.46
2017	0.03	0.00	6.01	6.0	3.28	-	-	7.15	6.81	10.80	0.01	0.13	566.02	12.81	(1.31)
2018	0.02	0.00	5.91	8.7	0.15	-	-	33.07	5.82	10.03	0.01	0.08	496.49	13.24	(6.09)
Total		1.26			11.64										

*Sub-debt has been issued in 2014 for first time
**The dividend payout ratio is calculated based on profits after tax and common share dividends
***BB provide exemption for maintaining capital against BDT 60.11 billion classified loans which requires to be kept next 10 years from 2019–2020
(*Source* Annual Report, 2018, pp. 170, 177)
Source Annual Reports of AB Bank Limited

in billions of BDT, year-on-year

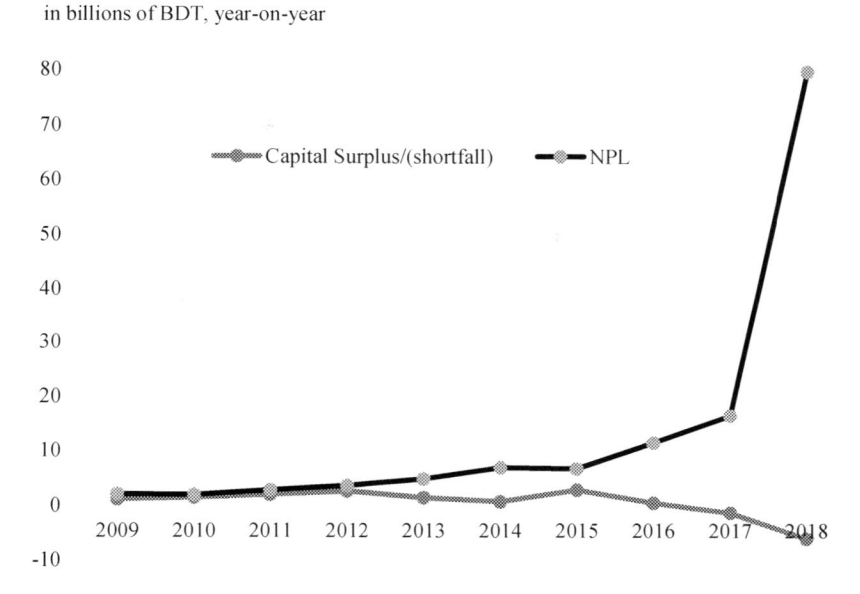

Fig. 7.2 Impact of ABBL's NPL on capital

Table 7.5 Total RWA of ABBL under Basel Framework (in billions BDT)

	2013	2014	2015	2016	2017	2018
RWA for Credit Risk	153.4	196.9	228.4	253.1	259.2	298.6
RWA for Market Risk	6.6	7.4	7.8	8.8	7.89	7.9
RWA for Operational Risk	13.9	16.6	19.3	22.1	22.64	22.6
Total RWA	173.9	220.9	255.5	284	289.73	329.1

pay no cost for their responsibility toward the bad assets and management performance. Rather bank has instrumentalized the sub-debt as Tier 2 capital and generous deferral facility to maintain the CRAR. In our view such malpractice has distort the core objectives of Basel framework and distort the incentives for ECAIs and professional bankers to improve their rating quality and efforts to improve the ROA, respectively.

The crux question is why a deferral facility of loan loss provision to the ABBL was provided. Such decision could be justified from the following perspective. Firstly, resist the erosion of public trust on deposit taking institutions. That is if ABBL would face the same situation in 2019 like FBL had faced in 2017, the erosion of public trust on financial system of the country would further down and there was high chance for another bank run in 2019. However, the flaws of such stance provide an opportunity to the economic elites of the country to doge accountability, shift responsibility and undermine the microprudential regulations of the banking system. Second, there is chance for a nexus among vested groups to support ABBL in an extraordinary way. Whatever the reason is, the ABBL case signals that PCBs owners are finally dominated over prudential regulations. Indeed, the concern from ABBL episode is that it exposed a weak supervision process and instrumentalizing of the sub-debt by the PCBs.

Janata Bank Limited Case

Janata Bank Limited (JBL), the second largest state-owned commercial bank of the country, commenced it business in 1972 after amalgamation of the then Union Bank Limited and United Bank Limited under Banks Nationalization Order of 1972 (JBL, 2019). The bank balance sheet size stood at BDT 895.38 billion as of December 2019 and have total 915 branches for deposit mobilization and resource allocation (JBL, 2019). JBL traditionally is one of the profits generating SCB and never experienced net loss in its 46 years of journey except in 2012 (see JBL, 2019). In fact, the profitability and efficiency of the bank have downgraded rapidly within few years in turn bank capital deficit in 2012 stood at BDT 20.12 billion which was surplus in previous years (see Table 7.6). Due to its continuous downward asset quality, the bank has also allowed for deferral facility to maintain its loan loss provision in subsequent years which helped the bank not to show the actual capital deficit under Basel Accord disclosure. Table 7.6 shows the last 10 years performance of JBL.

Table 7.6 shows that the CRAR has declined from 13.81% in 2009 to 10.09% in 2018. We shall note that the bank maintains CRAR above 10.0% despite its ROA dropped sharply, mainly due to recapitalization by MoF (see Figs. 7.3 and 7.4). In addition, the bank write-off huge bad loans from the balance sheet (see Table 7.6) and issue sub-debt as Tier 2 capital to maintain minimum CRAR in 2018 (see Table 7.6). In fact, if the bank would not avail the deferral facility for loan loss provision, the capital surplus that is shown in Table 7.6 would disappear.

Table 7.6 Performance of JBL (in billions BDT otherwise stated)

	Profit after tax	Common share dividend	Retained earnings	Outstanding balance of sub-debt*	Paid-up capital	Write-off loans during the period	Cash div. rate (%)	NPL ratio (%)	CET capital ratio (%)	Total CRAR (%)	ROA (%)	ROE (%)	Debt/Equity ratio (in times)	Capital surplus/(deficit)**
	1	2	3	4	5	6	7	8	9	10	11	12	13	14
2009	2.80	0.00	1.67	0	5.00	1.56	0.00	8.44	8.79	13.81	1.00	23.38	16.49	0.88
2010	4.91	0.01	3.33	0	5.00	1.45	0.20	5.24	5.65	9.19	0.77	27.80	14.05	0.60
2011	4.44	0.01	2.66	0	8.13	1.22	0.12	5.83	7.20	10.20	1.12	16.32	10.62	0.48
2012	(15.28)	0.00	(15.29)	0	11.00	2.47	0.00	17.42	1.85	3.70	(3.50)	(49.74)	24.09	(20.12)
2013	9.55	0.01	7.58	0	19.14	10.83	0.05	11.12	7.85	10.27	1.42	30.09	13.13	0.91
2014	3.81	0.01	2.75	0	19.1	1.84	0.05	11.69	8.07	10.30	0.61	9.66	12.08	1.05
2015	4.81	0.01	3.78	0	19.1	7.92	0.05	12.34	8.20	10.16	0.70	9.70	10.48	0.57
2016	2.61	0.01	2.02	0	19.1	1.52	0.05	14.73	8.85	10.69	0.33	5.22	11.86	2.78
2017	2.69	0.01	1.88	0	19.1	0.12	0.05	16.54	8.40	10.06	0.33	5.23	11.64	0.25
2018	0.25	0.01	0.06	15	23.1	0.24	0.04	33.72	6.57	10.09	0.03	0.46	11.38	0.50
Total		0.08				29.16								

*Sub-debt has been, issued in. 2018 for first time
**BB provide deferral facility for maintaining provisions against classified loans in 2015–2018, hence the capital deficit not reflect the actual deficit
(*Source* Annual Reports 2015–2018)
Source Annual Reports of Janata Bank Limited

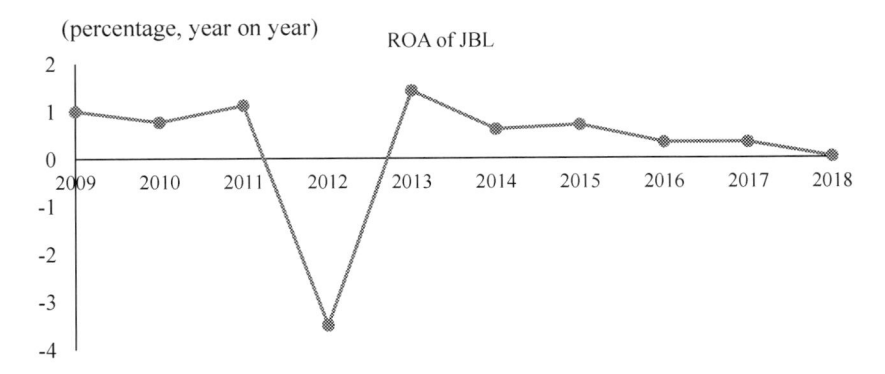

Fig. 7.3   High NPL adversely affect the bank's ROA

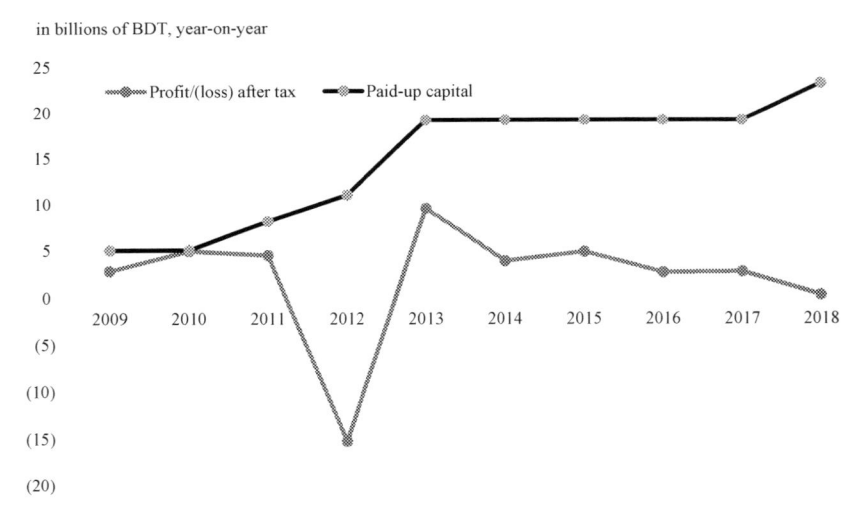

Fig. 7.4   Recapitalization to JBL to maintain CRAR

JBL case can be summarized as follows. The MoF has mandate on appointment of BOD and top management of all state-owned banks and financial institutions of the country. Hence as per tradition, when the new government was formed after the general election in 2009, the ministry has nominated new directors to JBL including chairman of the board. After taking over the charge, the chairman has reshuffled the board sub-committees (Executive committee and Audit Committee) by placing the new members to these committees. In fact, the bank performance has started deteriorating since 2012 when it aggressively lending to the corporate and drastically reduced its portfolio from the public sector (see Fig. 7.5). It is observed that NPL was climbed up by 199% in 2012 from the previous year which downgraded CRAR to 3.70% in 2012 from 10.20% in 2011 (see Table 7.6). To maintain the minimum CRAR, MoF has injected equity capital of BDT 6.0 billion between 2011 and 2012. However, the upward trend of NPL was not controlled, which reached at 33.72% as of December 2018. In fact, the NPL of the bank has increased 300% within 10 years. Later it has discovered that the bank's BOD had approved several corporate clients (such as Annontex Group and Crescent Group) while violating the single borrower exposure rule of BB between 2009 and 2014 (Prothom Alo, 2018; Sakib, 2018; Star, 2018). According to single borrower exposure rule, a banking company cannot lend more than a specific percentage (it combined with funded and non-funded exposure and sector wise exposures) of its paid-up capital to a single borrower. In fact, both the corporates had diverted and laundered the fund, and at the end, a majority portion of the exposures against Annontex Group and Crescent Group turned as bad loans in 2018. The outstanding balance of total loans of the two groups stood at BDT 91.22 billion as of December 2018 (see JBL, 2018, p. 247). Later it

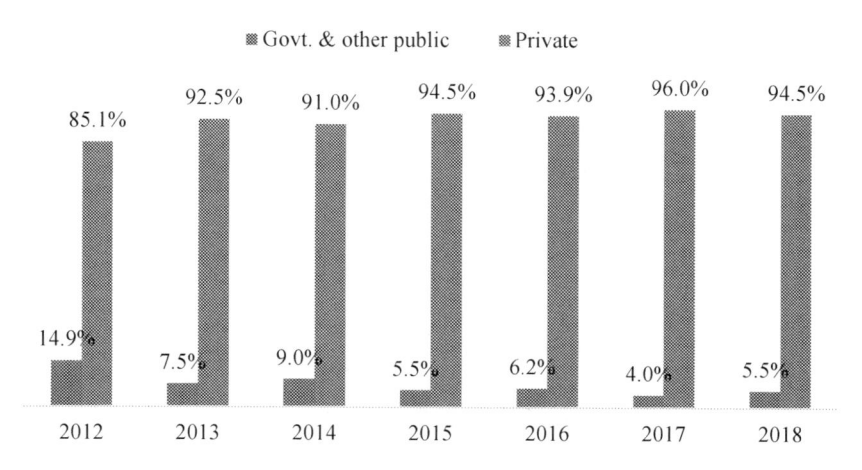

Fig. 7.5   Sector-wise percentage of loans and advances of JBL

has informed to the parliament that the total NPL of JBL stood at BDT 159.74 billion as of June 2020 (Express, 2020).

From the above episode it is evident that the newly appointed BOD in 2009 had took risky investment strategy. Besides, it is mysterious why a prominent SCB attempted to slash its public sector credit portfolio and eager to lend to corporates (see Fig. 7.5). However, as there are no official white paper reports have been published to the public on JBL's loan scams, no official evidence is available to us regarding details of the gross irregularities of JBL which occurred between 2009 and 2014. But it can be presumed that the board members and bank managers have ill-incentive to violate the single borrower rule in case of corporates because a state-owned banks' core objective might not maximize profit rather to support the national economic policies and create real employment. Indeed, when the SCBs allocate their resources to the corporates, it makes no sense to recapitalize the SCBs with public money. To sum up, the JBL case provides evidence that how the BOD and management of bank had underscored the enforcement of the banking regulations.

To conclude, it is evident from the above cases of bank distress that the country's microprudential regulation has failed to control the banks risk appetite. Besides, both the PCBs and SCB were following the standardized approach (SA) and ECAIs rating notch for quantifying the credit risk under Basel Accord; however, the asset quality of banks were not improved. Consequently, the banks were tapped into sub-debt trap. What is more, it signals the weakness of Bangladeshi mode of supervision to the regulated banks. Why it so, a crux query that readers might raise.

7.3   Concluding Remarks: A Critique of the BB Order 1972

It has been long debated on how we should design an appropriate financial architecture for preventing bank failures and bailing out troubled banks if occurred. It is widely recognized that the unbiased, coherent and consistent mode of supervising should be sought for prudential supervision. In this context, the concentration of responsibility in the regulatory body together with a well-designed 'check and balance' mechanism is considered as an important institutional setting. We should note the weakness in the concentration of responsibility in the Bangladeshi regulatory body, which may have undermined the prudential supervision by the BB.

Indeed, the concept of central banking in South Asia has started in 1930s. The Reserve Bank of India (RBI) was the first central bank in South Asia (now India, Pakistan, Bangladesh) under British colonial regime which established under Reserve Bank of India Act 1934 by the Great Britain. After independence from the Great Britain in 1947, RBI acted as central bank of India whereas 'State Bank of Pakistan' (SBP) has been established in 1948 under The State Bank of Pakistan Order 1948 (SBP, 1956). In 1972, the Dhaka Branch of SBP reorganized as 'Bangladesh Bank' under the Bangladesh Bank Order, 1972 right after the country's independence in December 1971 from Pakistan. After commencement of its operation in 1972 as central bank of the newly independent state, BB was a part of Ministry of Finance. The World Bank project namely 'Central Bank Strengthening Project' has been considered as the first comprehensive approach and milestone to reform the BB since its commencement in 1972 although there were few amendments in 1990, 1993 (Ahmed, 2007). The key objectives of the project were: (i) to strengthen the Bangladesh Bank (BB) to enable it to play its due role as the country's monetary authority and bank regulator and supervisor, and (ii) to enable Bangladesh Bank to lead the design and implementation of a medium to long-term reform program for achieving a sound and efficient financial system (WB, 2003, 2014).

However, the BB has not yet been strengthened enough to take the roles expected in the reform plan. We observe that the BB is still not independent from the MOF. For example, the article 9A(1) of BB Order 1972 allows the Council to coordinate the fiscal, monetary and exchange rate strategies and policies, while there is no clause to form or appoint an ad hoc committee within the BB for checking the coherence and consistency in regulation and supervision. The Council members are Minister for Finance, Minister for Commerce, Governor of BB, Secretary of Finance Division, Secretary of Internal Resources Division and a member from Planning Commission (see Bangladesh Bank Order, 1972). Besides, the Ministry of Finance has the mandate on the governance and administration over SCBs. This mandate includes the appointment and dismissal of Board of Directors, appointment of Managing Director, Deputy Managing Director and General Manager (see FID, 2010). In other words, the Ministry of Finance reserves an effective power of disciplining any senior management staff or the Board by taking visible punitive actions for irregularities and banking frauds in SCBs. As was suggested by the case study of JBL in which there was no legal action to be taken against the seemingly corrupted BOD of JBL, the banking inspection on SCBs by MOF is conducted at their discretion, so occasionally arbitrary. We would say that the governance on, at least, SCBs is not under the independent control of BB. Also we would say that the BB does not well work as a 'check and balance' mechanism for the banking inspection by MOF. We should note the structural problem in the Bangladeshi mode of supervision.

REFERENCES

AB Bank Limited (ABBL). (2018). *Annual Report 2018.* AB Bank Limited. https://www.jb.com.bd/about_us/annual_report.

Ahmed, H. A. (2007). *Bangladesh bank reforms: Changes and challenges.* Brac University.

Alo, J. N. (2018, December 21). Farmers Bank: Dramatic raise in loan default. *The Daily Star*, p. 1.

Bangladesh Bank (BB). (1972). *Bangladesh bank order, 1972* (President's Order No. 127 of 1972). Bangladesh Bank.

Bangladesh Bank (BB). (2013, November 7). *Write off Policy* (BRPD Circular No. 13). Banking Regulation and Policy Department, Bangladesh Bank.

Bangladesh Bank (BB). (2019, January 29). *Regarding the change of name "The Farmers Bank Limited" into "Padma Bank Limited"* (BRPD Circular No. 2). Banking Regulation and Policy Department, Bangladesh Bank.

Center for Policy Dialogue (CPD). (2018). *Bangladesh economy in FY2017–18 interim review of macroeconomic performance.* Center for Policy Dialogue.

Center for Policy Dialogue (CPD). (2019). *State of the Bangladesh economy in FY2019–20 first reading.* Center for Policy Dialogue.

Express, F. (2020, September 7). SoCBs' default loans stack up to BDT 410b. *The Financial Express*, p. 8.

Farmers Bank Limited (FBL). (2013). *Annual Report 2013.* The Farmers Bank Limited.

Farmers Bank Limited (FBL). (2016). *Annual Report 2016.* The Farmers Bank Limited.

Financial Institutions Division (FID). (2010). *Allocation of business 2010: Department of banks and financial institutions.* Retrieved June 28, 2020, from Financial Institutions Division, Ministry of Finance, Government of the People's Republic of Bangladesh: https://fid.gov.bd/site/page/e0e6e343-e4c8-4c86-a0fa-cad36b1175fc/Mandate-of-FID.

Islam, K. (2019, February 2). বন্দরের ১৭৫ কোটি টাকা ফেরতে অনিশ্চয়তা (Port's amount of BDT 175 crore is unsure to get back). *Dainik Purbokone*, p(s).1, 11.

Islam, S. (2018, January 22). Two Port authorities have Tk 235 cr. Deposit stuck at Farmers Bank. *Dhaka Tribune*. https://www.dhakatribune.com/

business/banks/2018/01/22/two-port-authorities-tk235cr-deposit-stuck-farmers-bank.

Islam, S., Kallol, A. S., & Kallol, A. S. (2017, December 15). Government worried about climate fund money in Farmers Bank. *The Daily Dhaka Tribune*.

Janata Bank Limited (JBL). (2018). *Annual Report 2018: Janata Bank Limited*. https://www.jb.com.bd/about_us/annual_report.

Janata Bank Limited (JBL). (2019). *Annual Report 2019: Janata Bank Limited*. https://www.jb.com.bd/about_us/annual_report.

Prothom Alo. (2018, December 26). জনতা ব্যাংকের খেলাপি ঋণ দুই বছরে বেড়েছে তিন গুণ. (Janata Bank's default loans raised by three times within two years). *The Prothom Alo*.

Rahman, S., & Uddin, A. K. M. Z. (2017, December 14). Farmers Bank: Scam fallout getting worse. *The Daily Star*, p. 1.

Sakib, S. (2018, December 6). জনতা ব্যাংকে বিশেষ নিরীক্ষা (Special Audit at Janata Bank). *The Daily Prothom Alo*.

Star. (2018, February 7). Janata Bank Loan Scam: Whole bank was in it. *The Daily Star*.

Star. (2019, August 25). Padma Bank struggles to return fixed deposits. *The Daily Star*. https://www.thedailystar.net/business/news/padma-bank-struggles-return-fixed-deposits-1790206.

State Bank of Pakistan (SBP). (1956). *State Bank of Pakistan Act, 1956*. State Bank of Pakistan.

Uddin, A. K. M. Z. (2018, December 24). Farmers Bank to take new name amid image crisis: Troubled bank seeks a fresh start. *The Daily Star*.

World Bank (WB). (2003). *Bangladesh Central Bank Strengthening Project: Project appraisal document*. The World Bank.

World Bank (WB). (2014). *ICR review on Bangladesh Central Bank Strengthening Project*. The World Bank.

CHAPTER 8

The Building Blocks to Design Robust and Effective Capital Regulation

8.1 Introduction

So far, we document that the realities of Bangladeshi banking sector between 2009 and 2018 are an ill-by-product of multiple institutional failures. To analyze the issue more specifically, we shed light on ECAIs regulations and sub-debt regulations which are discussed in Chapters 4–6 whereas Chapter 7 provides multiple cases of bank distress. At this point, the crucial question is how to build a robust and effective capital regulation for emerging economies like Bangladesh. Based on our findings and analysis, we develop several institutional reform policies for financial regulators to fix the banking sector malaise from institutional perspective. The structure of the chapter is as follows. Section 8.2 offers the detailed reform policies for ensuring the ECAIs rating quality based on best practices in the US. Section 8.3 presents the detailed reform policy prescriptions for tackling the sub-debt trap and building a resilient capital from Basel Accord philosophy. Section 8.4 is the concluding remarks.

8.2 Way Forward for Improving ECAI's Rating Quality

Trend of Institutional Reform in CRAs Regulation in the US

Several institutional reforms have been taken place by global regulators to monitor and supervise the CRA's activities during last two decades.

A K M K. Hasan and Y. Suzuki, *Implementation of Basel Accords in Bangladesh*, https://doi.org/10.1007/978-981-16-3472-7_8

The US, EU, Australia and Japan have taken initiatives to change their CRA regulations in line with global concerns (IOSCO, 2011). We attempt to briefly analyze the US reform activities instead of discussing all other countries reformation agendas as CRA's evolution history is mostly related with the US market context. The US has adopted the Sarbanes-Oxley Act in 2002 after the financial fraud scandal in the auditing and accounting services industry. Specifically, prior to the act, the audit firms were self-regulated and considered as 'gatekeepers' of investors (PAE, 2000). Why did the 'gatekeepers' fail? Several reasons are pointed out by contemporary scholars for 'failure of gatekeepers' such as 'de-professionalization' (Healy & Palepu, 2003), 'sale of consulting service' (Levitt, 2002), 'legal liability standard for auditors to combat its conflict of interest which mainly arises from its revenue generation model' (Coffee, 2006). In fact, Sarbanes-Oxley was a response to the failure of self-regulation of the auditing profession and principally designed to regulate auditors so that they will perform better as 'gatekeepers' (Coates, 2007). The Sarbanes-Oxley Act has responded to all academic debates except the legal liability of auditors and did not mention any comments on the role of CRA's in the accounting scandal. Possibly that was a major legal drawback of the Sarbanes-Oxley Act.

After the global financial crisis in 2007–2008, US regulators were responding to the failures of CRAs through the Dodd-Frank Act of 2010 (Partony, 2017) and acknowledged that CRAs are 'critical gatekeepers' in the US financial market (Dodd-Frank Act, 2010, 993(1)). Although transparency and disclosure for CRAs are highly stressed in the Dodd-Frank Act, the act failed to introduce any specific solution for CRA's accountability, related with their 'pay model' and reduce the reliance on CRA's rating (Patrony, 2017). We shall note that, the US SEC has confessed that, the commission is trying to explore the potential conflict of interest of CRAs when issuers are paying for ratings (USSEC, 2013). In fact, it is an unsolved problem in US institutions insofar as how to reduce the side-effects that are embedded within CRAs pay model. Besides, the European Commission (EC, 2016, pp. 82–84) in its latest report 'Study on the Feasibility of Alternatives to Credit Rating' has identified five alternative approaches to a CRA's rating. These are internal measures and rating, market implied ratings, accountancy-based measures, OECD country risk classification and central credit registers, but they could not find any alternative model to the CRA's rather they put it to the needs, circumstances and market participants (EC, 2016).

Some academics, however, offer to introduce an 'investor pay model,' i.e., in case of an ECAI, a bank will pay the fees instead of the firm. But simply turning back to an old payment system, i.e., 'investor pay model' may create the old problem in a new form, i.e., the 'free rider' problem. Some scholars such as Covitz and Harrison (2003) advocate for strengthening the compliance function of CRA's to reduce conflict of interest. Miglionico (2014, p. 60) mentioned that 'the compliance function in CRAs governance could stop the ratings from being a precondition for the sale of structured securities and reduce the CRAs' conflicts and it should be managed by appropriate regulatory oversight.' Darbellay (2013, p. 149) has mentioned three possible reforms to mitigate CRA's conflict of interest while referring to Weber and Bauman (2013) opinion. These are (i) separation of a CRA's analyst function from its other ancillary services function (ii) analysts' income should not depend on fee generation and (iii) establishing a 'Chinese wall' to avoid exchanges of sensitive information for rating analysts' conflicting mandates.

In summary, it is difficult to find an alternative to the 'issuer-pay' model, and rather the scholars opined on several defensive approaches to minimize the conflict of interest. This defensive approach includes increasing CRA's governance structure and bring more transparency to the operational structure along with meaningful disclosure. It is worth mentioning here that existing CRC rules of Bangladesh have allowed them to keep a compliance officer who will communicate with regulators (BSEC, 1996) but there is no provision for establishment of a governance and compliance department in CRAs. However, lapses in CRA's regulation can be compensated for if supervisors are taking initiative to minimize the conflicts of interest and enhance regulatory supervision to ensure the rating quality of ECAIs.

How Well Does the Supervision Process of ECAIs Work in Bangladesh?

We mentioned earlier that, Bangladeshi CRC/ECAIs have two regulatory supervisors, namely BB and the BSEC. While investigating the BSEC's supervisory structure, we have found that 'Supervision and Regulation of Intermediaries Department (SRI)' is the regulating department of CRCs. The organogram of the SRI is the Executive Director (ED) is the head of the department and reports to the commissioner of the BSEC whereas several officials work under ED. At the time of writing (October 2020), there is one executive director, one director, three deputy directors and

Table 8.1 Capital market intermediaries in Bangladesh

Sl. No	Name of the intermediaries	Total number of intermediaries
1	Stockbrokers and stock-dealers (we consider only stock exchanges)	2
2	Depository participants (we consider only CDBL)	1
3	Merchant bankers	63
4	Asset management companies (AMC)	47
5	CRC	8
6	Trustees	90
7	Fund managers	17
8	Custodians	19
	Total	**247**

Information available at BSEC website as of October 2020

two assistant directors who are assigned to the department and the SRI supervises all intermediaries of the capital market (as per information available at BSEC web portal). There are eight types of market intermediaries in the capital market, and within the intermediary segment, there are several participants. Major functions of the SRI include preparing all kinds of intermediaries' related regulations, supervision and inspection (BSEC, 2018). Table 8.1 shows in details about the market intermediaries.

The crucial question at this point is, is it possible to do justice to the regulatory and supervisory mission of the department with such limited manpower (only seven individuals)? We may recall that the US has only 10 NRSROs, and to monitor and supervise these CRAs, there is the 'Office of Credit Ratings' (OCR) at the US SEC since 2010 (U.S. SEC, 2018). However, while asking this question during interview to one of the commissioners[1] of the BSEC, he confessed that due to a shortage of human resources, the commission cannot properly monitor all market intermediaries and, one senior official of the SRI acknowledged that they do not do any investigations into CRAs until they get

---

[1] Commissioners are appointed by the government for full time and there are four commissioners are appointed by the govt. to the commission as of October 2020. See https://www.sec.gov.bd/home/commission.

a written complaint from the stakeholders. This means that the BSEC is simply issuing a 'regulatory license' to the CRC and depends on quarterly reports provided by CRCs to supervise and monitor. Hence, there is no instrument in hand for the BSEC to judge the CRAs rating quality except for the quarterly reports of CRAs. However, whatever the reason is, it is BSEC's supervisory responsibility and mission to verify the CRA's rating quality, especially considering how effective their bank exposure rating is, when the country suffers from huge non-performing loans in the banking sector.

On the other hand, quantifying the credit risk is the main responsibility of ECAIs under Basel Accord while harmonization of the credit risk among ECAI's grading and to check the accuracy of ECAI's risk quantification are the prime responsibility of the regulator (BB, 2014). The Banking Regulation and Policy Department of BB is officially assigned to make prudential regulations, guidelines to ensure a sound and stable banking system (see BB web portal, https://bb.org.bd/aboutus/dept/dept_details.php). On top of that the recognition and supervision of ECAIs are conducted by the BB. In an in-depth interview (regarding ECAI's pay model, competition and their supervision), one of the central bankers mentioned some constraints to take punitive measures against ECAIs. Those may be related with central bank independence and governance which is out of the scope of this study.[2]

Policy Recommendations for Improvement of Rating Quality of ECAI

The previous discussion in Chapters 4 and 5 can be explained by two broad headings:

(a) Moral hazard of ECAIs derived from two corners:

- Absence of a liability regime in the existing institutions in the sense that 'issuer-pay' model is creating a conflict of interest which leads to moral hazard and
- In the absence of incentive-based regulation and fierce competition in the market leads ECAIs to another moral hazard.

---

[2] See, for example, Andrie et al. (2020) in which they found that central bank independence and systemic risk have a robust, negative and significant alignment.

(b) Weak supervision has compounded ECAI's moral hazard.

Based on these two core issues, the possible way out can be two ways: firstly, reform the existing CRC rules and ECAI's recognition guidelines to address the moral hazard of ECAIs. While reforming the rule, two issues need to be solved in the proposed reform. One, introduce incentives in the regulation and another is to identify the civil liability of CRAs. And second, strengthen the supervisory capacity of the two national supervisors. Below we discuss those institutional reform policies in detail.

(i) Create incentives in the ECAIs institutions

While considering reform in the existing rules we need to consider the reality of competition in the CRA industry. In general competition law, it is argued that a competitive market ensures the maximization of societal welfare as there is no deadweight welfare loss (Jenny, 2008). As we argued earlier, the CDR/transition matrix of ECAIs in Bangladesh does not reflect the real picture of rating quality as it fails to capture the real credit risk, and hence it is difficult to claim that competition law is effective in CRA industry of Bangladesh. If a competitive market fails to deliver its expected benefits, either 'regulation' or 'exemption of competition law' can correct the market mechanism (Jenny, 2008, p. 3). Therefore, 'regulation' helps to incentivize the market players and the government should play a role in a proper functioning market mechanism. Competition law and governmental regulation should go together to correct market failure, in response to externalities and deal with information asymmetry (Geiger, 2010). Besides, CRAs are dealing with experience goods and compete for the market rather than in the market (Langhor & Langhor, 2008). Hence in case of CRAs we should consider a specific, sector-wise competition policy rather than general competition law (Darbellay, 2013). Another follow-up query may arise at this point, that is, can antitrust law correct the market behavior? Probably the answer is no. There is limited scope of antitrust law in the rating industry since CRA rating is used for market structure products and rating-based regulation (Darbellay, 2013). Antitrust laws against CRAs have not been implemented in the US due to insufficient evidence against CRAs (Partnoy, 2002). Hence although high competition in the market and the 'issuer-pay' business model of ECAIs document that they can uplift the actual rating of bank exposure, there is neither any published evidence to prove the claim from a civil liability perspective nor have the regulators conducted any empirical research to investigate this. Hence, if the BSEC tries to introduce an antitrust law against CRAs, it is difficult for the commission to bring enough evidence to support the claims. This is one of the major legal drawbacks in the existing CRA institutions in Bangladesh. Therefore, creating an incentive in the institutions/incentive-based financial regulation and regulatory intervention to capture the real credit risk in the ECAI's rating notch may be a pragmatic solution. The initiative should be originated from the central bank as it relies on ECAIs for financial regulation. We mentioned earlier that, there is no evidence that any ECAI has lost its recognition status due to its inflated exposure rating. Hence, its central bank's responsibility to find an answer as to why banking sector credit risks are not properly quantified by external credit assessment institutions. In other words, before blaming the ECAI's rating, BB should justify what incentives they provide to ECAIs for quantifying the credit risk as they promote competition in the ECAIs market. Because competition requires the alignment of incentives and if the regulators introduce incentive-based regulation, the market participants would adopt their behavior and competition will bring welfare to the industry (Darbellay, 2013).

(ii) <u>Install a sanction mechanism/create a liability regime in the institutions and transparency in disclosure of ECAIs</u>

There are strong opinions in favor of imposing a cost upon CRAs for a wrong rating, especially after the financial crisis of 2007 (see details in Dodd-Frank Act, 2010; Partnoy, 2017). Their main point based on the 'regulatory license' view is that as a CRA's notch is used for banking regulation CRAs enjoy some benefit for their rating and their mis-rating would create a systemic risk in the entire financial system (due to its regulatory uses). Some scholars argue that credit rating agencies play a public function role rather than transactional role (like lawyers or investment bankers) (Rhee, 2015). Coffee (2011) mentioned that the 'issuer-pay model' and the 'regulatory license' are the basic critique for rating agencies performance. While in our discussion we mentioned that institutions of ECAIs in Bangladesh have no room for a liability regime for ECAIs in the case of exposure rating. If CDR/transition matrix of ECAIs could be aligned with Credit Information Bureau (CIB)[3] of BB and the national supervisors of ECAIs monitored the surveillance rating, then it is expected that the CDR will reflect how efficiently an ECAI's rating has captured the real credit risk. Then it would be a more realistic solution to install a sanction mechanism in the institutions, i.e., civil liability of ECAI's quantification of credit risk.

In addition, disclosure is not a disclosure if it does not disclose anything (Hemraj, 2015). Most of the Bangladeshi ECAI's rating methodologies did not express material information. Insufficient disclosure and the internal governance of CRAs has created a gray zone in the institutions, in our view. What is more, institutions do not impose any liability upon the rating committee (RC) members. While conducting our investigation we found that there is no consistency in the number of RC members among CRAs and the RC's appointment and remuneration systems are not disclosed. Therefore, the users/consumers of an ECAI's rating do not know who is behind the rating and who assigned it or whose responsibility it is in the case of mis-rating. While installing the sanction mechanism these issues also need to be addressed.

(iii) Strengthen the supervisory competence and discretion

Both the regulators have explained the issue regarding their shortage of human resources in supervision of ECAIs while interviewing with us. As the Ministry of Finance is the competent authority of the BSEC and BB; the ministry should listen to the voice of the national supervisors and should not intervene in the supervisory process for the interest of the national economy and strengthen the capacity of the national supervisors to reach to their regulatory mission.

(iv) Nationalize or merge the ECAI and create a duopoly market

Besides the above recommendation, one radical option may be to nationalize all ECAIs or create a duopoly market by merging all ECAIs

---

[3] CIB is an online database, which established by BB in 1992, that includes credit information of borrowers having an outstanding amount of BDT 50,000 (equivalent to USD 625) & above and defaulted credit card information having an outstanding amount of BDT 10,000 & above (BB, 2019b).

into two or three. It is hard to implement but it is possible. The justification is that an ECAI's rating is widely used for banking regulation and supervision and any distortion in the rating process has to be replaced by a bailout plan and ultimately by tax-payers money. As we mentioned in the Chapter 7 that, the bail out for Farmers banks in 2018 was incredibly costly (the government had to inject 1.78 times the capital than the initial paid-up capital of the bank). In addition, deposit insurance only covers a maximum of BDT 200,000 (equivalent to USD 2,316) per depositor per insured bank. Therefore, from the viewpoint of public interest, the government can nationalize all ECAIs and make the rating a 'public good'. The government would pay the rating fees to all the ECAIs in favor of commercial banks and commercial banks will determine their RWA based on the ECAI's rating notch. This radical shift might reduce the moral hazard problem of ECAIs. However, it requires a strong political commitment and decision from the government to not interfere in the rating process in a later stage. Because if the government interferes in the rating process, after nationalization, then, it makes no sense, and the rating will lose its acceptance.

8.3 'Sub-debt Trap' and Way Out

Why do banks fall into the 'sub-debt trap'? In our view, the regulation that creates wrong incentive for banks is largely responsible. For example, in the 'Guidelines on Subordinated Debt' for inclusion of sub-debt as regulatory capital there is maximum limits however, the serious missing point in the institutions is, there is no direction regarding the frequency of issuance of debt and no coupon rate cap for sub-debt. Besides there is no clear-cut roadmap on how sub-debtholders (especially institutional investors) play a role in the market discipline. In other words, the regulations failed to produce an effective outcome in due course and failed to fix the yield of sub-debt and its high transaction cost/issuance cost as well. Consequently, opportunistic and short-sighted bank mangers fall under the moral hazard for proper credit risk management as they rely on the issuance of sub-debt to maintain their minimum capital requirement. In our view, sub-debt failed to correct bank's risk appetite rather it encouraged banks to expand loan exposure. To sum up, it appears that the Bangladeshi banks are in a 'sub-debt trap' while complying with the Basel Accord due to a failure of 'commission' by regulators. We mention below a few policy implications for national regulators.

(i) Eliminate the bank incentive for subordinated debt arbitrage

This can be achieved in two ways. First, set limits on the frequency of debt issuance by the amendment of existing regulations. For example, the clause can be added in the sub-debt regulations that 'before fully redeeming the existing debt, banks are not allowed to issue new debt as a Tier 2 capital instrument'. Hopefully, this adjustment can make a cushion against risk appetite and bankers can avoid the moral hazard of monitoring and supervision of credit. Second, the central bank may impose sanctions on the owners of the bank's equity holders. For example, a sanction (kind of a poison pill) on sub-debt issuing banks, that they cannot offer any cash dividends to the shareholders until the debt is cleared. Since the study documented that bank owners are taking cash out from the business as a form of cash dividend whereas they should bring fresh equity due to maintaining the minimum CRAR. In fact, a dividend policy for the banks should be aligned with CET 1 ratio of banks. That is, banks which have stronger CET 1 capital base would be allowed to provide higher dividend in the form of cash and stock. Hence, we strongly hold the opinion that the cash dividend facility should be revoked for the banks (which issued a debt for capital adequacy purpose) as a sanction mechanism to shareholders and bank manager's risk-taking behavior.

(ii) Reduce the transaction cost/issue cost of sub-debt and coupon rate

Our earlier discussion in Chapter 4 shows that the transaction cost of sub-debt is around 1% of the total issued although BB mentioned it is around 6% of the issue size (BB, 2019a). BB and the BSEC should make the issue cost of debt fixed. In addition, there is no methodology to fix the interest rate and BB determined it with ad hoc basis. However, the beneficiaries of the high interest rate on sub-debt are banks, other financial institutional investors and high net worth individuals. The point is that banks offer lower interest rates to working-class households against their hardcore savings although they offer high interest rates to the institutional investors, which ultimately creates inequality in society. In other words, social justice denied in this context. Therefore, to increase welfare in society it is urgent to bring the interest rate of sub-debt in line with savings deposit rate.

(iii) <u>Re-fix the CRAR</u>

We shall note that the international standard for CRAR was 8% in 2010 (now it is 10% including buffer); however, BB has fixed it at 10% since December 31, 2007 which was the prime reason to issue sub-debt by IBBL in 2007. Why has Bangladesh Bank introduced such stringent capital regulation in 2007 beyond the global standard set by BIS in Basel Accord II? In our view, there is no rationale to introduce this stringent capital ratio beyond the international standard upon the domestic banks (in fact Basel regulation was prepared for internationally active banks). Hence one of our radical recommendation is to re-fix the CRAR in Bangladesh so it aligns with the international standard (or below). That is, reduce the CRAR from 12.5% to 10% (or below). This is a quite simple remedy to overcome the 'sub-debt trap' of Bangladeshi banks. In such a case, the central bank may conduct a fresh quantitative impact study (QIS) with the help of academic and professional experts to determine the actual CRAR required for Bangladeshi domestic banks rather than simply following on the BIS framework.

8.4   CONCLUDING REMARKS

In fact, as a public economic institution, it is the central bank's responsibility to formulate a robust prudential regulation to ensure financial stability in the market. To sum up, we attempted to decipher the anomalies of the Bangladeshi banking sector through Basel framework with two key findings. First, in our view, sub-debt did not bring resilience in the banking industry or enhance the quality of capital (as well as CRAR which aims to absorb the shock of systemic risk or bank run or unexpected loss in the banking industry). The danger of sub-debt is that it creates a systemic risk and chance for chain bankruptcies as sub-debts are funded by the industry players themselves. Earlier we document that the industry ROE (especially in the case of private commercial banks) tends to be increased while CRAR is maintained by issuing sub-debt. Second, the ALCO and credit risk management system of banks should be held responsible for expansion of loan exposure and subsequently accumulation of NPL. We strongly view that bank managers should act professionally rather than seeking short sighted profit/incentive or with 'animal spirit'. It is their professional obligation to be aware of the quality of an ECAI's rating instead of naïvely relying on an ECAI's rating notch and simply being a Basel standard compliant bank. If they naïvely rely on ECAIs rating, then what is the *raison d'être* of a bank in society? The study offers a set of institutional reforms in the existing ECAIs regulations to ensure ECAIs' rating quality. However, to what extent the ECAIs credit information/rating is adroit to tackle the 'fundamental uncertainty' of business could be a counter-argument from Post-Keynesian tradition. Perhaps the debate will be left as a future research agenda.

Finally, to improve the country's vulnerable banking sector and reap the expected outcome from adoption of the Basel regulation we provide a set of policy measures in this chapter. However, in case of 'enforcement' capability of microprudential regulations/policies, it might require bringing structural institutional reform in 'Bangladesh Bank Order 1972'. For instance, to establish a separate 'regulatory authority' either under the roof of central bank or outside the roof of central bank to oversee the banking prudential regulations and supervisory affairs (like the PRA at the Bank of England).

References

Andrie, A. M., Podpiera, A. M., & Sprincean, N. (2020, December 6). *Central bank independence and systemic risk* (BOFIT Discussion Papers 13/2020). The Bank of Finland Institute for Economics in Transition (BOFIT). Retrieved June 23, 2020 from: https://www.suomenpankki.fi/en/media-and-publications/publications/.

Bangladesh Bank (BB). (2009, October 14). *Guidelines on Subordinated debt for inclusion in Regulatory Capital* (BRPD Circular No. 13). Banking Regulation and Policy Department, Bangladesh Bank.

Bangladesh Bank (BB). (2014, December 21). *Guidelines on Risk Based Capital Adequacy (Revised Regulatory Capital Framework for banks in line with Basel III)* (BRPD Circular No. 18). Banking Regulation and Policy Department, Bangladesh Bank.

Bangladesh Bank (BB). (2019a). *Comprehensive framework on the development of the bond market in Bangladesh*. Bangladesh Bank. https://www.bb.org.bd/pub/publictn.php.

Bangladesh Bank (BB). (2019b). *Annual Report 2017–2018*. Bangladesh Bank.

Bangladesh Securities and Exchange Commission (BSEC). (1996). *Credit rating companies rules 1996*. BSEC. https://www.sec.gov.bd/home/lbook.

Bangladesh Securities and Exchange Commission (BSEC). (2018). *Annual Report 2017–2018*. BSEC. https://www.sec.gov.bd/home/annual_reports.

Coates, C. J. (2007). The goals and promise of the Sarbanes-Oxley Act. *The Journal of Economic Perspectives, 21*(1), 91–116.

Coffee, J. C. (2006). *Gatekeepers: The professions and corporate governance.* Oxford University Press.

Coffee, J. C. (2011). Rating reforms: The good, the bad and the ugly. *Harvard Business Law Review, 1*, 231–278.

Covitz, D. M., & Harrison, P. (2003). *Testing conflicts of interest at bond ratings agencies with market anticipation: Evidence that reputation incentives dominate* (Board of Governors of the Federal Reserve System Research Paper Series No. 2003-68). Board of Governors of the Federal Reserve System. https://www.federalreserve.gov/econres/feds/2003.htm.

Darbellay, A. (2013). *Regulating credit rating agencies.* Edward Elgar.

Dodd-Frank Act. (2010). *The Dodd-Frank Wall Street Reform and Consumer Protection Act* (Pu.L. 111-203, H.R. 4173). House of Congress.

European Commission (EC). (2016). *Study on the state of the credit rating market: Final Report.* European Commission. https://doi.org/10.2874/625016. https://ec.europa.eu/info/system/files/state-of-credit-rating-market-study-01012016_en.pdf.

Geiger, R. (2010). The development of the world economy and competition law. In R. Zach, A. Heinemann, & A. Kellerhals (Eds.), *The development of competitive law.* Edward Elgar.

Healy, P. M., & Palepu, K. (2003). The fall of Enron. *Journal of Economic Perspectives, 17*(2), 3–26. https://doi.org/10.2139/ssrn.417840.

Hemraj, M. (2015). *Credit rating agencies self-regulation, statutory regulation and case law regulation in the United States and European Union.* Springer International Publishing.

International Organization of Securities commissions (IOSCO). (2011). *Regulatory implementation of the statement of principles regarding the activities of credit rating agencies: Final Report* (FR04/11). IOSCO. https://www.iosco.org/publications/?subsection=public_reports.

Jenny, F. (2008). *The "coming out" of abuse of superior bargaining power in the antitrust world.* Ad-Hoc Expert Group on the Role of Competition Law and Policy in Promoting Growth and Development Geneva.

Langhor, H. M., & Langhor, P. T. (2008). *The rating agencies and their credit ratings what they are, how they work and why they are relevant.* Wiley.

Levitt, A. (2002, January 17). Who audit the auditors? *The New York Times.* https://www.nytimes.com/2002/01/17/opinion/who-audits-the-auditors.html.

Miglionico, A. (2014). *Recasting credit rating agencies' responsibility: Suggestions for reform* (Doctoral Dissertation, University of London). https://qmro.qmul.ac.uk/xmlui/bitstream/handle/123456789/12986/Miglionico_Andrea_PhD_Final_260216.pdf?sequence=1.

Panel on Audit Effectiveness (PAE). (2000, August 31). *Report and recommendations*. The Public Oversight Board. https://www.iasplus.com/en/binary/resource/pobaudit.pdf.

Partnoy, F. (2002). The paradox of credit ratings. In R. M. Levich, G. Majnoni, & C. M. Reinhart (Eds.), *Ratings, ratings agencies and the global financial system* (pp. 65–84). Kluwer Academic Publishing.

Partnoy, F. (2017). What's (still) wrong with credit ratings. *Washington Law Review, 92*(3), 1408–1472.

Rhee, R. J. (2015). Why credit rating agencies exist. *Banca Monte Dei Paschi Di Siena SpA, 44*(2), 161–175.

U.S. Securities and Exchange Commission (U.S. SEC). (2013). *Report to congress credit rating agency independence study*. U.S. Securities and Exchange Commission.

U.S. Securities and Exchange Commission (U.S. SEC). (2018). *Annual report on nationally recognized statistical rating organizations*. U.S. Securities and Exchange Commission.

Weber, R. H., & Bauman, S. (2013). Conflicts of interest and risk management practices. In J. Kleineman & L. Gorton (Eds.), *Credit rating agencies*. Stockholm Center for Commercial Law.

CHAPTER 9

Conclusion

9.1 Introduction

Scholars argued that financial stability is required for long-term economic growth (Lin & Huang, 2012; Moshirian & Wu, 2012). BB formally implemented the Basel Accord II in 2009 to bring financial stability to the country's financial system (BB, 2014). Hence, the study investigates the banking sector performance between the period 2009 and 2018 to examine to what extent the Basel framework was able to bring financial stability to Bangladesh. We observed during our investigated period that, the banking industry was more volatile, non-performing loans soared rapidly, the country had experienced a bank run situation and tax payers' money was wasted to recapitalize the inefficient state-owned banks. In addition, about BDT 225 billion in banking money was lost due to major bank scams, irregularities and heists within this period (CPD, 2018). The study found evidence that several imprudent initiatives had been taken by local regulators while implementing the Basel regulation. For example, enhancing 'competition' among ECAIs without creating appropriate 'incentive' in the institutions, consenting to the issuance of bulk amounts of sub-debts without considering its ill-impact, and repeatedly reviewing the loan rescheduling policy and relaxing the bad loans written-off policy. Those initiatives have created a moral hazard in the industry. In a word, country's microprudential banking regulations have failed to bring financial stability and financial discipline to the market which created a 'banking lost decade' for the banking and financial system of Bangladesh. This chapter summarizes the central theme of this academic work why microprudential banking regulations, specifically, the Basel Accords II and III implementation failed to bring financial stability to the Bangladeshi banking sector. The structure of the chapter is as follows. Section 9.2 describes the overall summary of the research findings which decipher the anomalies we raised in Chapter 1. Section 9.3 presents future research issues and concluding remarks.

9.2   SUMMARY OF THE RESEARCH FINDINGS AND DECIPHERING THE ANOMALIES

Research Findings Associated with Anomaly (i)

To explain the anomaly, (i) the study addresses from the institutional perspective, an analysis of ECAIs' regulations and examines the ECAIs' rating quality. We argue that due to ECAIs' low quality of credit information, the Basel regulation has a positive impact on loan growth. We hypothesized that ECAIs' ratings might not reflect the real credit risk of exposure. The follow-up question is why so? To answer this, the study stepped in to analyses of the institutions of ECAIs from two perspectives: (i) incentive structure and (ii) liability regime.

(i) Incentive structure

Scholars argued that regulatory use of ratings and the absence of 'competition' in the credit rating industry have reduced the CRAs' incentive for quality rating (Darballay & Partnoy, 2012; Mariano, 2012) which suggests that competition can provide 'incentives' for CRAs as market forces will determine the rating quality (the logic is CRAs will strive for 'reputation' and will not compromise with quality to increase their market share). However, some argued that when a CRA's rating is used for regulatory purposes, then 'competition' would provide the 'wrong incentive' and CRAs will fall under a 'race to bottom' in the sense of quality of the rating (Coffee, 2011; Darbellay, 2013). Their main point is that, due to regulatory arbitrage, CRAs lost their incentive for quality rating, especially in the US, and hence, CRAs became a triple A (AAA) producing factory (Coffee, 2011; Darbellay, 2013). Furthermore, the European Commission (EC, 2016, p. 95) opined that the impacts of competition in the credit rating markets remain unclear. Based on these contemporary academic theories and debate, we investigate the existing institutions of ECAIs in Bangladesh.

In our research, we have found that there is a crowd in the rating industry as eight domestic CRAs are recognized by BB as ECAIs. We attest that, as the Bangladeshi capital market is underdeveloped, CRAs/ECAIs lion's share of revenue is derived from bank exposure ratings. In addition, central bank has instructed the ECAIs to follow the unique pricing system for credit rating which limits ECAIs' ability to allocate necessary resources for quality rating and there is no visible yardstick to compare the rating quality among ECAIs. As a result, existing institutions failed to create any 'incentive' for ECAIs regarding quality ratings. Hence, in our view, these major structural loopholes within the institutions distort the ECAIs' incentive for quantification of the actual credit risk associated with bank exposure.

(ii) Liability regime

As ECAIs' rating is used for regulatory purposes, it provides an incentive for ECAIs to expand their businesses based on 'regulatory license' rather than 'reputational capital' and this regulatory reliance on ECAIs demands that 'credit rating agencies owe a duty of care to use reasonable skills and care when issuing rating' (Miglionico, 2019, p. 264). Besides, ECAIs' rating has a general public interest in the sense that when banks accumulated huge NPLs due to loan default or in the case of bank failure (e.g., FBL case), CRAR failed to capture the market shock. In turn, public money needed to recapitalize the SCBs or to bailout the private commercial bank. In our investigation, we have found such evidence in Bangladesh's case. Therefore, if there is no liability regime for ECAIs regarding bank exposure ratings in the institutions, the 'duty of care' (Miglionico, 2019) of ECAI or 'public interest' might be neglected.

The study critically analyzing the existing institutions, however, found that there is incentive for borrowers (firms) to be unrated after the initial rating, and hence, transition matrix of ECAIs failed to capture the real default rate of the rating. As a result, there is no evidence of ECAIs' mis-rating and subsequent loan default based on the transition matrix. Hence, we argued that 'reputation capital' is not enough to ensure the rating accuracy of ECAIs in the context of Bangladesh, as there is lacuna in the existing institutions to hold ECAIs responsible for their negligence in 'duty of care' or 'public interest.' However, ECAIs can escape this from two perspectives: (i) lack of proper information (especially financial information) for borrowers and (ii) small ECAIs who have little market share may use the excuse of inability of resource allocation for the accumulation of credit risk screening skills. To respond to the first claim, our view is that BB should make accessible its CIB database for ECAIs so that borrower's previous financial records can be matched with the central bank data warehouse. Regarding their second claim, the fact is, ECAIs' profit should be derived from rating the accuracy/quality of credit information which is used for regulatory purposes. Hence, our view is that 'incubation' cannot be justified in such a case. Our findings are similar to Miglionico (2019) who stressed this issue and after reviewing the UK, the US, the EU and Australian institutions regarding CRAs' liability regime, argued that 'civil liability regime' is still a missing point in the developed countries' CRA institutions as well.

However, we have discussed a possible way out, which includes creating 'incentives' in the institutions for ECAIs, revoking the ECAIs' remuneration so that market forces will correct ECAIs' rating quality and install 'sanction' mechanisms in the institutions to specify the liability regime of ECAIs. Besides this, we suggested that, to reduce excessive 'competition' in the rating industry of Bangladesh, either merge the ECAIs and create a duopolistic market or nationalize all the ECAIs to make credit ratings public goods.

In summary, as a 'quasi regulator,' ECAIs have a responsibility to take utmost care to verify financial information and quantify the credit risk accurately that is embedded in each exposure. On the other hand, the quality and accuracy of rating can be questioned from the existing institutional framework as "CRAs enjoy their reputational capital and regulatory reliance on rating as long as there is no clear-cut evidence of intention or gross negligence of inflated rating ... every rating may be justifiable within the domains of inexact qualitative analysis, based on its probabilistic nature, or on the basis of confidential information" (Miglionico, 2019, p. 272). In short, failure to create 'appropriate incentives' and define a 'civil liability regime' for ECAI in the institution, in our view, is a failure of 'omission,' and this a unique factor in the special context of Bangladesh that hampers obtaining the potential benefits derived from the adoption of Basel framework.

Research Findings Associated with Anomaly (ii)

The second anomaly that observed in the Bangladeshi banking industry has been examined from the real impact of sub-debt on banking performance which we termed as the 'sub-debt trap.' We strongly argue that sub-debt has provided ill-incentive to banks to adopt a 'leveraging' strategy and enhance ROE. We also critique banks' ALCOs for their imprudent funding in sub-debt which created a funding risk in the entire financial sector. We have found that Bangladeshi banks could not build up retained earnings (which is an important component in Tier 1 capital) due to loan loss provisioning and paid out cash dividends to the equity holders. As a result, banks tend to increase Tier 2 capital and subordinated debt is the only option at hand in such a case. From our empirical investigation, we have found that there is a strong positive relationship with ROE, cash dividend and CRAR when sub-debt is considered as Tier 2 regulatory capital. We presume that banks are using sub-debt to enhance their ROE and Bangladeshi banks are using sub-debt as an instrument for a 'leveraging' strategy to take more risk or extend their loan portfolio. Besides, sub-debts are not issued through public offerings and not traded on the stock exchanges (except one sub-debt); hence, debt yield failed to control banks' risk-taking behavior. We observed that Bangladeshi banks fell into the 'sub-debt trap' (as they have multiple incentives to issue sub-debt), which creates systemic risk in the financial system since banks and other financial institutions hold the sub-debts of each other. In our view, this failure of 'commission' creates a potential systemic risk to financial stability and market discipline. We offer several policy measures to tackle this unique problem which includes reducing the bank's incentive to use sub-debt, issuing sub-debt through public offerings and trading in the stock exchanges, stop pay out cash dividend and so on.

One important observation from issuance of sub-debt is that two SCBs (Janata Bank Limited and Rupali Bank Limited) have issued sub-debt for BDT 21 billion between 2009 and 2018. The reason for low amount of issuance of sub-debt is, during the investigated period, SCBs were recapitalized by the MoF from budgetary allocation to maintain minimum CRAR. For instance, the paid-up capital of Sonali Bank Limited,[1] the largest state-owned commercial bank in Bangladesh, has

---

[1] Annual Report 2018 of Sonali Bank Limited is available at https://www.sonalibank.com.bd/.

been increased by 403.33 percent from 2010 to 2018 (paid-up capital was BDT 9,000 million in 2010 which reached at BDT 45,300 million in 2018). However, the IMF (2020, p. 12) in its recent 'Staff Report' recommends to the competent authorities that 'a clear definition of the public mandate with transparent budget support' is required while recapitalization of SCBs. We shall note that the four SCBs' (Sonali Bank Ltd., Janata Bank Ltd, Agrani Bank Ltd. and Rupali Bank Ltd.) 92.7% loans and advances go to the private sectors and only 7.3% disbursed to the SOEs/public entities as of December 2018 (see the annual reports for the year 2018 of the said four SCBs). ECAIs' ratings are used while computation of the RWA of SCBs under the Basel Accords and their credit portfolios are dominated by the private sectors. Hence, credit risk quantification-related discussion can be discussed with the PCBs and SCBs in the same/single framework. However, the comprehensive evaluation of asset quality of SCBs should also be discussed with the political economy landscape as the MoF has mandates on SCBs administration and governance (see FID, 2010). To sum up our observation regarding SCBs is, so far as BB applies the Basel-type capital adequacy requirement to supervise the category of state-owned commercial banks and specialized banks, too, it would make sense of investigating their performance in the same/single frame of discussion. The regulator should offer a different criterion which requires the capital adequacy seemingly necessary for each category of banks.

9.3   Future Research Issues and Concluding Remarks

The institutional approaches adopted in the study will help to understand the reasons for the banking sector malaise from an unconventional point of view. However, we have acknowledged that there are a couple of limitations to the study. Those can be considered as the pathway for future research. First, further research on ECAIs' cumulative default rate (CDR) should be conducted for the sake of public interest and social welfare of the country, as without accurate CDR data, it is not feasible to create incentives or identify the civil liability regime of ECAIs in the existing institutions. Central bank can take initiative to digitalize all ECAI databases with the CIB and compute actual CDR of ECAIs on bank exposure. Second, when subordinated debt is considered as regulatory capital, the yield of the sub-debt is the crux for market discipline. As yield is not disclosed in the banks' annual report and the sub-debts are not traded in the market, it might be the regulator's responsibility to conduct empirical research into what extend sub-debt yield acts as market discipline and restrains the banks from taking more risk. Third, in fact, we have a few alternatives at hand to substitute the regulatory uses of CRAs/ECAIs ratings (Darbellay, 2013; EC, 2015). We shall note that common equity to Tier 1 capital is still fixed at 6% in Basel framework, which shows that banking firms are highly leveraged. Hence, to maintain financial stability and control banks' risk appetite, we should rather fix a standard ratio considering the capital charges under supervisory review process (SRP). In this regard, Bangladeshi decision makers, regulators and other stakeholders of the industry should have envisioned for fully implementing the Basel Accord with a comprehensive mind as banks are still struggling to comply with capital charge under pillar I of Basel framework.

In fact, "required minima meant that they provide not much a buffer against (unexpected) loss, instead the buffer was provided by the margin that the banks voluntarily carried in excess of those minima" (Goodhart, 2011). However, the reality is, the Bangladeshi banking industry has a total loan loss provision (which is maintained to cover expected loss of the banking industry) shortfall of BDT 66.1 billion as of December 2018 which was surplus of BDT 3.1 billion in 2009 (see BB, 2018, p. 117). Besides, country's Deposit Insurance System (DIS) coverage limits only a maximum amount of BDT 200,000 per depositor (see BB, 2020; FID, 2020). This means that the expected loss (loss against non-performing loans) is still not covered by the banking sector's loan loss provision and the DIS has guaranteed only a little amount of household deposits in banks. Most importantly, after implementation of Basel Accord, one should review carefully that does it contribute to improving the quality of banks capital in a meaningful way, enhancing resilience of the banking sector and bring market discipline in Bangladesh? This is a deeper and more complex question from an efficiency and social welfare perspective. Hopefully, this quest for inquiry will open many windows for future research.

REFERENCES

Bangladesh Bank (BB). (2014, December 21). *Guidelines on Risk Based Capital Adequacy (Revised Regulatory Capital Framework for banks in line with Basel III)* (BRPD Circular No. 18). Banking Regulation and Policy Department, Bangladesh Bank.

Bangladesh Bank (BB). (2018). *Financial Stability Report, 2018, Issue 9.* Financial Stability Department, Bangladesh Bank.

Bangladesh Bank (BB). (2020). *Annual Report 2018–2019.* Bangladesh Bank.

Center for Policy Dialogue (CPD). (2018). *Bangladesh economy in FY2017-18 interim review of macroeconomic performance.* Center for Policy Dialogue.

Coffee, J. C. (2011). Rating reforms: The good, the bad and the ugly. *Harvard Business Law Review, 1,* 231–278.

Darballay, A., & Partnoy, F. (2012). *Credit rating agencies and regulatory* (Working Paper). University of San Diego School of Law.

Darbellay, A. (2013). *Regulating credit rating agencies.* Edward Elgar.

European Commission (EC). (2015). *Study on the feasibility of alternatives to credit ratings: Final Report.* European Commission. https://doi.org/10.2874/370060. https://ec.europa.eu/info/publications/study-feasibility-alternatives-credit-ratings_en.

European Commission (EC). (2016). *Study on the state of the credit rating market: Final Report.* European Commission. https://doi.org/10.2874/625016. https://ec.europa.eu/info/system/files/state-of-credit-rating-market-study-01012016_en.pdf.

Financial Institutions Division (FID). (2010). *Allocation of business 2010.* Department of Banks and Financial Institutions. Retrieved June 28, 2020, from Financial Institutions Division, Ministry of Finance, Government of the People's Republic of Bangladesh: https://fid.gov.bd/site/page/e0e6e343-e4c8-4c86-a0fa-cad36b1175fc/Mandate-of-FID.

Financial Institutions Division (FID). (2020). *Draft Amanat Surokka Ain 2020 (Deposit Protection Act 2020).* Department of Banks and Financial Institutions. Retrieved February 4, 2021, from Financial Institutions Division, Ministry of Finance, Government of the People's Republic of Bangladesh: https://fid.gov.bd/sites/default/files/files/fid.portal.gov.bd/draft_law/b55929ed_9767_4cd9_8f5b_b5b8cad36862/%E0%A6%B8%E0%A7%81%E0%A6%B0%E0%A6%95%E0%A7%8D%E0%A6%B7%E0%A6%BE%20%E0%A6%86%E0%A6%87%E0%A6%A8.pdf.

Goodhart, C. (2011). *The Basel Committee on Banking Supervision: A history of the early years 1974–1997.* Cambridge University Press.

International Monetary Fund (IMF). (2020). *Requests for disbursement under the rapid credit facility and purchase under the rapid financing instrument: Press release; staff report; and statement by the executive director for Bangladesh* (IMF Country Report No. 20/187). International Monetary Fund.

Lin, P.-C., & Huang, H.-C. (2012). Banking industry volatility and growth. *Journal of Macroeconomics, 34*, 1007–1019.

Mariano, B. (2012). Market power and reputational concerns in the rating industry. *Journal of Banking and Finance, 36*, 1616–1626.

Miglionico, A. (2019). *The governance of credit rating agencies regulatory regime and liability issues.* Edward Elgar.

Moshirian, F., & Wu, Q. (2012). Banking industry volatility and economic growth. *Research in International Business and Finance, 26*, 428–442.

ANNEXURES

See Tables A.1, A.2, A.3, A.4, and A.5.

A K M K. Hasan and Y. Suzuki, *Implementation of Basel Accords in Bangladesh*, https://doi.org/10.1007/978-981-16-3472-7

Table A.1 Country-wise financial soundness indicators (FSIs) of banking sector (percent, end of Q4)

Countries	Regulatory Capital to Risk-Weighted Assets				Regulatory Tier 1 Capital to Risk-Weighted Assets				NPLs to Total Gross Loans				Return on Assets				Renin on Equity			
	2016	2017	2018	2019	2016	2017	2018	2019	2016	2017	2018	2019	2016	2017	2018	2019	2016	2017	2018	2019
Majen South Asian Economies																				
Bangladesh	**11.1**	**10.7**	**105**	**11.6**	**8.1**	**7.5**	**6.8**	**7.7**	**8.9**	**8.9**	**9.9**	**8.9**	**1.3**	**1.4**	**0.9**	**1.1**	**16.7**	**19.0**	**12.9**	**16.6**
India	13.0	12.8	12.9	15.4	10.7	11.0	11.9	14.7	9.2	10.0	9.5	9.2	0.4	0.3	–	0.2	5.1	4.5	– 0.2	2.7
Pakistan	16.3	15.8	16.2	17.0	13.1	12.9	13.2	14.0	10.1	8.4	8.0	8.6	1.3	0.9	0.8	0.8	14.4	11.5	10.7	11.2
Sri Lanka	14.3	15.2	15.1	16.5	11.4	12.4	12.0	13.0	2.6	2.5	3.4	4.7	19.0	2.0	1.8	1.4	24.5	24.7	20.3	16.0
Advanced Economies																				
Japan*	16.2	16.7	17.0	17.3	13.4	14.2	14.8	15.1	1.4	1.2	1.1	1.1	0.3	0.3	0.3	0.2	8.3	8.1	7.3	6.1
United States	14.2	14.5	14.8	14.7	13.2	13.5	13.8	13.7	1.3	1.1	0.9	0.9	0.4	0.3	0.4	0.3	3.2	2.9	3.4	2.9
United Kingdom	20.8	20.5	21.4	N/A	16.9	17.1	17.9	N/A	0.9	0.7	1.1	N/A	0.3	0.5	0.5	N/A	3.8	7.6	7.5	N/A

*Japan data represent Q3 each year **-Not available
Source IMF, Retrieved on 26 June 2020

Table A.2 Banking sector performance between 2009 and 2018

Types of Banks	NPL radio									
	2009	2010	2011	2012	2013	2014	2015	2016	2017	2018
State Owned Commercial Banks	21.93	15 66	1137	23.87	19.76	22.23	21.46	25.05	26.52	30
Specialized Banks	25.91	24.15	24.55	26.77	26.78	32.81	23.24	26.02	23.39	19.5
Private Commercial Banks	3.92	3.15	2.95	4.58	4.54	4.98	4.85	4.58	4.87	5.5
Foreign Commercial Banks	2.27	2.99	2.96	3.53	5.46	7.3	7.77	9.56	7.04	6.5
All Banks	9.21	7.27	6.12	10.03	8.93	9.69	8.79	9.23	9.31	10.3
	ROA									
State Owned Commercial Banks	0.96	1.11	1.34	−0.56	0.59	−0.55	−0.04	−0.16	0.21	−1.3
Specialized Banks	−0.37	0.19	0.03	0.06	−0.82	−0.63	−1.15	−2.8	−3.49	−2.8
Private Commercial Banks	1.55	2.14	1.59	0.92	0.95	0.99	1	1.03	0.89	0.7
Foreign Commercial B anks	3.18	2.87	3.24	3.27	2.98	3.38	2.92	2.56	2.24	2.61
All Banks	1.37	1.78	1.54	0.64	0.88	0.64	0.77	0.68	0.67	0.3
	ROE									
State Owned Commercial Banks	26.15	18.83	19.66	−11.87	10.93	−13.46	−1.47	−6.02	3.45	−29.6
Specialized Banks	−171.68	−3.17	−0.92	−1.06	−12.04	−5.97	−5.79	−6.94	−17.19	−13.5
Private Commercial Banks	20.95	20.94	15.69	10.17	9.76	10.26	10.75	11.09	12.01	11
Foreign Commercial Banks	22.38	16.99	16.99	17.29	16.93	17.29	14.59	13.08	11.31	12.4

(continued)

Table A.2 (continued)

Types of Banks	NPL radio									
	2009	2010	2011	2012	2013	2014	2015	2016	2017	2018
All Banks	21.72	17,02	17.02	8.2	10.8	8.09	10.51	9.42	9.6	3.9
	CRAR									
State Owned Commercial Banks	9	8.9	11.7	8.1	10.8	8.3	6.35	5.86	5	1.9
Specialized Banks	0.4	−7.3	−4.5	−7.8	−9.7	−17.3	−31.95	−33.67	−35.5	−31.7
Private Commercial Banks	121	10.1	11.5	11.4	12.6	12.5	12.38	12.36	12.5	12.8
Foreign Commercial Banks	28.1	15.6	21	20.6	20.2	22.6	25.6	25.37	24.9	26
All Banks	11.6	9.3	11.4	10.5	11.5	11.3	10.84	10.8	10.8	10.5

Source Suzuki and Hasan (2018) and several issues of BB quarterly review

Table A.3 ECAI's Credit Rating Categories Mapped with BB's Rating Grade

BB Rating Grade	Equivalent Rating of S&P and Fitch	Equivalent Rating of Moody	Equivalent Rating of CRISL	Equivalent Rating of CRAB	Equivalent Rating of NCR1	Equivalent Rating of ECRL	Equivalent Rating of ACRSL	Equivalent Rating of ACRL	Equivalent Rating of WASO
1	AAA to AA	Aaa to Aa	AAA, AA+, AA, AA-	AAA, AA1, AA2, AA3	AAA, AA+, AA, AA-	AAA, AA+, AA, AA-	AAA, AA+, AA, AA-	AAA, AA+, AA, AA-	AAA, AA1, AA2, AA3
2	A	A	A+, A, A-	Al, A2, A3	A+, A, A-	A+, A, A-	A+, A, A-	A+, A, A-	Al, A2, A3
3	BBB	Baa	BBB+, BBB, BBB-	BBB1, BBB2, BBB3	BBB+, BBB, BBB-	BBB+, BBB, BBB -	BBB+, BBB, BBB-	BBB+, BBB, BBB-	BBB1, BBB2, BBB3
4	BB to B	Ba to B	BB+, BB, BB-	BB1, BB2, BB3	BB+, BB, BB-	BB+, BB, BB-	BB+, BB, BB-	BB+, BB, BB-	BB1, BB2, BB3
5	Below B	Below B	B+, B, B, CCC+, CCC, CCC-, CC+, CC, CC-	B1, B2, B3, CCC1, CCC2, CCC3, CC	B+, B, B-	B +, B, B-	B+ , B, B-, CC+, CC,CC-	B+ , B, B-, CCC	B1, B2, B3, CCC
6			C+, C, C-,D	C, D	C+ C, C-, D	D	C+, C, C-, D	CC+, CC, CC-, C+, C, C-, D	CCI, CC2, CC3, C+, C, C-, D
Short-Term Rating Category Mapping									
SI	F1+	PI	ST-1	ST-1	N1	ECRL-1	ST-1	AR-1	P-1
S2	F1	P2	ST-2	ST-2	N2	ECRL-2	ST-2	AR-2	P-2
S3	F2	P3	ST-3	ST-3	N3	ECRL-3	ST-3	AR-3	P-3
S4	F3	NP	ST-4	ST-4	N4	ECRL-4	ST-4	AR-4	P-4
S5, S6	B, C, D		ST-5, ST-6	ST-5, ST-6	N5	D	ST-5, ST-6	AR-5, AR-6	P-5, P-6

Table A.4 ECAI's Credit Rating Categories Mapped with BB's SME Rating Grade

BB SME Rating Grade 01	Equivalent Rating of BDRAL	Equivalent Rating of CRISL	Equivalent Rating of CRAB	Equivalent Rating of ECRL	Equivalent Rating of ARGUS 03	Equivalent Rating of ALPHA 04	Equivalent Rating of NCRL 05	Equivalent Rating of WASO 06
SME 1	SE1, ME 1	CRISL Me-1/Se-1	CRAB-ME 1/SE 1	ESME 1	AQSE 1/AQME 1	ARSME-1	NSME-1	WCR SE 1/ME 1
SME 2	SE2, ME 2	CRISL Me-2/Se-2	CRAB-ME 2/SE 2	ESME 2	AQSE 2/AQME 2	ARSME-2	NSME-2	WCR SE 2/ME 2
SME 3	SE3, ME 3	CRISL Me-3/Se-3	CRAB-ME 3/SE 3	ESME 3	AQSE 3/AQME 3	ARSME-3	NSME-3	WCR SE 3/ME 3
SME 4	SE4, ME 4	CRISL Me-4/Se-4	CRAB-ME 4/SE 4	ESME 4	AQSE 4/AQME 4	ARSME-4	NSME-4	WCR SE 4/ME 4
SME 5	SE5, ME 5	CRISL Me-5/Se-5	CRAB-ME 5/SE 5	ESME 5	AQSE 5/AOME 5	ARSME-5	NSME-5	WCR SE 5/ME 5
SME 6	SE6, SE7, SE0, ME 6 ME 7, ME 8	CRISL Me-6,7,8,9,10/Se-6,7,8,9,10	CRAB-ME 6,7,8/SE 6,7,8	ESME 6,7,8	AQSE6,7,8/AQME 6,7,8	ARSME-6,7,8	NSME-6,7,8	WCR SE 6,7,8/ME 6,7,8

Source BB (2014, pp. 23)

Table A.5 Exchange rate (Taka/USD)

2009–2010	69.18
2010–2011	71.17
2011–2012	79.10
2012–2013	79.93
2013–2014	77.72
2014–2015	77.67
2015–2016	78.26
2016–2017	79.12
2017–2018	82.10
2018–2019	84.03

Source BB, Monthly Economic Trend, November 2019

Appendix: History of CRAs in the US and Regulatory References of Their Rating Notch by the US Regulators

Introduction

The history of credit rating to some extent is related with the sovereign bond issuance history of Europe in seventeenth century and US corporate bond rating history in the nineteenth century. In Europe, mainly the Dutch had developed a significant government bond market in seventeenth century to finance wars and other large-scale projects while in the US, government bonds played vital role in financing the railway industry (Scalet & Kelly, 2012). However, CRAs' evolution history is much more linked with the nineteenth and early twentieth century's US economy. Hence, this historical background of CRAs in the US will help us to understand the initiation of using CRAs' rating notch for regulatory purposes.

In the 1800s, CRAs mainly provided credit information to merchandisers in the US and Europe, who used the information to minimize their merchandising risk. CRAs were the necessary information brokers through informal sources to formal appointees. The mercantile agencies established the concept of 'rating' and published printed reports for its subscribers during this period. On the other hand, in the early 1900s, CRAs had produced reports mainly to rate the US securities which were used as a chief source of capital for the US railway reconstruction project. Therefore, CRAs' historical background in the US can be categorized into two broad timelines such as before 1907 and after 1907. The period before 1907, may be termed as the 'classical period' of credit reporting agencies whereas, the story after 1907 can be termed as the 'modern era' of credit rating (see Table A.6 for developments in these two periods). In the following sections, we discuss the historical evolution of the US CRAs in detail.

CRAs in Classical and Modern Period

Role of CRAs in the 'classical period'

Until the nineteenth century, American merchandisers relied on personal contact and commitment for credit information of other parties (Madison, 1974). The credit agent's profession grew to be popular with the merchants as they provided borrowers personal creditworthiness (Madison, 1974). Wholesalers in New York had first hired credit investigators for their business in the 1820s; however, this attempt was not sustained due to coordination problems. Later in the 1830s, the American society invented a 'credit reporting agency' to coordinate all information of a client from various sources and disseminate the information to the merchandisers (Olegario, 2001). In fact, the unavailability of financial and moral information of the individuals was the prime reason for the emergence of the credit reporting agencies in the US in the early 1830s (Beckman, 1930; Harold, 1938; Lynch, 2009). The credit reporting process was in fact a kind of 'hub and spoke' system (Klein, 2001). The agency did not provide any written report to the merchants and rather verbally described the report while maintaining high confidentiality (Klein, 2001). The financial crisis in 1837 had also played an important role for creation of credit rating agencies as the merchants began to realize that the lack of information was one of the major reasons for the financial crisis (Darbellay, 2013). In the classical period, we have found two major credit reporting agencies namely the 'mercantile agency' which was founded by Lewis Tappan in 1841 and the 'Bradstreet agency' founded in 1849 by John M. Bradstreet (Madison, 1974). The mercantile agency is considered as the founder of modern CRAs in the US (Darbellay, 2013). Below we discuss in detail the 'Mercantile Agency' to portray the CRAs' picture in the 1800s US market.

'Mercantile Agency' the first CRA in the US

In 1841, Lewis Tappan first established the 'Mercantile Agency' with aims to sell 'creditworthy information' of businesses to the US lenders (Sylla, 2002). Lewis Tappan may fairly be called the originator and father of

Table A.6 Timeline of CRAs evolution in the US

Before 1907							
1820s	*1830s*	*1840s*	*1850s*	*1860s*	*1870s*	*1880s*	*1890s*
New York Credit investigators	Credit reporting agency	Mercantile agency	Mercantile agency's reference book	HV Poor started to published annual report on railroad			
	Financial crisis in the US	Bradstreet agency					

After 1907										
1900s	*1910s*	*1920s*	*1930s*	*1940s*	*1950s*	*1960s*	*1970s*	*1980s*	*1990s*	*2000s*
Moody established		Fitch established. Standard published first rating report		Standard and Poor merged as S&P			NRSRO' rule incorporate	New rating agencies enter in the market		

the mercantile agency system (Vose, 1916). After his retirement from the agency in 1849, his brother Arthur Tappan and Benjamin Douglass took over the business. In 1854, Mr. Douglass assumed sole ownership of the mercantile agency from Arthur Tappan and made Robert Graham Dun a partner (Vose, 1916). In 1859, Mr. Douglass retired and sold his entire share to his partner Robert G. Dun (p. 77). In this way the entire ownership of the company had transferred to Dun, a non-sponsor of the firm. The first credit rating report (named as 'Mercantile Agency's Reference Book') was published by the agency in 1859 which contained 20,268 clients name from the US and Canada with their respective ratings (Vose, 1916). Subsequently its next versions were published in 1864 and 1866 with 123,000 and 200,000 client's names, respectively. The invention of the typewriting machine in the 1870s in the US made the printing job smoother and faster and made it easier to record client's information (Jeong, 2016). The agency had 300 correspondents in 1844 and reached to more than 10,000 by the 1870s, and by the end of 1900th century it produced around 2,000 volumes of credit reports (Jeong, 2016). This bulk volume of reports documents how rapidly the mercantile agency's business had expanded in the US market. The agency entered the Mexican market and expanded its business in several South African cities like Cape Town, Durban, Port Elizabeth, all states of the German Empire, Austria-Hungary and the Netherlands in 1901–1914 (Jeong, 2016). According to Vose (1916), Lewis Tappan established the mercantile agency in 1841, Benjamin Douglass strengthened it to a national level, Robert Graham Dun expanded it to the entire US and Canada, and finally Robert Dun Douglass made it accepted worldwide in the early 1900s. 'Dun & Bradstreet' of the US is the current version of the 'Mercantile Agency.'

However, the road of the classical period was rocky, and several hurdles had to be passed to gain market confidence. For instance, lawsuits from rated businessmen to the agency, and business houses attempting to pass regulatory legislation against the agency (Darbellay, 2013). However, most of the verdicts in the 1800s were in favor of the agency which helped them with acceptance of their credit rating reports among the business community during this period (Madison, 1974). Another major problem of CRAs in the 1800s the improvement of the quality of credit reports which arose due to a low paid system and part-time correspondent (Madison, 1974). The reporting quality was improved by recruiting full-time paid reporters in most cities of America in the 1870s and contacting businessmen directly with some set of questions (like a modern questionnaire) to prepare more reliable and active credit reports (Madison, 1974). Gradually, overcoming the internal weaknesses and legal threats, CRAs became a reliable center for providing creditworthiness information of businesses in the 1890s.

The Role of CRAs in the 'modern period'

The US government had issued railroad bonds to finance the railroad construction project in the 1800s (Mundy, 1907). CRAs' roles had changed in the beginning of the twentieth century as the agencies had started to do securities rating considering the experience of commercial credit rating (Darbelly, 2013). John Moody published the first security rating (using rating symbols) book 'Analyses of railroad investment' in 1909 based on his prior working experience as a financial analyst on railway bond-related financial information (Harold, 1938). His source of information and inspiration came from the then two contemporary books 'The Earing Powers of Railroads' published by Floyd Mundy in 1903 and 'American Railways as Investments' published by Carl Snyder in 1907 (Harold, 1938). The main limits in both publications were: No rating symbols were used in the books and the bond and security of American railroad ratings were not published together. John Moody classified the railroad securities according to their value and marketability and rated all railroad bonds of the country, which was the most attractive part of his book to the investors (Harold, 1938, p. 12). The business grew rapidly, and Moody had covered one hundred percent of US bond rating by 1924 (Partnoy, 1999). Poor's publishing company was the second that published security and bond ratings by its prominent analyst Freeman Putney in 1916 (Harold, 1938). Standard Statistics Company, Inc. facilitated interpretation of the data and condensed their language into symbols and ratings, meaning that eventually they published their first version in 1922 with the initiatives and work of Harold G. Parker and R.S. Dana (Harold, 1938). Standard Statistics merged with Poor's to form 'Standard and Poors' in 1941 (West, 1973) and today's 'S&P Global,' is the latest version of the company. The security rating industry got its fourth entrant in 1924 as 'Fitch Publishing Company,' an extended business wing of Francis Emory Fitch Inc. (West, 1973).

According to Harold (1938), the attitude of investors toward the rating publication companies in 1900–1924 was mixed. Some bond traders who had the intelligence to analyze security and bond profitability had coldly welcomed the publishing of ratings of securities and bonds as they considered that this would cut their speculative profit (Harold, 1938). However, it was welcomed by commercial banks and investors as the rating symbols expressed the judgment of investment quality (Darbellay, 2013). Some institutional investors' financial analysts seemed to feel pressured, as the 'psychological value of confirmation' of their own judgment on a specific security and bond compared with the rating published by rating agencies, due to fearing the loss of incentive from the corporation to rate their instrument too high (Harold, 1938). Overall, the rating book published by the agencies acted as a 'source of information' and 'trust' during this period and 'reputational consideration' was the most important driver of CRAs' behavior in order to gain market share during 1920–1930 (Darbellay, 2013; Partnoy, 1999). In summary, 'competition' within the industry and 'communication' within the stakeholders of securities and bonds helped the rating agencies to build 'reputational capital' which helped CRAs to gain acceptance of their ratings by US regulators.

REGULATORY REFERENCES OF CRAS RATING NOTCH AND ITS IMPACT

The two US regulators, the Office of the Comptroller of the Currency (OCC) and the U.S. Securities and Exchange Commission (U.S. SEC), considered CRAs' rating notch for regulatory purposes in different occasions. First, on the heels of a sharp decline in credit quality in 1931, the OCC ruled that banks holdings of publicly rated bonds had to be rated 'BBB' or better by at least one rating agency if they were to be carried at book value; otherwise, the bonds were to be written down to market value and 50 percent of the resulting book losses were to be charged against net bank capital (Cantor & Packer, 1994). If a bond was not rated 'Baa' or better, its short-term price action would have an impact on the adequacy of bank capital, regardless of whether a loss was realized (West, 1973). In addition, in 1936, OCC and the Federal Reserve again revised the rules and prohibited banks altogether from holding bonds not rated triple B ('BBB') or above by at least two agencies (Cantor & Packer, 1994). Due to the difference between an investment grade bond and speculative bond, the rating of bonds became crucial for investment by banks, pension funds and mutual funds as well (Cantor

& Packer, 1994). The National Association of Supervisors of the State Banks also issued a similar resolution in 1949. The National Association of Insurance Commissioners began equating the term 'investment grade' as bonds having 'Baa' or better in 1951 (West, 1973). This trend continued until the 1970s when bond ratings were considered an essential part of the financial regulation (Darbellay, 2013). Second, the U.S. SEC rules while incorporating 'Nationally Recognized Statistical Rating Organization' (NRSRO) in 1973, making credit rating a regulatory role which allows the broker dealers to calculate their net capital requirements based on credit ratings from a NRSRO certified by the SEC (Pinto, 2006). It indicates that the NRSRO rating is a legal instrument that is used for mapping the capital requirement. The NRSRO concept was widely accepted by other context in federal and state legislation.

Although the US regulators were significantly using the CRAs' rating notch for regulation purposes, the rating agencies in the US market were limited to three until 1975 and the market was getting more competitors in the 1980s (Cantor & Packer, 1994). Currently there are ten NRSROs which are recognized by the US regulators (U.S. SEC, 2018). However, scholars are severely criticizing the regulatory uses of CRAs' ratings. Abdelal (2007), while quoting the comment of the US Justice Department, noted that the NRSRO designation was inherently anticompetitive and 'it does not maintain any form of ongoing oversight.' Partnoy (1999, 2006) more precisely mentioned that, 'in these ways credit rating agencies were granted a regulatory benefit, one kind of 'regulatory license' to generate economic rent by US governmental agencies.' In fact, the consequence of the regulatory uses of CRAs' ratings had switched the pay model of CRAs and created an opportunity to enjoy economic rent.

Switching the Pay Model of CRA
Investors were paying the rating agency assessment until 1970 (House of Lords, 2009); however, the revenue model/fee paying model of CRAs had changed to 'issuer pay' during the 1970s. There are two reasons behind this historic move of pay model from 'investors pay' model to 'issuer pay' model. Firstly, the default of Penn Central in 1970 for $80 million commercial paper caused a panic in the industry and the issuers of the commercial paper were seeking ratings from CRAs to calm down the market and reassure the investors (Cantor & Packer, 1994). Some academics referred to it as 'restoration of confidence of the investors' (Darbellay, 2013). The second is the 'free rider problem' of the investors

pay model. Some investors pay the rating fees directly to the agencies and others are getting the information without any cost (Partnoy, 1999). To solve this problem, agencies started to charge their rating fees to the issuers considering it as 'public goods' and from the issuers perspective as the rating is used for 'regulatory purposes' as well, they have incentive to pay the rating fees to the agencies (Partnoy, 1999). Indeed, rating-based regulation played a key role in changing the rating fees model from 'subscribers' to 'issuers' (Darbellay, 2013).

Moreover, due to growth of structured finance or securitization in the US market, a new door had opened for corporate rating for CRAs (Hunt, 2009) and lead the US CRAs' majority revenue to be derived from structured finance (Coval et al., 2009). Investors are heavily dependent on CRAs' ratings and assessment (as third-party assessments of the riskiness of securitization products) on various structured capital market products due to their complex structure; the contents of the underlying asset pool were frequently not revealed (House of Lords, 2009). Considering this role of CRAs, some scholars mentioned them as the 'gatekeeper of capital' in the US financial market (Coffee, 2006; Hunt, 2009). To sum up, the regulatory references of CRAs' rating notch have two great implications on CRAs' business. First, it changes the initial business model and second, the reliability/trust in CRAs rating had increased significantly among US investors.

CONCLUSION

To conclude, the above-mentioned historical context document that CRAs started their business in the 1800s in the US for providing information about the creditworthiness of business entities. Once their rating had been accepted by investors; CRAs gradually accumulated 'reputational capital.' US financial regulators are extensively using the CRAs' rating notch for regulatory purposes from this 'reputational capital' point of view which CRAs had built over their century-long experiences in the market. However, we cannot deny that such regulatory reference has created an economic rent for the US credit rating agencies.

REFERENCES

Abdelal, R. (2007). *Capital rules: The construction of global finance*. Harvard University Press.

Beckman, T. N. (1930). *Credit and collection in theory and practice*. MC Graw Hill Company.

Cantor, R., & Packer, F. (1994). The credit rating industry. *The Journal of Fixed Income, 5*(3), 10–34.

Coffee, J. C. (2006). *Gatekeepers: The professions and corporate governance*. Oxford University Press.

Coval, J. D., Jurek, J., & Stafford, E. (2009). The economics of structured finance. *Journal of Economic Perspectives, 23*(1), 3–25.

Harold, G. (1938). *Bond rating as an investment guide, an appraisal of their effectiveness*. The Ronald Press Company.

House of Lords. (2009). *Select committee on economic affairs, banking supervision and regulation, 2nd report of session 2008–09 Volume 1: Report*. Authority of the House of Lords.

Hunt, J. P. (2009). Credit rating agencies and the 'worldwide credit crisis': The limits of reputation, the insufficiency of reform, and a proposal for improvement. *Columbia Business Law Review, 1,* 4–74. https://doi.org/10.2139/ssrn.1267625.

Jeong, S. (2016, April 21). Credit bureaus were the NSA of the 19th century. *The Atlantic.* https://www.theatlantic.com/technology/archive/2016/04/mass-surveillance-was-invented-by-credit-bureaus/479226/.

Klein, D. B. (2001). Credit-information reporting: Why free speech is vital to social accountability and consumer opportunity. *The Independent Review, 5*(3), 325–344.

Lynch, T. E. (2009). Deeply and persistently conflicted: Credit rating agencies in the current regulatory environment. *Case Western Reserve Law Review, 59*(2), 227–304.

Madison, J. H. (1974). The evolution of commercial credit reporting agencies in nineteenth-century America. *The Business History Review, 48*(2), 164–186.

Mundy, F. W. (1907). Railroad bonds as an investment security. *The Annals of the American Academy of Political and Social Science, 30,* 120–143.

Olegario, R. (2001). *Credit-reporting agencies: Their historical roots, current status, and role in market development*. http://siteresources.worldbank.org/INTWDRS/Resources/4773651257315064764/2429_olegario.pdf://rld bank.org/INTWDR.

Patnoy, F. (2009). *Overdependence on credit ratings was a primary cause of the crisis* (Research Paper No. 09-015). Legal Studies Research Paper Series, University of San Diego.

Partnoy, F. (2006). How and why credit rating agencies are not like other gatekeepers (University of San Diego Legal Studies Research Paper Series No. 07-46). In Y. Fuchita & R. E. Litan (Eds.), *Financial gatekeepers: Can they protect investors?* Brookings Institution Press & the Nomura Institute of Capital Markets Research.

Pinto, A. R. (2006), Control and responsibility of credit rating agencies in the United States. *The American Journal of Comparative Law, 54*(1), 341–356.

Scalet, S., & Kelly, T. F. (2012). The ethics of credit rating agencies: What happened and the way forward. *Journal of Business Ethics, 111*(4), 477–490. https://doi.org/10.1007/s10551-012-1212-y.

Sylla, R. (2002). An historical primer on the business of credit rating. In R. M. Levich, G. Majnoni, & C. M. Reinhart (Eds.), *Ratings, ratings agencies and the global financial system* (pp. 65–84). Kluwer Academic Publishing.

U.S. Securities and Exchange Commission (U.S. SEC). (2018). *Annual report on nationally recognized statistical rating organizations.* U.S. Securities and Exchange Commission.

Vose, E. N. (1916). *Seventy-five years of the mercantile agency R. G. Dun & Co. 1841–1916.* Printing House of R.G. Dun & Co.

West, R. R. (1973). Bond ratings, bond yields and financial regulation: Some findings. *Journal of Law and Economics, 16*(1), 159–168.

Printed in the United States
by Baker & Taylor Publisher Services